STORIES FROM
JERUSALEM

STORIES FROM JERUSALEM

by

DAVID SHAHAR

Translated by Dalya Bilu and others

PAUL ELEK   LONDON

First published in Great Britain in 1976 by
Elek Books Ltd
54–58 Caledonian Road
London N1 9RN

The following stories in this volume have previously
been published in English:
"The Death of the Little God" in *Retrievements: A Jeru-
salem Anthology*, edited by Dennis Silk. Israel Uni-
versities Press, Jerusalem 1968.
"Bruria" in *Ariel, A Quarterly Review of Arts and Let-
ters*, Spring 1972. Published by the Cultural and
Scientific Relations Division, Ministry for Foreign
Affairs, Jerusalem.
"Moses and the Negress" in *Orot, Journal of Hebrew
Literature*, Number 13, June 1972.
"The Proposal" was printed by the Institute for the
Translation of Hebrew Literature, Tel Aviv, in 1965.

ISBN 0 236 40033 9

Printed in Great Britain by Unwin Brothers Limited
Old Woking, Surrey

CONTENTS

Grateful acknowledgment is made to The Institute for the Translation of Hebrew Literature Ltd. for its kind help in making possible the translation of several stories into English.

STORIES FROM
JERUSALEM

1

THE FORTUNE TELLER

As WILL BECOME readily apparent, it's not the fortune
teller that I want to talk about here, but my uncle Kalman.
The fortune teller was no more than a kind of railway junction that redirected the train of my uncle Kalman's life onto
tracks which led nowhere—or nowhere, at least, that anyone
could see. I have compared the fortune teller to a railway
junction because, like a railway junction, he didn't know
what he was doing. As a matter of fact, the fortune teller did
nothing: it was his absence that led to what happened. If he
had stayed where he was supposed to be—that is, chained to
his wife's bedside—then whatever it was that did happen
wouldn't have happened.

Twenty-five years ago, when I was a boy of nine, the fortune teller lived in our house. It seems strange, and even a
little frightening, that I already have clear memories of things
that took place so long ago—a quarter of a century ago! But to
get back to our story: over the window of his room, facing the
street, hung a sign on which the words "Fortune Teller" were
inscribed in the old-fashioned style of Torah scribes, letters
with soft rounded corners and sharp pointed tips like thorns.
Also painted on the sign was the head of a man with a black
tarboosh and a glazed look in his eyes, as if he were gazing
into the depths of the future; and all around the face were
little drawings interspersed with flying letters. Over the years

most of the drawings had faded away, but the letters could still be deciphered. In winter the sign would creak in the wind and bang against the ancient stones of the wall, and drops of rain would flow like tears from the glazed eyes into the mossy cracks in the wall.

The fortune teller lived with his wife for two years in the little room in the corner of our yard, and at the end of the second year, about a week after Kalman was released from prison and came to live with us, we woke up one morning to find that both of them, the fortune teller and his wife, had disappeared, simply run off with seven months' rent still due to us. During the two years that he spent in our house there probably wasn't a single soul in the whole neighborhood who hadn't come to have his fortune told at least two or three times. In this respect, the fortune teller resembled old Dr. Weinstein, who was intimately acquainted with the pains and the heartaches of everyone in the neighborhood: like him, the fortune teller had four or five ready-made formulas for every occasion, and like him he had two or three steady customers who had need of him every two or three days. One of these was Rahamim, the old stonecutter. Rahamim himself could not remember how old he was, and when anyone asked him he would say, "Old enough, Praise the Lord, much older than seventy . . ." and his tongue would dart in and out, trembling all the time, like a snail peeking out of its shell this way and that to have a look at the wide world. He used to consult both Dr. Weinstein and the fortune teller regularly on the question of his virility. And then there was the old Bukharan crone, so fat she was incapable of rising from a sitting position without assistance, who used to sit at the door of her basement all day long, muttering to herself in the language of Bukharan Jews and sucking at the mouthpiece of her narghile. She too used to come to the fortune teller at regular intervals to ask him when the letter was due to arrive. The secret of the letter was known only to the two of them. And I remember the fortune teller's wife too, and her two brothers, both of whom rose in the world to become taxi drivers on Ben Yehuda Street, and eventually even managed to acquire a taxi of their own. As for the fortune teller himself, I never laid eyes on him.

"Hanna's tied her husband to the bed again," said my uncle Kalman to my mother, and he laughed. I loved my uncle Kalman more than anyone in the world. He was a good, happy man and he used to sing all kinds of songs—Yiddish songs from the days when he was a Yeshiva student, and German songs from the days when he was a student at the "Lemel" School, and French songs from his schooldays at the "Alliance Israelite" and the records of Maurice Chevalier, and even Turkish songs which had somehow remained in his memory from the days of his early childhood. But I couldn't understand why he laughed when he said that Hanna had tied her husband to the bed again. Hanna's husband was the fortune teller. And whenever the two of them quarreled, she would tie him to the bed. To my mind there was something obscure and vaguely threatening about the whole situation. How could a woman struggle with a man, overcome him, and even tie him to her bed! Why, it was impossible—or else the fortune teller must be a very small man, a sort of midget. Obviously, a fortune teller couldn't be an ordinary person. He was a midget then, sitting on a pillow in the middle of his wife's big bed, sipping Turkish coffee from a tiny cup and telling his clients their fortunes in a hoarse, piping voice.

"How can Hanna tie him to her bed?" I asked Kalman. "After all, she isn't so very strong!" "Strong enough for the purpose, it seems," said Kalman, "and he's evidently quite content to let her have her way."

What he said made no sense to me at all, but I didn't argue

with him. In those distant days I hadn't yet developed the urge to argue with everyone, and certainly not with my uncle Kalman. I always agreed with everything he said, drinking his words in thirstily even when I had no idea of what they meant. It was only years later, when I was already a student of philosophy, that I was drawn into an argument with my uncle Kalman, once when he was expounding the main tenets of his system of thought to me. And the "philosophical" discussion I had with him then has since become one of my most painful memories. I shall never forgive myself for it. As befitting one of my philosophy professor's most "brilliant students," I was self-satisfied, conceited, and intolerant, and had in full measure the special kind of arrogance which characterized all the diligent disciples who had grasped the main tenets of their master's teaching and learned from him how to turn everything into a game of words and triumph over any thinking, feeling human being trying to express himself by these means. So I crushed my uncle Kalman simply by reducing everything he said to words, and then asking for the precise definition of every single one of them. But the main thing I shall never forgive myself for is that in the depths of my heart I was angry with him. Yes, angry with him—just as I was angry with anyone who dared express an opinion on "professional" philosophical matters without having taken the trouble to study the latest discoveries in the field of logic and semantics. This particular stage in my life, however, has nothing to do with my uncle Kalman.

What was Kalman doing in our house twenty-five years ago when the fortune teller was still living in the room in our yard? As a matter of fact, he wasn't doing anything at all. True, when the urge took him he used to help my mother with the housework—emptying the garbage pail in the morning, going on urgent errands to the grocer or greengrocer or butcher, washing the dishes, and even mopping the floors. Once his industry reached such lengths that he got up early in the morning, polished all our shoes and placed them in a straight line on the bench outside for us to see when we woke. These attacks of energy, however, were neither lasting nor frequent. In this, as in other matters, Kalman was a little peculiar. If he really felt like it, no work was too hard for him— he was ready to turn the closets upside down and scrub their backsides. But when he was in the grip of idleness, nothing in the world could make him budge from his place on the couch. He would lie there, sprawled across it, his head resting on a pillow propped against the wall, his feet, with shoes on, crossed on the only upholstered chair in the house, one hand holding a cigarette and the other an ashtray, his eyes fixed on the ceiling with a calm, distant gaze. When he reached the higher degrees of idleness he didn't even take the trouble to find an ashtray and would drop cigarette ash all over his shirt and trousers, on the floor and in the water jar. No wonder that by the end of the week he spent in our house before moving into the fortune teller's room, he had managed to burn holes in all my father's shirts. The miracle was that he didn't set his bed on fire, for he fell asleep with a burning cigarette in his mouth on more than one occasion. He used to fall asleep stretched out on his back, his hollow cheeks sunken as if he were sucking them in his sleep and his prominent nose, more prominent than ever, emitting an ill-humored snore. It was my father's shirts he burned holes in, because when he came to our house he had only the shirt on his back and that was thrown into the rubbish bin soon after his arrival, where it was followed by his trousers, his underwear, and even the battered little suitcase whose contents have remained unknown to this day because my mother threw it away without even bothering to open it. In those days the people of our

neighborhood were in no hurry to throw old clothes away, and
if Kalman's garments had been treated in this summary manner it was only because there was absolutely no alternative.
On that day he looked like a fierce, plucked bird. A bird set
free, whose heart was still beating wildly within him. Altogether, there was something sharply birdlike about him, and
when he put on my father's clothes, which were much too big
for him, this impression became even more pronounced. All
his life, in fact, Kalman wore trousers which were too big for
him, since the trousers in the shops were all too wide for his
narrow hips and he never had the means or the inclination to
have any made to measure. It was because of these baggy
trousers, I think, that he acquired the hopping, sidling gait
that was characteristic of him.

On the day of his arrival, even before crossing the threshold,
he said to my mother, "Give me some of Eli's old clothes and
throw mine straight into the rubbish bin. Do you have any
carbolic soap?" Eli, of course, was my father, and my mother
understood at once that her brother Kalman was full of lice
and bugs. Before he was caught and put in jail, Kalman had
been hiding for weeks in the cellar of Levi the mad Georgian
porter who never spoke anything but Yiddish although he
was a Sephardi Jew. And he had come to our house straight
after spending twenty-one days in jail. Everything had con-
spired against him at once—all his creditors had descended
upon him and taken him to court just when the judge had
ordered him to pay five pounds a month for his wife's support.

He sought refuge in Levi's cellar, hiding first from the court
clerk who was trying to deliver the summons, then from the
law enforcement officer who was trying to serve him with the
first and then the final warning notice, and lastly from Trachtenberg, the policeman who had been ordered to arrest him.

Trachtenberg the policeman lived in the same house as Levi the porter and about once a week he would go down to the cellar to talk to Kalman about women and politics. Before taking his departure he would complain about his harsh fate and mention the great dangers that lay in wait for him should the English police officer ever get to know, Heaven forbid, that the sentenced criminal Kalman was hiding in his own house. He, the policeman Trachtenberg, would be fired and put into prison as well. Whenever this imminent peril was mentioned, Kalman would thrust his hand into his trouser pocket, take out some coins, and slip them to the policeman. Once when he could no longer find a single copper in his pocket, he borrowed ten piasters from Levi the porter. After a few weeks Kalman got sick of the whole situation and gave himself up to the police. Then he sat for twenty-one days in prison, appearing twice before the Arab judge, to whom he spoke of matters of the spirit. The judge enjoyed these conversations so much that he found mitigating circumstances for all Kalman's transgressions of the law and ordered him to pay off his debts at the rate of only twenty-five piasters a month; he even reduced the sum he had to pay to his wife from five to three pounds a month.

The whole matter of Kalman's wife requires some explanation or, perhaps it would be better to say, justification. The truth is that I don't really remember his wife at all. Not because I never saw her, but simply because she made no impression on me. In fact, if I had parted from her and then bumped into her again by chance half an hour later, I doubt if I would have recognized her. All I remember is that she was considerably taller than Kalman, that her voice was rather deep, and that she was always talking about "support." She wasn't a bad woman, and if it had only been a question of "support," she probably wouldn't have taken Kalman to court at all, but would have tried to supply whatever was lacking herself. After all, what did a woman need in those days? I think that most of the women in our neighborhood didn't even know that electric refrigerators existed. Pots that had to be kept cool were wrapped in wet cloths and left standing on the window sill in basins of water, and all the housewives were quite content with this arrangement, including Kalman's wife. She would probably never have become involved in shameful, distressing legal proceedings if it hadn't been for the energetic interference of her family. She had a secret fear of my uncle Kalman. He frightened her with his opinions, his talk, his sudden bursts of activity and prolonged bouts of idleness, and his behavior in general. In time, she even grew afraid of his singing, his laughter, and the look in his eyes. For some years she contrived to hide her fears from her family and neighbors, and she would even defend her husband, whom they regarded as a loafer of the worst sort, from their attacks. He liked sitting with the drunken British soldiers and policemen who frequented the cafés in the vicinity of the Edison Cinema. When she was asked what her husband did for a living, she used to say he was an "agent," and once when she was pressed to be more specific, she said he was a "dry goods agent." For some reason, this branch of commerce had a particular importance in her eyes, and during the five years of their life together, she did her utmost to make Kalman open a dry goods shop. Her father was even willing to rent a shop and fill it with the requisite goods, but the person chiefly concerned, namely my uncle Kalman, flatly refused to rise to such heights. He was quite content with his own way of making a living, which consisted of writing letters for people and filling out documents for them in the languages he had acquired at the Lemel school and the Alliance Israelite. His wife—and here I realize that not only have I forgotten what she looked like, I can't even remember her name—claimed that she would have been prepared to make ends meet even on this meager income, if only it had been steady. He, however, preferred to read useless books or lounge in cafés. Finally things came to such a pass that she felt it was better for him to be sitting in a café than to be lying on his back in the yard chatting with the neighborhood children. His café sessions could at least be explained by the fact that he was "negotiating . . . you know . . . business deals." She never dared admit her fears and anxieties even to herself, until one day her mother arrived at the house to "have it out with her," "call a spade a spade," and save her from her husband before it was too late. As luck would have it, her mother turned up precisely on the ill-fated and disastrous day that had seemed to start out so well with Kalman in a particularly good mood and intent, or so it appeared, on effecting a reconciliation between them. After a long period of estrangement, he had approached her and embraced her in a manner that moved her to the point of tears. He said that it was impossible to continue in this way and that something had to be done. Her heart began to beat wildly in anticipation of the fulfillment of her dream, of a dry goods shop and the end of shame and the beginning of prosperity and respectability. But slowly something in his words began to jar and trouble her, reawakening all her anxieties. Suddenly she realized that he was speaking of his own suffering, saying that he was "rotting away," that he had "no one to talk to about really important things," and that he lacked "proper conditions for study and reflection." She was struck dumb, unable to utter a word. That very evening she agreed with her mother that the time had come to "take action."

My mother had no carbolic soap, but she did have laundry soap in plenty. She lit the two big Primus stoves and heated up water for Kalman to bathe in. At that time there was no running water in the whole of the neighborhood and we used to draw our water from the cistern in the courtyard. In the corner of the yard, next to the fortune teller's room, stood a little wooden hut which was used both as a bathroom and a laundry, the big washtub doing double duty as a bathtub when the occasion arose. Kalman scrubbed himself in the washtub, singing Maurice Chevalier's "Beneath the Roofs of Paris" at the top of his voice. Then he emerged wrapped in mother's dressing gown, and asked if there were any sardines in the house. We had gefilte fish and meat and other products of my mother's cooking, but Kalman wanted sardines and I had to run to the shop and buy some for him. After squeezing a whole lemon over them, Kalman ate the sardines straight from the tin, standing in the kitchen, and washed the lot down with a glass of cocoa. During his twenty-one days in jail, he told me, this was the meal he had longed for. When he had finished eating, he fell onto the couch in his usual position, flat on his back with his head resting on a pillow against the wall and his feet crossed on the only upholstered chair in the house, and immediately fell asleep. He slept for ten consecutive hours.

About a week after Kalman was released from prison and came to live in our house, the fortune teller vanished from his room together with his wife and our last hopes of ever obtaining the seven months' rent they owed us. A long time later we heard that he had settled down in the Arab quarter of Tiberias where, it was rumored, his affairs prospered. When the fortune teller disappeared, Kalman moved into his room.

I have already mentioned that Kalman had the look of a bird about him, with his wizened, beaky face and darting, beady eyes. He was about forty-five years old when he was released from jail and set up house in the fortune teller's room.

Something had happened to him there in prison, and I am not referring to the more or less respectable way of life which he adopted on his release: the Arab judge, as will be recalled, had ordered him to pay back his debts at the rate of twenty-five piasters a month and pay support for his wife at the rate of three pounds a month. Thus he had to earn at least six pounds a month in order to pay all his debts and provide for himself as well, which he did by translating letters for the orphanage nearby, spending no more than three hours a day at it. As I say, I am not referring to his way of life which was more or less normal and respectable, nor even to the fact that he played gladly with the neighborhood children and sang songs for them; he had always been a friendly, good humored man. Something had happened to him there in prison, something very different from anything we can imagine. For instance, he would often lie flat on the ground for hours on end, watching a line of ants winding their way from a crack in the paving stones to some mysterious destination of their own and back again; and he would be so entranced by what he saw that I could sit down on his back and he wouldn't even realize that I was there. All living creatures fascinated him; not necessarily lions and tigers and exotic beasts in the zoo, but the cats and dogs in the street, the sparrows on the roof, and the little lizards that crawl into your hand. And not only creatures but also plants, and even the simplest most ordinary things. On the day he went down to live in the fortune teller's room—you had to go down seven steps to reach it, but it wasn't called a basement because its windows were high enough to overlook the street—he gave my mother a real fright. When she came in to see how he was getting on she found him sitting cross-legged on the floor, staring at a stone—an ordinary, undressed stone. And when she asked him whether he wouldn't like to stay with us a little longer until his room could be properly whitewashed, he made no response at all because he neither saw nor heard her. Mother was afraid that he was ill or that he'd fainted, and it was only after she had shaken him and shouted, "Kalman, Kalman, what's the matter with you?" into his ear that he came out of his trance and answered her in a surprised tone of voice, "But I told you, there's no need to have the room whitewashed."

Years later, when I was already a student of philosophy, he said to me (in the course of the conversation to which I have already referred) that in his opinion a person could "grasp the essence of things by rapt contemplation, by the annihilation of the self," and that it didn't matter what the object of contemplation was, even a piece of stone. "Once you grasp the essence you no longer see anything as separate or whole, beautiful or ugly, good or bad." And later in the course of that same discussion he also said, "The suffering of a child is the punishment which God inflicts on himself when he awakens from the intoxication of his love of himself in individuals and time."

And all this began in the prison cell. One night, when he was sitting on his mattress, he became aware of a drop of water suspended from a projecting stone in the wall. It took on the typical pear shape, full and extended to the utmost, of a drop of water just before it falls. Only it didn't fall, it remained hanging there. The drop seemed very near and very far away. It was the center of all things, and all things were related to it and far removed from it. The cell expanded immeasurably, and everything was engulfed in an infinite calm, and Kalman became part of this living calm. From that moment on, he felt that he could no longer understand the anxiety, the worry, the anger, the irritation, the fuss, and the bother of the people around him, in the prison and outside it.

Once he had installed himself in the fortune teller's room,

Kalman became a fortune teller himself. On the first day he opened his eyes in that room, the old Bukharan woman rolled in, puffing and panting and muttering to herself, to discuss the matter of the letter. She was not at all put out to find that the fortune teller had changed his form and countenance and denied that he was himself. On the contrary, she was glad of an excuse to go over the whole history of the letter again from beginning to end without omitting a single detail. Kalman listened to her patiently and told himself that he must remember to remove the sign over the window facing the street. On second thoughts, however, he decided that it wouldn't make any difference if he did, and that in any case it wasn't worth the trouble. To this day, I believe, the sign is still there, creaking in the wind.

To the Bukharan woman he said, "The letter will arrive in seven days and seven nights and seven hours and seven minutes and seven seconds."

"Blessings on your head," she said, and the blessing immediately materialized, not on his head exactly but in his hand, in the form of a loud moist kiss followed by a five-piaster coin.

"It's not necessary, really it isn't," he said, referring to both aspects of the blessing, the one of sentiment and the one of substance, but she firmly refused to take the coin back. Seeing that she seemed offended, Kalman reconsidered and decided that in the long run, in the ultimate reckoning of what was good for her own soul, he should take her money. When she had gone he decided to sit down and write the letter at once so that she would get it in time, but on second thoughts he realized that he would be doing her more harm than good if he put an end to her hopes by fulfilling them, so he did nothing.

She had barely departed when the other one came—Rahamim the old stonecutter. Rahamim was a suspicious old Jew.

As soon as he glanced in at the doorway and saw the figure of my uncle Kalman, he raised his eyebrows and pursed his mouth in a petulant question mark, but he made no move to retreat.

"Please come in," Kalman called. "Come in, sir, please." The stonecutter did not wait for any further invitation. "I am the servant of a servant," explained Kalman, "the apprentice of an apprentice of him who sees the end in the beginning, reads the history of the generations before it is written, and remembers the future because it is past."

These words, clear as the sun, pure as the moon, and fragrant as myrrh and frankincense, immediately set the mind of the stonecutter at ease and completely dispelled his suspicions. At once, without any preliminaries, speaking as man to man, he launched forth on the long, hard problem of his virility, and since his lips trembled as he spoke and his tongue protruded like a soft snail poking its head out of its shell, the problem grew longer and harder to follow with his every word.

"I see," concluded Kalman, "that the happy turn of events is near. It will happen as it must and will stand firm in its glory when Miriam cometh."

The stonecutter extracted a ten-piaster coin from the folds of his striped sash, slapped it down on the table, and said, "Your honor will understand, as usual—the rest on account."

"How much on account?"

"Fifteen piasters, no more. That's what we always pay, the cash and fifteen on account."

"And the others, the Bukharan?"

"I always get a discount," the stonecutter explained. "I haven't had a job now for over twenty years."

"Why, that old woman cheated me," Kalman thought to himself and began to laugh aloud until tears came to his eyes. The stonecutter stared at him in concern, bade him farewell, and hurried away.

Well, said Kalman to himself, this seems easy and enjoyable work; he liked listening and not being listened to, seeing and not being seen, getting others to talk and putting their minds at rest. Strange how it was only his own wife's mind that he was unable to put at rest. Or perhaps it wasn't so strange after all, for in order to put her mind at rest he would have had to change into another person, and that was patently beyond his powers. The mistake lay in his ever having married her in the first place. But then he had only married her in order to put her mind at rest. Well it certainly seemed easier to tell other people their fortunes . . . Suddenly he felt that he was losing his own peace of mind, that he was becoming involved, that he was lying. He tried to concentrate on the water jug on the table, but the great calm did not descend to envelop him again. He rushed out to the corner of the street and slipped the fifteen piasters he had received from his clients into the blind Yemenite beggar's box. Then he wandered about the alleyways of the neighborhood until sundown repeating to himself, without knowing why, "the dark night of the soul, the dark night of the soul." He sensed something horrible threatening him, something not connected with anything in his immediate surroundings. The fifteen piasters he had taken for telling fortunes had opened a thin crack for the dark night to seep into his soul.

As the sun began to set he returned to his room, sat down, and waited. From the first moment he knew, from the moment her shadow in the doorway blocked out the rays of the setting sun. She was beautiful and dignified even in her distress. Very restrained and delicate, almost apologetic at troubling others—even if it was only a fortune teller whose business it was to be troubled—with her pain and suffering. The very fact that she had come to a fortune teller could have only one meaning, so clear that further explanations were superfluous—it was the end. There was no hope. Her eleven-year-old son

Gili had cancer of the glands. She had come to him furtively in the dusk, embarrassed and ashamed of herself for coming, and her eyes were imploring, tearless, and stretched wide open.

"You are Mrs. Greenfeld," he said to her, "Dr. Greenfeld's wife."

Her husband was a lecturer in biochemistry. Once when Kalman had been waiting in the courtroom to have his detention period renewed he had seen Dr. Greenfeld and his wife appearing as plaintiffs in a case involving an accident in which a truck driver had lost control of his vehicle, hit a child, and finally smashed into their little black Morris.

Her eyes gleamed with hope, as if she was standing before the advent of a miracle.

"I know your name because I happened to be present at your court case. There's nothing to wonder at."

"My husband must never know that I've come to you," she said apologetically.

"Yes, of course. He doesn't believe in fortune tellers and miracles and suchlike superstitions," he replied. "Neither do I. I'm not a fortune teller. It's a mistake. A lie. Once a fortune teller did live here, but he's gone now. I'll take down the sign tomorrow."

She sat still on the stool, shrinking as if she had just received one blow and was waiting, resigned, for the next. Kalman looked at her. The darkness in the room deepened. Since he was facing the door, she looked to him like a silhouette with only the glass buttons on her blouse glistening in the dark.

"If so, I must go," she murmured at last, but she remained seated.

"I'd better light the lamp," he said.

He lit the kerosene lamp, and the little flame leaped and flickered until the whole wick caught, and then it steadied itself into a tongue of light. One of the glass buttons on her blouse reflected the radiance faintly, sending little rays of light in all directions with every breath she took. Suddenly the button became fixed, a motionless center like the drop of water in the prison cell, and everything ebbed away from him in a smooth rapid movement, calm and full of life.

"If you don't mind," he said, "I'll come with you to the hospital." He felt that he ought to see the child with his own eyes.

Again she stirred expectantly. They walked quickly and silently, side by side, through the streets. The full moon had already risen and the shadows of the houses were sharp and clear like a woodcut. Three weeks had passed since the doctors had concluded that it was "the end, only a matter of days." But the body refused to die. The boy lay wrapped up on his bed, behind a screen separating him from the other two patients in the room whose condition was not so desperate. He was small and shriveled, like a little skeleton, and only his swollen neck and belly protruded. Every once in a while he would quiver in a spasm of pain. His mother sat on the chair by the bed and looked at him with wide-open eyes. The night nurse peeped into the room. "The doctor said that tomorrow they'll give him another blood transfusion," she said to the mother. She was evidently trying to cheer her up. So long as they were giving blood transfusions there was still hope.

Kalman went out of the ward on tiptoe. He knew that he ought to say something encouraging to the mother. She needed the lying encouragement of the fortune teller more than the fat old woman or the feeble old man, more than any other human being, but he could not bring himself to say a single consoling word to her. He wandered about the streets for hours on end, with no notion of the passing of time, until he became aware of the fact that he was walking in circles around the prison. He returned home after midnight and fell onto his bed like a stone. When he awoke in the morning he knew at once that he had to hurry to save a life in danger. He jumped out of bed and hurried to the blood bank to donate blood for the child Gili Greenfeld. "We must do everything necessary, everything known, everything possible," he said to himself as his blood dripped into the fat-bellied bottle, and all the time he knew that at best the blood transfusion would do no more than prolong the child's agony for another few hours or days.

A child's pain. What greatness, what glory, what power, and what goodness was there in the world, in all the worlds, in all the vast space of lightyears, in all the galaxies, in all creation, in God himself, if he allowed a single child to suffer such awful pain? These terrible torments, why were they created, for what purpose did they exist?

"You can have a cup of coffee and then get a meal in the hospital kitchen," the nurse said as she undid the rubber tube on his arm.

"Thank you, I'll just have the coffee," he said. He swallowed the cup of coffee in one gulp and rushed out as if he were in a great hurry. But in fact he had nothing to do, nothing at all. There was nothing to do. That night he returned to the hospital and the porter let him in as soon as he mentioned the child's name—the special privilege of the families of the dying, thought Kalman, they can get into the hospital outside visiting hours. In the courtyard, on a bench beneath a tall pine tree, the boy's mother sat weeping quietly while his father walked up and down giving vent every now and then to a muffled groan. Kalman went straight to the mortuary, drew back the sheet and looked at the child's face for a long time. He looked as if he were sleeping soundly. All the lines of pain had faded from his face. His body, that had now once again become part of the whole of existence, had nothing whatever to do with the anxiety, fear, sorrow, suffering, and pain of living in individuals and time. On the other side of the little barred window, the branch of an olive tree glowed in the light of the street lamp, and the soul of Gili did not need to go anywhere. It existed.

Kalman left the mortuary with a strange feeling of release, and as he went out of the hospital he felt a great hunger. He went into Abulafia's restaurant, ordered a plate of *humus*, and then a double portion of shishlik and kebab and pickles, which he swallowed down with the assistance of a glass of cognac, and finished his meal with a cup of Turkish coffee. When he rose from the table he was slightly dizzy and his knees felt weak. "So giving blood does weaken you after all," he said to himself aloud. "They take three hundred grams of blood, I believe, from your body . . ."

As soon as he reached home, he fell onto his bed in his usual position, his head resting on a pillow against the wall and his feet crossed on a stool. On the wall opposite him was a large black nail upon which the fortune teller had once hung a big calendar illustrated with the signs of the Zodiac. Kalman's eyes now fastened themselves on this nail. Instantly, as though struck by a beam of pure light, he became aware of the great calm of life in its essence and its nothingness, and he knew that it was greater than the God who had created life in individuals and in time. In the beginning God created the universe as a mirror to give him back his own reflection so that he could preen himself, and as soon as he wanted to see his own image in a mirror he fell to the level of the pettiest of tyrants trying to get his picture in the newspapers. And the way is open for me to be greater than he, great as the great calm of life in its essence and its nothingness, which is greater than the God who created life in individuals and in time. The calm which has no separate parts or differences, and no past and no future, because it is the eternal glory of the present moment.

The blackness of the nail expanded until it enveloped him entirely and he fell into a deep sleep.

Translated by Yehuda Hanegbi

2

UNCLE ZEMACH

OUR FAMILY always had its fair share of gifted members, but for some reason fortune failed to smile on them. Some of them never took the trouble to develop their talents, which remained hidden in the depths of their beings to haunt them all their lives; in others talent bloomed early, but on reaching the crucial point suddenly turned off the main road to lose itself in crooked byways, while still others spread their talents out over so wide a field that in the end they lacked all substance. Take, for instance, my uncle Lippa. When Lippa went to America to study political economy and statistics, there was no one in the whole of the old settlement who was even aware of the fact that sciences such as these existed. He was twenty years old when he received his first degree and started preparing for his Master's, and then his evil genius got the better of him and persuaded him to improve his performance on the violin instead. In his childhood Lippa had played all sorts of tunes on the violin, such as "Hatikvah" and "There in the Land of our Fathers' Longing," but he had never studied music and played only by ear. When he decided to develop this talent, he abandoned economics and statistics and all other pursuits of this nature, and devoted himself entirely to the violin, but by then it was too late and he was left the loser on both counts. Lippa's brother might have had it in him to become a great writer if only his peculiar ideas had not led him astray. Since he had been brought up in Yiddish at home he decided to write in this language only. In fact, all the children of his generation (except the children of Eliezer Ben Yehuda) had spoken Yiddish at home and this had not prevented the new Hebrew literature from coming into being, but he thought otherwise. He argued that it was unnatural to write in a language that you had not learned at your mother's knee. Therefore he wrote what he wrote in Yiddish. He might have had it in him to become a great writer in Yiddish, but his laziness prevented him. He spent his life sunk in a kind of philosophical laziness which led him to regard himself and everything around him with disdain. Because of this philosophical laziness he wouldn't even send the few manuscripts in his possession to the editors of the Jewish papers in America, and those stories which were published were only published thanks to his wife, who copied them out in her fair hand. His name was Nechemia and he died destitute.

Unique among all the talented members of the family was my uncle Zemach, who was endowed with a practical turn of mind as well. He decided to become a successful man with a position in society. Being younger than his brothers, he took the lesson of their lives to heart and made up his mind to keep his talents under control and direct them into the channels of material profit. He had a great talent for painting and even spent two years studying fine arts at the Bezalel School of Art. One of his paintings, a landscape in oils of the country around the Arab village of Abu Gosh, hangs in our house to this day. We have many other paintings of his too, only there is no room on the walls to hang them. And even if there were room, my mother would refuse to hang them because she says they send cold shivers down her spine.

When he was still a young boy, Zemach made a name for

himself in the town, not as a great artist but as a national hero. This happened three years after the British arrived in the country when he was a lad of about seventeen. He was visiting his cousin Shmuel in Nes Ziona when he heard that several hundred Arabs had staged a demonstration against the Jews at the Jaffa Gate. That same evening he bought a German revolver from one of his uncle's Arab workers for 50 Egyptian grush and went up to Jerusalem. A few months later the Arabs rioted on the holiday of Nebi Moussa. It was a Friday. In the morning he went to Bezalel and within an hour rumors that the Arab rioters were collecting at the Damascus Gate reached the school. "I'm off," he said to his friend. "Where to?" "To stop them. I've got a revolver." The friend looked at him and paled. "I'm coming too," he said. "What?" said Zemach. "Unarmed?" "I'll swipe the shoub'ria."

The shoub'ria was an ancient Arab dagger with a finely wrought silver haft, one of the exhibits on display in the principal's office. Zemach's friend stole the dagger and the two of them left the school courtyard and set out for the Damascus Gate. On their way they discovered that the rioters were closing in on Meah Shearim. They made a detour around the Abyssinian Road and entered Meah Shearim. There was an oppressive quiet in the quarter. The shops were shuttered, the houses were locked, and not a soul stirred in the streets. From the synagogues rose the sound of voices chanting psalms. They walked down the length of the main street and then climbed onto the roof of the flour mill. Now they could see the rioters coming, armed with knives and sticks, and hear their shouts. Suddenly they stopped to dance a sword dance around their leader, who was riding shoulder high and waving his sword with sinuous, rhythmic movements. A number of British policemen in steel helmets stood watching the

spectacle with enjoyment. When the rioters reached the first
Jewish shops they started breaking into them with iron bars
and sticks. Zemach took the revolver out of his briefcase,
loaded it, and without taking aim fired one shot into the
crowd. There was an uproar. All the British policemen lay
flat on the street, as if in response to a command. Zemach
fired four more shots one after the other, and when he paused
to reload the revolver he saw that all the Arabs were running
for their lives. The next day it became known that in the
attack on Meah Shearim one Arab had been killed.

The reputation he gained as a hero caused Zemach much
satisfaction, but it didn't go to his head. He wanted to be an
artist and worked diligently in pursuit of this aim, refusing to
join the Hagana, which was then being organized, and not
even taking part in discussions on socialism and Jewish labor
and the kibbutz. In his second year of studies at Bezalel his
brother Nechemia died, leaving a widow and four destitute
children behind him. A few months later his brother Lippa
returned from America with a B.A. in statistics and a violin,
and after a long period of unemployment succeeded in finding a job as a violinist in the Café Tamar. The evening that
Lippa made his debut in the Café Tamar Zemach made up
his mind to leave Bezalel and go to study law at the law school
established by the mandatory government. Better, he said,
to be a second-rate lawyer than a fourth-rate artist. This
should not be taken to mean that Zemach was modest and
failed to give his artistic talents their due. He regarded his
fellow students as inferior to himself, and even his teachers
and instructors as fifth- and sixth-rate artists. Unlike his
brother Lippa, Zemach was proud.

My first clear memories are connected with the period preceding his journey to England. He was then about twenty-
five years old, and to me he seemed a fully mature man in

every respect. After graduating from law school he decided to continue his studies in England so that he could come back and be the most famous and distinguished lawyer in the country. To the farewell party he gave he invited only the most superior of his friends, and in everything scrupulously observed the rules laid down in an English book he had purchased called *Etiquette,* a book bound in blue covers and decorated with gold lettering, which contained all the forms and usages and obligations of politeness in good society.

He studied this book assiduously and even set himself exercises and practiced how to eat fish balls and how to eat meatballs, how to wipe his mouth and how to blow his nose, which hand to use when helping a lady upstairs, and which hand to use when opening the door for her, which people to invite to a big party, and which to a small one.

In the matter of the guests invited to his farewell party he aroused my mother's wrath. He refused to invite his cousin Shmuel from Nes Ziona who had come to spend a week in our house. Shmuel was a good lad, but there was no denying that brains were not his strong point. He had a weakness for cockfights, and whenever he came across two cocks he would provoke them to a duel.

"Since there won't be any live cocks at the party there's no point in inviting Shmuel," said Zemach to Mother with a smile. Mother was not amused. "Imagine that you were staying at Shmuel's house in Nes Ziona and he gave a party and didn't invite you to it. How would you feel?"

Zemach smiled tolerantly with the air of a man obliged through no fault of his own to listen to inanities and reply to them. He had fine white teeth, a small fair mustache, and an engaging smile which disarmed his listeners and prevented feelings of anger and resentment from gaining the upper hand.

"How many times do I have to tell you," he said in reply to my mother, "that you can't make comparisons between people? The basic mistake on which social life is founded today is that people are born equal. It's not only a mistake, it's a denial of reality. People are not born equal. People are born tall and short, clever and stupid, strong and weak, handsome and ugly, and so on and so forth. You can't dump them all into the same category and expect them to live according to the same conditions. Shmuel's affairs are of no interest to me and his friends aren't my friends, and just as I would feel out of place at a party he gave for his friends, so he would feel out of place at the party I'm giving for my friends. For his own good, he shouldn't be invited to the party."

"All your fine words can't justify your deeds," Mother said angrily. "If you behaved according to natural manners and not the artificial manners in your holy book, you wouldn't hesitate for a single minute before inviting Shmuel to your party. Shmuel is a good boy with a warm heart. As for his cockfighting, I don't think the boxing matches you're so crazy about are any better than cockfighting."

Zemach turned away before Mother had finished what she was saying. He always claimed to know in advance what people were about to say to him, so that there was no need for him to stand and listen to the end, except in cases where the etiquette book demanded it. Mother sent a hurt, angry look after him, and he went off twirling his cane in a dandyish fashion. About two weeks before the journey to England he bought a silver-knobbed cane in Stiletzky's shop in Jaffa Road, and on the first day he had it he already knew how to perform all sorts of tricks with it. He could transfer it deftly and elegantly from one hand to the other and twirl it between two fingers only, the index finger and the thumb, with surprising speed; and once when he was standing alone in his room I saw to my astonishment how he balanced it carefully on the tip of his nose, spread his hands out on either side of him, and walked the length of the room with the wobbling cane about to topple off his nose at any moment. The sight of this sport filled me with shame and I blushed. I couldn't understand how a grown-up man, a lawyer who knew all the right answers, could be attracted to such childish tricks. Since I didn't want to catch him red-handed, I turned on my heel and saw my uncle Lippa with his violin in his hand.

"Why are you so red?" he asked loudly and clapped me on the shoulder. Before I could reply, Zemach emerged from the room. My uncle Lippa looked at him inquiringly and the shadow of a smile crossed his face. He was ten years older than Zemach and adopted rather a patronizing attitude toward him. "What's happened to you to make your nose so red and your eyes full of tears?" he asked Zemach. Zemach's nose was not only red, it was also swollen from the weight of the cane.

"It's nothing," said Zemach. "A slight cold."

My heart pounded. All my respect for Zemach vanished in an instant. His childishness I forgave him, but not his lie.

"That's not a cold!" I shouted suddenly. "He was standing in the room all this time and balancing his cane on his nose."

My uncle Lippa burst out laughing. "Never mind," he said. "Young lawyers are allowed to have a little fun sometimes too. As far as I know there's no law in the etiquette book to stop them from balancing a cane on their noses whenever they feel like it."

"That's right," said Zemach, "and there's no law either to prevent graduates in statistics and economics from earning their living by playing the violin in cafés for the entertainment of His Majesty's drunken soldiers."

Zemach considered it beneath Lippa's dignity to play in a

café. He would avoid passing the Café Tamar in order to escape the painful sight of my uncle Lippa playing the violin in front of the British soldiers and policemen who were its habitual customers. Lippa even made friends with them and drank with them at the bar. Perhaps all this would not have wounded Zemach so much if Lippa hadn't possessed a B.A. in the economic sciences. He couldn't forgive Lippa for abandoning the path of science and failing to obtain a respectable position in society. Lippa regarded his younger brother's lofty ambitions and arrogant ways with fatherly tolerance and a shade of mockery.

Lippa came late to Zemach's farewell party. He worked until ten at night and there was no possibility of his appearing before half past ten. Zemach awaited his arrival with an eagerness which was tinged with anxiety. Despite all their quarrels and disagreements, in the depths of his heart Zemach admired his older brother's personality, but at the same time he was never free of the apprehension that Lippa's nature was such that it might lead him to do things that would lower his dignity in the eyes of others.

When my uncle Lippa arrived at the party at a quarter to eleven he was not alone. He was holding his violin under one arm, and in the other my cousin Shmuel, who was a head taller than all the other guests and in a state of great bewilderment and agitation, looking nervously about him in all directions to see where help might lie. Lippa himself was slightly tipsy. He had already had a few brandies in the Café Tamar before coming to the party. Zemach looked at him and smiled and his heart sank inside him. Among the guests were three lecturers from the law school and one British judge called William Benton. The judge was a habitué of the Café Tamar, and Lippa went up to exchange a few words with him.

"Phillip," said the judge, "play something in honor of our

host." Phillip was what the English called my uncle Lippa. Zemach wasn't sure whether the judge knew that Lippa was his brother, or if perhaps he imagined that he had been invited to the party to play the violin. Lippa went to the center of the table, pushed the bottles and plates aside, and then leaped up onto it to the accompaniment of cries of encouragement and clapping. Zemach stood at the end of the hall leaning against the wall with his arms crossed, and Lippa turned to him, waved his bow in the air, and began to make an emotional farewell speech. He spoke of law and lawyers, of justice and injustice, of the society of man and of man in society, of the littleness of man and his greatness, of good and evil and of what lies beyond good and evil. He concluded his speech with a quotation from the poet: "This above all—to thine own self be true." He bowed and everyone burst into applause except for Zemach, who remained standing in his place blushing deeply. Lippa bent down, filled a glass, poured it down his throat, and began to play. He played folk tunes and dances and everything he played vibrated with a strain of sadness and longing. He got down from the table and moved about among the dancers with his violin, and he went on playing after all the guests had one by one departed. Only Zemach and Shmuel were left in the hall. Shmuel was completely drunk and sat dozing and crooning to himself with his head bowed between his shoulders, and Zemach continued standing against the wall with his arms folded on his chest. During the entire party he had hardly taken a drop to drink.

Lippa stood playing the violin and Zemach stood staring into space and dreaming about the future. Suddenly he shook himself, glanced at Shmuel who had ceased his mutterings and started to snore, and then looked at Lippa who could hardly keep on his feet. He left his place by the wall, took up his silver-knobbed cane, and said to Lippa, "I ought to thank

you for the fine speech you made this evening in my honor
and reply in kind, but since I doubt whether your present
condition would enable you to listen to a speech, and even if
you weren't drunk I don't expect you would agree with what
I have to say, I'll content myself with an allusion to the
words of the poet. I want you to know that, as for me, I can
dream and yet not make dreams my master, and I can think
and not make thoughts my aim. My aim is to succeed and all
roads leading to success are right."

My uncle Zemach spent four years in England and he returned with the degree of Doctor of Jurisprudence and with
a wife. I remember his first visit to our house on his return.
It was Saturday night. Outside the rain poured down and the
wind howled at the windows. He came with his wife in a
hired taxi. In those days it was unusual to hire a taxi for any
purpose at all, let alone a short trip from one part of Jerusalem to another, and it seemed conceited even more than
extravagant of Uncle Zemach to drive up to our house in this
fashion. The first thing that struck me about him was his
smell. As soon as he came into the house the air was filled
with a strange smell, the smell of British soldiers and policemen. At first I didn't realize that this smell was the aroma of
the smoke coming out of the English tobacco in his pipe.
His shoulders were broad and he filled the house with his
strong and manly presence. He had grown fatter and more
robust in England. He had also shaved off his fair mustache
and now walked without a stick—apparently canes were no
longer in fashion. His voice had changed too; it had become
deep and full and strange. In contrast to him his wife seemed
an insignificant sort of creature. She was wrapped in furs
and only her meager face was revealed to the world. She
couldn't have been called pretty, but she wasn't ugly either.

She made neither a good nor a bad impression. Her eyes were big and her nose long and thin. She sat where she was without moving until he hinted that it was time to go. She said nothing, because the only language she knew was English. When he addressed her occasionally in English she answered briefly and rhythmically, and then it transpired that she had a soft, melodious voice, pleasing to the ear. From then on, whenever I heard her voice I felt surprised and anxious. It was always somehow unexpected and not like other voices. When I read the words of the poem:

> *Hark, listen: from the depths of the silent forest*
> *As if frightened and ashamed the song of the nightingale*
> *slowly steals . . .*

I heard her voice. I read this poem at least two years after her death, and suddenly her voice echoed in my ears and my heart leaped inside me. I didn't know whose voice it was, but I felt that it was a voice which was not of this world. Even when she was alive her voice had not matched the rest of her. Her name was Stella.

Stella was born in Liverpool and was the daughter of a wealthy Jewish family. She loved Zemach very much, and she used to keep the sketches and water colors he painted in his spare time and scattered everywhere in an engraved wooden box. He himself knew nothing of this collection until he went through her belongings after her death and came upon the box. I think it must have been love at first sight for Stella. When Zemach came back from England I was a boy of about twelve and it was only then that I realized how handsome he was. He was not very tall but broad-boned and sturdy, with chestnut hair and blue eyes piercing in their look and full of the joy of life. They had a gay, mischievous, and rakish glint in them as if hinting at some joke hidden behind the seriousness of all things. Stella's heart must have pounded when he appeared before her for the first time in the university corridors. She loved him even when she knew that he had married her for her family's money, and her heart may have told her this even before their marriage. She was exceedingly well behaved and reserved. Even when she was most excited she remained outwardly calm; only her musical voice would tremble like a little bell. I shall never forget her on the day I went with her to show her the main Post Office building. It was a few weeks after her arrival from England. She was scrupulous in observing the traffic regulations and would only cross the street where she was supposed to, at the traffic islands. All the way she held my hand as if I were a small child who might get run over, or some sort of deposit which she must return to its owner in full. On the way we went into a café to have something to drink. It was early in the afternoon and the service was slow and unwilling. Stella waited patiently until the waitress finally made up her mind to give us her attention. She ordered two cups of tea with milk and cakes. The moment the waitress heard the English words the sulky expression on her face vanished and she smiled sweetly at us.

On our way back from the Post Office we went to visit Zemach in his office. His office was in Mamilla Road next to the Government Land Administration Department. The office, which was on the second story, had two entrances and three rooms. On the stairs Stella let go of my hand and I broke away from her and ran up the steps and burst into the office from the side entrance straight into his room. Zemach was standing and embracing a full-fleshed woman who was pressed against the wall. She was wearing glittering white earrings and holding a burning cigarette between her fingers and she didn't let go of it even when Zemach kissed her.

Before Zemach could shake off the intoxication of his embraces I fled for my life. I ran down the steps as quickly as my legs could carry me, afraid that he would call after me. I met Stella coming up the stairs and ran past her into the street. When I reached the corner of St. Julien Street I stopped running and started feeling qualms. I remembered Stella and felt like a soldier who deserts the battle and leaves his wounded comrade to face the enemy alone. I felt I should stand by her and fight for her but I didn't know how to, or who the enemy was. I remained standing miserably on the street corner watching the passersby, Jewish government clerks with bald heads and glasses, and Arab government clerks with oiled hair glistening in the sunlight, and English government clerks with pipes and healthy-looking bodies. I looked at them and wondered if they too did in their offices what my uncle Zemach did in his. I looked at the women walking past and paired them off with the men. For some reason I imagined that only handsome men and beautiful women were capable of making love. It would be somehow against nature for a middle-aged clerk whose looks were nothing to write home about to suddenly clasp a flabby woman to his paunch and whisper loving words in her ear. Suddenly I knew that everyone—all the men and women passing in the street—was full of lust and lewd thoughts. Everyone— except Stella, for Stella loved Zemach. And therefore he should love her in return, because no other woman loved him so much. I felt a hand holding mine and I saw Stella. She was calm and serene as if nothing had happened, and she took care to cross the road at the traffic islands only. She bought a pair of sunglasses in a department store and put them on even before we left the shop. At first I thought of promising her never to tell anyone what I had seen, but I soon realized that it wasn't necessary. Stella was continually shocked by Zemach's behavior. She was shocked and she forgave him, but she never forgot. She accepted him as he was without trying to change him or to force herself on him. From that day forth she tried to avoid visiting him at his office, and when it was necessary for her to do so, she would telephone beforehand to tell him that she was coming.

Once she telephoned to tell him that she felt unwell. He promised to come home straight away, but he was so busy that he couldn't get away until six o'clock in the evening. When he got home he saw a violin lying on the table in the hall, and he knew that Lippa was already sitting at her bedside. Whenever anyone in the family was ill, Lippa was immediately summoned. Lippa was a bachelor and he always said that to marry a woman and bring children into the world was a responsibility so heavy that it terrified him. It wasn't that he was irresponsible; on the contrary, his sense of responsibility was too great. Stella lay in bed looking very pale and Lippa sat on a chair next to her bed leafing through a magazine. There were little bottles and packets of medicine standing on the bedside table. Zemach breathed a sigh of relief. He knew that Lippa had already done everything that was required. Lippa did everything that was required during all the six months of Stella's illness, the same six months which saw Zemach rise to his greatest social and economic heights. Zemach was full of suppressed anger at Stella for deciding to be ill precisely at this point in his life. Not only was he in the midst of consolidating and expanding his own private practice, but also he had been appointed legal adviser to the Government Land Administration Department at a full salary. He spent his days between his own office and the offices of the government department, and his nights in conferences. And now Stella's illness had come to upset his routine. When Lippa appeared on the scene to rescue him, Zemach wasn't surprised and didn't even find it necessary to thank him in his heart.

Stella had some sort of heart disease. Sometimes she felt quite well and got out of bed and walked about and did what healthy people do, and sometimes she felt ill and stayed in bed for days on end. When she was feeling well and Lippa was working in the evening, she would go out alone to the Café Tamar and sit there at one of the tables and order her usual tea with milk, and Lippa would play her favorite songs for her. The British soldiers and policemen thought that she was Lippa's mistress. Jewish girls kept away from the café on the whole and those who did enter it were usually semi-prostitutes. Even if the British habitués hadn't imagined her to be Lippa's mistress, they wouldn't have attempted to approach her. It was immediately obvious to them that she was a "lady." She would sit for hours until Lippa finished working and accompanied her home. Sometimes he would stop work at nine and take her to the cinema, and whenever there was a concert in Jerusalem Lippa would take the night off and dress himself up in the dark blue suit he had acquired in the days of his studies in America and tie a bow tie around his neck, and Stella would wrap herself in her furs and the two of them would take a taxi to the concert hall.

One day Zemach decided to come home early from work. That morning Stella had seemed in the best of health and had been very gay and Zemach had kissed her on the cheek before leaving for the office and promised her to be home not later than five o'clock. At four he left the office and started walking down Mamilla Road. When he reached the corner of St. Julien Street he turned right in the direction of Jaffa Road, and here, through the haze of his preoccupations, he saw a blond woman coming toward him and smiling. He didn't recognize her and thought she must be one of his clients. He responded to her smile of greeting with a polite nod and was about to continue on his way when she seized hold of his sleeve and cried, "Zemach! Don't you recognize me?" At the sound of her voice he remembered who she was. She had been a fellow student of his at Bezalel. A thin, long-legged girl from one of the country towns, Petach Tikva or Zichron Ya'akov, who dreamed of Paris. Without being particularly gifted, she had been a steady worker and a diligent student, and although she had been advised to take up commercial art, she had insisted on fine arts or nothing. Zemach gazed at her in amazement and admiration. "You've grown pretty," he said. "Lord, you've grown pretty."

More than ten years had passed since he had seen her last. She was his age, about thirty, and had developed into a statuesque woman with full limbs and amorous eyes.

"And you, Zemach, you've grown into a real man. Actually," she added with a smile, "you were always something special. I hear that you received a doctorate in England. Doctor Sharon!"

"And you? Are you still painting?"

For some reason she blushed. "Didn't you see in the newspaper?" she said, putting her head on one side with a half-serious, half-arch look, as if she were only pretending to be serious, or mocking her own seriousness. "There was a review of an exhibition of mine at the Artists' House."

He looked at her and wondered how to answer. There was a suppressed excitement in her which bubbled up and broke out in every movement, look, and smile. He wondered if she were married or not, if she had been living in Jerusalem all these years or if she had spent them wandering about the world.

"Come and let me show you some of my canvases. I live close by." He wanted to tell her that he was in a hurry to get home, but he found himself following her instead. She was living on the second floor of a big Arab house in Mamilla Road. She had a spacious well-lit room with a balcony overlooking the Moslem cemetery as well as a kitchen and a hall which served as another room. He saw with surprise mingled with admiration that her apartment was neat and tidy and devoid of the chaos usually associated with artists' studios. She seated him on a low oriental divan and hurried to the kitchen to prepare something to drink.

"Tea or coffee?" she called out from the kitchen.

He was infected by her excitement. While they drank he allowed her to show him one big canvas smeared with bright oil paints after the other. He expressed enthusiasm for what he saw. And then suddenly he went up to her, gripped her shoulder with one hand, removed the painting she was holding with the other, put it down on the table, and said, "Leave that now. Come and tell me what you've been doing with yourself all these years." She trembled and turned her face toward him and he pressed a kiss onto her lips.

When he left her and went out into the street there were stars in the sky and the street lamps were lit. As he walked his steps grew longer and longer until in the end he was running. He reached his house breathing heavily, with his heart pounding and his temples roaring. He ran inside and saw a violin lying on the table in the hall. Hoping that he had not come too late he burst into Stella's room. She had died in the early hours of the evening of a heart attack.

At Stella's funeral Zemach walked erect and angry. He looked straight in front of him with lips compressed as if he resented the presence of all the other mourners. One of them, Dr. Kronnenberg, walked next to him and from time to time patted his shoulder and mumbled in English, "Yes, my boy, that's the way things are, my son." And Zemach refused to look at him and strode ahead with an angry face. There were a lot of people he didn't recognize at the funeral. They must have been his business acquaintances and professional colleagues. Two women who were walking arm in arm never took their eyes off him and kept on whispering to one another. "I didn't know he was so handsome," said one. "He's not so handsome, but he's very masculine," said the other, "I hear she left him ten thousand." "Ten thousand?" her friend repeated in great astonishment, rolling a pair of painted eyes about in her head. "What do you say! They say he betrayed her right and left. Ah, ah. . ." She sighed and shook her head. The second took out a handkerchief and blew her nose loudly. I found myself walking next to Lippa, who seemed depressed and utterly exhausted. His back sagged and he suddenly looked to me like a weak old Jew. He grasped my hand and whispered, "She was a good girl. A good, quiet girl." He must surely have meant Stella and I couldn't understand why he called her a "girl." From time to time I heard suppressed sobs escaping from my mother's mouth. All the way her eyes flowed with tears and she would wipe them away with a handkerchief and her eyes would fill with tears again. There was a strange feeling in my heart. As if Stella too were amongst us following her own coffin to the grave. It wouldn't have surprised me to see her suddenly appear beside Zemach and whisper something in his ear in her melodious voice. I looked at Zemach and I couldn't make him out. He was opaque and strange. From the day he decided to become a lawyer he had turned into a different man, and with every passing year his strangeness increased. He was no longer the young Bezalel student, brave and happy and friendly. A hidden barrier stood between us and it had grown increasingly wider since his return from England. I think that he himself didn't realize how mocking and arrogant he was, for all his manners and his engaging smile. Stella in her own quiet and reserved way had been the link between him and us. She had wanted to feel part of the family. After her death we seldom saw Zemach, and when we did he looked harassed and preoccupied, overburdened with work and sparing of his time. In addition to his expanding private practice and his government post he began, to our surprise, to concern himself with communal affairs. To our surprise, I said, because we knew that not only had he never shown the faintest interest in serving the community himself, but also he had always detested the type of person who did so. Up to now Zemach had been, so to say, nonpolitical and even, in a certain sense, non-Zionist. Now all of a sudden he was revealed to us in a new light as a man who made speeches at public meetings, sat on various committees, and appeared before the authorities as a representative of the National Executive.

It began some six months after Stella's death. Zemach was by then a respected and well-known lawyer. He had taken possession of his wife's estate and benefited to the extent of almost seven thousand pounds. In those days this was a sum which placed its owner in the ranks of the rich, enough to ensure both his own future and that of his sons after him. He also remained in sole possession of the four-roomed house in Beth Hakerem. One night he was looking through Stella's things and he discovered the box in which she had kept whichever of his paintings and drawings had fallen into her hands. At the sight of this box gloom descended on Zemach. During Stella's lifetime it had never even once occurred to him that she might take an interest in his artistic gifts and that his drawings were dear to her. "Why didn't she say so?" he asked himself. "Why didn't she at least hint?" More than sorrow he felt anger at her for her silence and submissiveness.

She had never attempted to express her ideas or feelings and had wrapped herself about in silence. There was a meek, frightened look in her eyes. She would look at him some-times with the look of a little girl afraid of losing everything dear to her by a wrong word or deed. She had never even had the courage to show her love without reservations. Per-haps she was shy, perhaps she felt unworthy of the happiness that had fallen to her lot. Things had never even reached the stage of a quarrel between them. If he lashed out at her she immediately held her words back and looked at him like a supplicant begging for her life. How many times had he lost his temper with her? Once or twice, perhaps three times—even this had been denied her. She had been like an object to him, a piece of furniture. Zemach sat looking at the draw-ings one after the other. There were landscapes in charcoal and water colors, and also a few portraits. "She probably wanted me to paint her," said Zemach to himself with a bitter smile on his lips. This idea that Stella had wanted him to paint her portrait and never dared to ask would not let him be. She must have thought about it often and tried from time to time to ask him, had second thoughts at the last moment and put it off to another time. He began recalling all the times she had been about to start on this subject and then suddenly fallen silent. She had a habit of starting to talk about something that was bothering her and then suddenly changing her mind and stopping. The more he thought about it the more strongly the idea took hold of him that until her dying day Stella had dreamed that one day he would come home from work and say to her, "You know, Stella, a funny idea has come into my head. I want to paint a big portrait and call it 'Stella.' You'll sit like that, in the armchair, turn-ing a little to the right, to face the light from the window . . ." Perhaps this was what she had thought on the last day of her life when he had promised her to come home early from work. Zemach was overcome with horror. He quickly replaced the pictures in the box, banged it shut, and ran out of the room. He went into the kitchen to put the kettle on to boil and all the time he asked himself how the idea of painting her had never once occurred to him. Not even of making a little pencil sketch. Without even thinking about it, he had made hundreds of drawings of all sorts of people, but he had never seen any necessity for putting her image down on paper. Suddenly it came into his head that if he had drawn her face once, even if it were only on the back of the electricity bill, Stella wouldn't have died. Zemach fumbled in his pocket and pulled out a fountain pen, tore a piece of paper out of a small black notebook lying on a shelf, and tried to sketch a few lines. In great fear he realized that he couldn't remember what she looked like. He had even forgotten how she wore her hair. Only her soft, musical voice came back to his ears like the distant murmur of waves. A strange, incomprehensible, continuous murmur without beginning or end. He closed his eyes and tried to recall her features. Only the sound of her voice emerged from the darkness. "Stella," he said suddenly, "what's the time?" He hoped to hear a reply from the murmur of sound. He thought that the sound of her voice speaking clearly would bring her image before him. His cry died away in the night. He called again "Stella!" this time in a loud voice that reverberated in the empty house.

"First sign of old age," said Zemach to himself. "I'm beginning to talk to myself." He tried to smile and couldn't manage it. "The neighbors will think I've gone out of my mind. Doctor Sharon stands in his kitchen in the middle of the night and calls out loud for his dead wife."

Next morning Zemach rose scowling and bad-tempered.

Before going to work he had another look at the box and came to the conclusion that he must do something about it. He took out the drawings and looked at them and saw that Stella had arranged them according to their dates: each drawing with its date neatly written on the back of the page. She had kept even little pieces of crumpled paper. "It doesn't mean a thing," said Zemach to himself. "It proves nothing but the pedantry of a woman. Of an Englishwoman. All these papers will have to be burned." He decided to burn the whole collection on his return from work.

This wise decision was forgotten the moment he reached his office. As soon as he crossed the threshold of his room he discovered a big spider hanging from a thin thread in the left corner of the ceiling. Its web had spread all over the entire corner. "Rachel," he called to the typist in a voice of thunder. "What's this?" He pointed to the spider and kept staring fixedly at it. The typist looked at Zemach in amazement. She thought that there was something the matter with his hand.

"Doctor Sharon," she asked tremulously, "what's the matter?"

"Nothing's the matter with me," shouted Zemach, and felt immediately that his anger was unjustified without being able to control himself. "Look at that spider! What's that bloody spider doing in the office? Why don't you see that the old Arab does her work properly? I might easily have found it in my tea! I might find cockroaches in my desk!"

The affair of the spider might have become the topic of the day in the office if something even stranger had not followed close on its heels. Zemach visited the Land Administration offices and left a file on the desk of a high-ranking Arab official. As soon as he closed the door he heard the official call a messenger boy and say to him in Arabic, "Run after the Jew and give him this file." The boy came out of the office and presented the file to Zemach with a polite smile. Before he knew what he was doing Zemach threw the file in the terrified lad's face and yelled at the top of his voice, "Tell the bloody Arab I've got a name." The shout ran through the offices on both sides of the corridor like a thunder clap. Doors were thrown open and the heads of bored clerks eager for a scandal peeped out of them. The Arab emerged from his room with a very pale face. A son of the well-known Nashashibe family, he had risen swiftly, despite his youth, to a very high post in the government bureaucracy. Zemach fixed him with a pair of wrathful eyes and saw an excess of self-confidence in his lowered chin. Suddenly it became clear to him that he had always felt a deep hatred for this chin. "This chin," said Zemach to himself, "embodies the rooted-ness of the Arabs, their profound and all-embracing arrogance, and their hatred and contempt for the Jews." On the chin was a mole, and Zemach looked at it and was overcome by a deep desire to flatten it with a punch, when Nashashibe suddenly bent down and picked up the file and handed it to him. "Doctor Sharon," he said in English, "I beg your pardon, sir." And he went back into his office slamming the door behind him. Zemach stood rooted to the spot holding the file, and the doors lining the corridor started closing one after the other. "I've never heard Doctor Sharon shout before," said one of the clerks to her friend. "I suppose he must still be upset by the death of his wife." These words reached Zemach's ears but failed to penetrate his mind. He was still enflamed by the mole on the Arab's chin. He turned toward the stairs with feelings of animosity toward Nashashibe in particular and the Arabs in general still burning in his breast. What angered him most was the impertinence of the Arabs. The Jews, so they thought, would forgive them everything out of rabbit-hearted righteousness. His mind seethed with recollections of affronts and sneers he had received at the hands of various Arab officials and passed over in silence. Once he had bumped into a little Arab messenger boy on the stairs, a cheeky little bastard of about seventeen, who instead of stepping back and giving Zemach the right of way, had remained standing on the whole width of the step, forcing Zemach to stand aside and let him pass. And he also remembered how once during the afternoon break a group of officials, Jews and Arabs, had started talking about the Turkish sultan and the Ottoman regime on the eve of the First World War, and old Anton, a Christian Arab from Bethlehem, had remarked that the Jews had tried to buy Abdul Hamid with money, and that it was they who had betrayed to Jamal Pasha the twenty Arab dignitaries who were hanged at the Jaffa Gate and Damascus. The Jews wanted to buy power and a land with money, but the Arabs shed their blood in the battle for the conquest of the land under the hero Hussein the Hashemite, the Sheriff of Mecca, and his noble sons, as the Englishman "Ourouns" had written. He meant of course Lawrence, and Zemach burst out laughing at his ridiculous mistake. Neither Zemach nor any of the other officials present had made any attempt to defend the truth which had been falsified. Then he laughed but now the memory aroused him to fury. For a moment he considered going back to the office and teaching the Arab a lesson. "He deserves to be flogged," said Zemach to himself and went furiously on his way. "If I had any self-respect . . ." But instead of going back to the office he went into a café and shouted at the waiter in English, "A cup of black coffee please, and hurry up about it. I haven't got any time to waste." The alarmed waiter hurried off to comply with his order and Zemach struck a match and scowlingly lit his pipe which had gone out. The whole of that day he didn't return to his office and wandered aimlessly about the streets. Once he found himself ascending the stairs to the artist's apartment in Mamilla Road, but when he realized where he was, he was overcome with fear and rushed off again.

In the evening he returned home with a heavy heart. He opened all the shutters and doors and sat by the window. His anger began to subside and in its place came feelings of regret. The whole affair seemed pointless and even ridiculous, only he couldn't laugh. In his mind's eye he saw how he had thrown the file in the messenger boy's face and how a tremendous shout had escaped his mouth, and how all the clerks had watched him to see what he would do next, and all for nothing. In the end, after all, the official had begged his pardon in public, apologizing in an absolutely unambiguous manner.

By nature Zemach was a man of quick decisions. His inability to free himself of misgivings about his behavior in the Land Administration Department offices therefore caused him great anguish of mind. After much hesitation he sat down at midnight to write a letter of resignation to the Director of the Land Administration Department. After writing it he felt a sense of relief. He explained his resignation by "reasons of health." "It's true," said Zemach to himself, "I'm not in good health. It's clear as day. I'm feverish, I've got a temperature . . ." A cold wind blew in from all the open windows and doors and Zemach shivered. He wrapped himself up in a woolen blanket and closed everything up again, made himself a cup of coffee and went to bed.

For a long time he couldn't fall asleep. Old memories of his boyhood and childhood began to take hold of him. It would never have occurred to him that a person could remember events from the distant past in such clear detail. His memories brought him neither satisfaction nor amusement.

He took them seriously and they filled him with sorrow and shame.

He remembered how he had once, about fifteen years ago, slandered a poor girl who was, if anything, on friendly terms with him. Simply slandered her for no reason at all. He said that he had seen her kissing a British officer in a doorway, and the rumor took wing and spread rapidly with various embellishments which it gathered on its way. When it reached her she burst into tears in the art-school courtyard. She put her face in her hands and her shoulders shook. A group of boys and girls collected around her. One of them taunted her—if it was a lie, why was she crying? Everyone laughed loudly. Zemach too stood there roaring with laughter, but now he was eaten up with remorse. What had happened to that girl? A strange idea came into his head. He must find her and ask her forgiveness. He didn't even remember her surname. He remembered clearly what she was wearing—a "tartan" skirt with big checks and pleats going all the way around her waist. She was good at making woodcuts. When she hid her face in her hands and cried, Zemach saw the cuts and scratches on her fingers from the stylus, and these now rose up clearly before his eyes and filled them with tears of pity. She had forgiven him on the same day and the whole incident had been forgotten. He lay thinking about her and wondered why she had forgiven him. She should have prosecuted him . . . "If only she had prosecuted me," he said to himself. "She ought to have prosecuted me, and then things would have looked altogether different . . ." All this time he knew that the incident was insignificant and his thoughts absurd, and still he couldn't suppress the clamorous feelings which the memory awoke in him. He even allowed himself to hope that the next day when he came to work he would find a summons from the court on his desk for insulting Miss. . . (on no account could he remember her name). He would have answered the summons eagerly. He would have put on his best clothes and appeared in the court and found it crowded with people. Everyone would be there—all his fellow students from Bezalel, and the teachers too, and the principal himself, and even the old janitor with the mustache like His Majesty the Emperor Franz Josef's, and at the last moment Lippa too would push his way through the crowd with his violin in his hand. And she would stand up in her place and accuse him of libel, and she would be wearing the same checked skirt and holding a stylus and a piece of wood in her hand. She would demand ten thousand pounds in damages, and he would jump up and say: "Madam, seven thousand pounds you will receive at once, and the other three thousand in promissory notes to be redeemed within a month . . ." Before he could finish speaking, Lippa would jump up and rush forward to the judge's rostrum, seize his hammer and bring it down twice with a bang, and there would be silence in the court. He would push the papers and the inkwell to one side, climb up onto the rostrum, take his violin out of its case, and begin to play Gershwin's "Rhapsody in Blue" . . . Zemach was wild with anticipation. He felt a great need to find her that same night, but how? Maybe he should go to Bezalel and search through the old files from fifteen years back? Since then she had probably changed her address ten times over. She had changed her name too, and he didn't remember her name. The artist from Mamilla Road came into his mind; without a doubt she remembered the incident. Perhaps they were still friends.

In the morning Zemach woke feeling limp and exhausted and made up his mind to go to see a doctor. When he had finished shaving he saw to his satisfaction that his face was as rosy and shining as ever and showed no trace of his sleeplessness, but he decided nevertheless to order a taxi to take him to town—he was afraid of the bus and the unavoidable meetings with acquaintances traveling to work. Before leaving the bathroom he heard the maid coming into the house on tiptoe. She was a quarter of an hour late and she made straight for the kitchen.

"You're late again," Zemach yelled at her, and the sound of his voice filled the house. "Hurry up and get breakfast ready." When she put his breakfast before him he took a sip of the coffee and pushed the tray away from him in disgust. In the past even when he had found it necessary to reprimand her he had done so gently and politely, and this was the first time that he had ever shouted at her. He noticed that her hands were trembling, and he wanted to conciliate her, but instead of conciliatory words he found himself raising his voice again.

"Phone for a taxi." She started nervously paging through the telephone directory, but before she could find the number Zemach took the book out of her hands and found it himself, and she ran away and hid in the kitchen until the taxi came. In the taxi he gave himself over to reflections on his condition. It was clear to him that he had been suffering recently from hypersensitivity. At night this sensitivity found expression in immeasurable sadness and in the daytime it made him a prey to attacks of uncontrollable rage. He fortified himself with the thought that his sensitivity was temporary and that with a little patience he would be able to overcome it. Firmly resolved to be ruled by his head rather than his heart, he entered his offices and said good morning to his typist and his articled clerk. This budding lawyer was a young man who admired Zemach greatly and tried to imitate him in everything: his speech, his dress, his manners, and even the way he lit his pipe. He was also a great flatterer and sycophant by nature. He hurried forward to take Zemach's hat.

"Please give this to the Director of the Land Administration

Department in person," said Zemach, removing the letter of resignation he had written at midnight from the inside pocket of his coat. For some reason he didn't want to give it to the typist to type.

Zemach glanced at the three women sitting in the waiting room and felt a sudden fear. He went into his room like a soldier burdened with his kit marching to the front with dread in his heart. The first woman's business was matrimonial. She had come to claim alimony from her husband. Zemach knew this even before she opened her mouth. She came in with mincing little steps and lips pursed in self-importance. She closed the door carefully behind her and looked left and right as if to make sure that none of her husband's agents was lurking in the corners. Before sitting down she examined the chair, and after satisfying herself that it was quite steady and that there were no crumbs on it, she lifted her skirt a little and sat down on its edge. She opened with a few general remarks suitable to the learned legal company in which she found herself, touching on the high cost of living and the price of Tnuva butter in comparison to imported Australian butter and local Arab butter. At the beginning she spoke quietly and even smiled, but as the conversation proceeded and she came closer to the point of her visit the smile vanished from her lips and she embarked on a violent tirade against the hardheartedness and cruelty of her husband. She told hair-raising tales of his ill-treatment of the children, burst into tears several times, blew her nose, and in the end declared that she could bear it no longer and demanded that he be locked up for three years at least.

"Three years . . . three years . . . how terrible!" said Zemach to himself without quite knowing what was so terrible, or what the meaning of three years was. He fell into a profound depression which remained with him for the rest of the day. He remembered his decision to see a doctor, but he didn't know to whom to go. He hardly ever needed a doctor: he had always enjoyed remarkably good health and doctors to him were mysterious, ill-boding beings. In the afternoon he finally went to see a doctor who was an acquaintance of his. He hinted, among other things, at his hypersensitivity and depression. After all the routine tests had shown him to be perfectly healthy, the doctor came to the conclusion that Zemach's nervous tension was due to overwork and told him to take a holiday and "stop worrying."

When Zemach left the doctor it was evening and the storm in his breast had not abated. He mingled with the passersby in the street and he felt very lonely. It seemed to him that for many years now he had not come into contact with people who were close to his heart. On the contrary; he tried as hard as he could to avoid his friends and most of the people with whom he had daily dealings aroused no feelings whatsoever in him. He felt a great need to see someone to whom he could speak frankly, to whom he could tell one or two little things in the certainty of finding attention and sympathy. For example, the girl in the "tartan" skirt. Perhaps Lippa still remembered her name. Lippa had a great talent for remembering small details. Not for nothing had he studied statistics. He remembered hundreds of numbers—telephone numbers and street numbers and the populations of small towns in America. Zemach remembered that he had to talk to Lippa. For a long time now he had had to talk to Lippa about an important matter, a very important matter concerning large sums of money. An important and urgent matter which would suffer no delay; a matter, in effect, of life and death.

Without feeling any surprise at himself, Zemach went into the Café Tamar, whose very name had once caused him agonies of shame. Lippa wasn't there. Zemach sat down by the bar and in the mirror opposite he saw old Benton sitting in a corner with a tankard of beer in front of him. Benton had once been a judge, later a lecturer at the Law School, and was now retired. He was an old Englishman of about seventy-five who had come to the country for obscure religious reasons. An intelligent man with a shrewd, subtle sense of humor, who was at the same time naïve and full of faith, he seemed somehow typical of a certain kind of Englishman. Since his return from England Zemach had hardly seen him. When he was a student at the law school he had conversed with him frequently, and he had even invited him to the farewell party he gave before leaving the country. Benton, who spent every evening at the Tamar, knew Lippa well. Zemach stood up and went across to the old man.

"Hello, Benton," he said in a hearty voice. He tried to appear gay and nonchalant.

"Perhaps you know what's happened to my brother Phillip to prevent him from showing up here tonight?"

Benton lifted his head slowly in the way of old men suddenly disturbed in their ruminations and finding it difficult to adjust themselves to the voice of the speaker. "Why it's you, Doctor Sharon. Please sit down. Well, well, I'm glad to see you. I'm very sorry I wasn't able to come to Stella's funeral. I seem to remember sending you a letter. Walking is difficult for me nowadays. Such is life—time is the great healer, but at the same time it brings you closer to the grave. Well, let's leave time to take care of itself, and I'll tell you a funny thing. This week I received a letter from my sister in Kent and she tells me that two weeks ago on Sunday evening the ghost appeared again. You know, nearly fifty years ago, a ghost came to settle in our house in Kent. He appears at least once every six months on Sunday evening. They say he's the ghost of poor Richard who killed himself for a girl." The old man laughed hoarsely and took a sip of beer from the tankard standing in front of him. Zemach ordered cognac, finished it in one gulp, and ordered another.

"Did you yourself ever see the ghost?"

The old man looked at him sharply, as if wondering what lay behind the question, and then said slowly, "Once, thirty years ago, I heard him. He kicked up a bit of a racket in the cellar opening cupboards and moving chairs, knocked over a jar of honey, and then disappeared into the garden."

"Are you sure it was Richard's ghost?" asked Zemach with great interest. His face was red from the second cognac and he was about to gulp down a third. Zemach was not in the habit of drinking hard liquor and on the few occasions when he did so he lost his head easily.

"I can't say for sure whether it was or not. You know, it's a matter of faith. Believers believe, and nonbelievers explain unusual phenomena by way of common sense and natural laws. It's quite possible that it was only a cat which got into the cellar. In those days I had a tendency to go into supernatural phenomena, and so I believed that I had indeed heard Richard's footsteps. This tendency came on me after I suffered a severe defeat in a competition for the heart of a beauty who preferred my rival (not the better man in this case) to me. In any case, it's a matter of tradition and there's no harm in it. It adds interest to life."

"You know," said Zemach excitedly, leaning toward the old man, "you British are lucky people. You've got a tradition. Now I, for example, am a man with no tradition. This may seem strange to you, but it's the truth. I, whose ancestors were singing psalms in the Temple when your ancestors were still swineherds in Kent, I who was born in the holy city to parents devoted to maintaining a tradition over three thousand years old, I am a man with no tradition. Our tradition has buried itself in prayer books and religion, and no new one has come to take its place."

The old man looked at Zemach in some concern. Zemach was holding his sixth cognac in his hand and his eyes were bloodshot. "I think you're exaggerating," he said, referring to the number of glasses on the table, but Zemach paid no attention to him and went on with his confession.

"I'll tell you a secret that you probably know already. A secret known to everybody, but especially to my brother Phillip who for some reason is taking his time in getting here tonight. Like everybody else who suddenly finds himself without a tradition, I acquired a tradition of my own." He poured the sixth cognac down his throat and wiped his mouth on his sleeve, something he would never have done if he had not been drunk. "An ancient tradition which came into the world the moment people's eyes were opened to the knowledge of good and evil. This tradition, my learned friend, is the tradition of those who worship the golden calf."

Benton looked vaguely in front of him and said, "That's it. We all of us worship the golden calf in one way or another, only sometimes it changes its face to such an extent that it becomes unrecognizable."

"That's not so!" shouted Zemach. "Phillip never did it, nor did Nechemia. I was the only one of all my brothers who did it, and I'll go on doing it. In my case it's a matter of deliberate choice. The deliberate cult of the golden calf. Have you ever heard of a cult, a religion, originating in cold, hard calculation and not in emotional excitement? It's the most widespread religion in the world, far ahead of all the others—the religion of getting rich."

"There are riches and riches," said Benton. "Some people spend their lives looking for Eldorado, and some spend their lives looking for Utopia." "I don't want Utopia," shouted Zemach and pounded on the table. "I want a good life in this world. For three years I went hungry; during the First World War when this country was under Turkish rule, I was a child and I went hungry. Hundreds of children went wandering about the streets with their bellies swollen with hunger until they died. Wisdom didn't help the wise, and courage didn't help the brave, but money helped the rich. They always know how to get what they need. It's what they've all got in common—all the mean and contemptible of this world, and I'm one of them. Yes, I count myself as one of them." Zemach beat his breast violently and drunkenly and Benton regarded him anxiously. "The worms, the vermin, all the fools who've never heard of Thomas More and haven't the faintest idea what makes engines work. They're fools as long as their interests aren't affected, but the minute they themselves are dragged into the current you suddenly discover that they know very well how to swim ashore. They've got a talent for survival that pulls them through all the vicissitudes of life."

"Can the Ethiopian change his skin or the leopard his spots?" suddenly said Lippa, who had been standing for some minutes next to the table and listening with a smile to Zemach's lecture. "The vermin you've been making speeches about always remain vermin. The trouble starts when they try to be lions." Zemach and Benton both turned to face Lippa at once.

"Don't try to turn the Tamar into a philosophical debating society," said Lippa to Zemach without a hint of reproach. "Now that you've finally decided to come here—a decision, by the way, which I, for one, regard as an important turning point in your life—you must abide by the rules of the house and do as the Romans do by drinking wine and speaking of women and art—two subjects which in a certain sense are both about the same thing."

"The lad's had more than enough to drink already," said

Benton, indicating the empty glasses and Zemach who could hardly sit on his chair. "Sit down and I'll tell you something interesting. I've had a letter from my sister in Kent who tells me that two weeks ago on Sunday evening Richard's ghost appeared again."

Lippa burst into loud and hearty laughter. "Really," he said, "I shall have to pack my bags and go and visit your sister as soon as I possibly can. All my life I've longed to see a ghost. I wouldn't be surprised if Richard put on a special performance in my honor. By the way," he said with a sly smile and a wink, "what's your sister like?"

"She got rid of her first husband without any trouble. He was as brave and tough as they come, but that didn't stop her from enslaving him from the first day of their married life. She'll be able to keep you for the rest of your life. She's older than you by twenty years, but I warn you in advance not to count on that. She's exactly like her Aunt Peggy, and Peggy outlived her second husband by fifteen years and died when she was a hundred and one years old."

Zemach sat leaning over the table and supporting his bowed head on his hands. He was very red and looked as if he felt nauseous.

"It's time I was going," said Lippa and stood up. He was about to start playing the violin, but Zemach suddenly woke up and took hold of his hand.

"Don't go, Lippa," he said. "I'm saying it for your own good. Don't go. If you must see ghosts then come to me and don't go to Kent, and don't dream of marrying that old Englishwoman. She's quite capable of dying before you." Lippa and Benton looked at Zemach and saw to their amazement that his eyes were full of tears. It wasn't clear to them whether they were drunken tears or not. Lippa sat down again and waited anxiously to hear what his brother would say.

"Every night there's a ghost in the bedroom. You know

whose ghost it is? Stella's ghost! She comes to reproach me for not painting her when she was alive."

"I think you'd better go home to sleep," said Lippa with concern.

"To sleep!" exclaimed Zemach angrily. "What do you mean to sleep? She doesn't let me sleep." He suddenly reached for Benton's tankard of beer which was still half full and started drinking avidly, holding it with both hands. He put it down only when he had drained it to the dregs. "Lippa," he cried when his brother rose to go, and seized hold of his lapel. "Has it ever occurred to you that I'm a coward? Benton," he turned to the old man and gripped his shoulder, either in a demonstration of affection or because he needed the support, and thus he stood and spoke with one hand clinging to Lippa's lapel and the other to Benton's shoulder. "My brother Lippa will bear witness that I've always been a brave man. I was braver than your old sister's husband. I was braver than all my friends. Lippa, tell him the truth! Tell him how I repulsed an attack of Arab rioters when I was only a boy of seventeen! But I can't fight ghosts. Benton, my friend, can a man fight against a ghost?" Zemach let go of Lippa's jacket and hung onto the old man with both his hands. "Tell me, isn't your sister afraid of Richard's ghost?"

The old man sat down in his chair. "Sit down, my boy," he said to Zemach. "You'll find it easier to talk sitting down."

Zemach obediently sat down. "But why should she be afraid of Richard?" he continued. "She's not to blame for his death. No one's to blame for his death. He killed himself because it was in his nature to kill himself, not because some girl didn't return his love. Hundreds of people suffer disappointments in love and they don't kill themselves. No one is to blame for Stella's death. Do you hear, Lippa"—he suddenly turned with a great cry to his brother who was sitting stunned on the edge of his chair—"no one is to blame for Stella's death. She died of a heart attack. She always had a weak heart, organically weak. You hear, she had an organic defect in her constitution. I spoke to Dr. Kronnenberg to get it clear. I asked him if there was anything in all these theories about heart diseases being influenced by the mental state of the patient. He said again and again that in Stella's case it was a constitutional defect, and that sooner or later she would have died of it. He showed me the X rays and explained the whole thing to me. And as for our constitution," he suddenly turned to Benton again, "for some time now I've been thinking of writing an article on the need to do away with the death penalty. You'll help me to investigate a few precedents from the seventeenth century. I imagine the Royal Society *Quarterly* will agree to print it, there's no reason why they shouldn't. It's a very important issue, very important. You know, it's more important for those who remain alive. There's always a need to get one or two things clear, and when the person's dead, then you can't get them cleared up any more, and then the ghost of the dead person appears. But the constitution doesn't recognize the validity of dead people's evidence. They aren't eligible to bear witness." Zemach stopped speaking and closed his eyes.

"I won't be able to play tonight," Lippa said to Benton. "I'll go and tell the boss. I must take Zemach home." He got up and went into a side room. Zemach opened his eyes and looked for his brother.

"Don't imagine that I'm afraid for my life, that I'm afraid of death," he continued, as if he were defending himself against an unjust accusation. "I'm afraid of ghosts. I'm afraid of what lies beyond life and death. At night I get frightened of the very existence of the intangible and ungraspable. If I knew that the ghost wanted my death I wouldn't be afraid of it, believe me. But the ghost doesn't want my death, it wants my life. It wants something I can't do and won't be able to do. Only a man of superhuman courage can fight a ghost. You know, Benton, my friend, I want to write an article about this. An article about the heroes of the spirit. You know who I would put at the head of these heroes? I'd put Poe. Edgar Allan Poe dared to dream dreams that no mortal dared to dream before. There's no greater heroism than that." Zemach pounded the table with his fist and was about to continue speaking, but at that moment Lippa appeared and put his hand under his brother's elbow.

"Get up, Zemach, let's go."

"Yes, let's go together," said Zemach, "and let's take Benton with us, too."

The three of them got up and left, Zemach leaning on Lippa's arm and Benton shuffling along behind them. In the taxi Zemach leaned his head against the back of his seat and his face was bathed in sweat. "Lippa," he cried suddenly, "you know what she wanted? A little thing which was never granted her in her lifetime. What do you think, wouldn't there be something cynical about it if I painted her now, when she's already dead? Would it be the hypocritical self-righteousness of a coward?"

All night Zemach's teeth chattered and he shivered feverishly. In the morning Lippa called the doctor, who diagnosed pneumonia. "It's a funny thing," said the doctor. "Only two days ago he came to see me and I couldn't find anything wrong with him. He complained of depression. He must have already been suffering from a cold which developed very rapidly during yesterday; he must be taken to the hospital."

Zemach refused pointblank to go to the hospital. Lippa gave in to him and hired a private nurse, and the doctor

called twice a day. For three weeks Zemach lay with a high
temperature and twice he passed through severe crises when
his life seemed to hang in the balance, although the doctor,
who put his faith in Zemach's strength and vitality, was sure
that he would recover. For days at a stretch he suffered
from hallucinations and muttered incessantly in his fever.
His excitement was most pronounced when Lippa came to
relieve the nurse. Sometimes he imagined that he was standing in the dock accused of murdering Stella, and then he
would call on Dr. Kronnenberg to appear as a witness for the
defense. Once he seized Lippa's hand, sat up in bed, and
said: "Lippa, why don't you tell His Honor that on the evening of Stella's death I wasn't at home at all? I was with the
lady from Mamilla Road. She's an old friend of mine from
years ago. Yes, many years ago . . ." At midnight his temperature rose and he wept like a child. "I can't remember her
name," he said. "Whose name?" asked Lippa. "The name of
the girl in the tartan skirt. You must have known her. She
was good at making woodcuts." Just before dawn he fell
asleep.

The next day his temperature dropped a little. He was
very weak and he experienced great difficulty in speaking,
but it seemed as if the storm in his soul had abated. In the
early afternoon he suddenly asked the nurse to send for
Lippa as quickly as she could. He didn't know that Lippa
was sleeping in the next room after watching over him all
night. The nurse was unwilling to wake him and after an
hour had passed Zemach became very angry and demanded
that she call him at once. After much hesitation she decided
at last to wake him. When he came into the room Zemach
asked the nurse to leave them alone. She went out and closed
the door behind her and Lippa sat down by his bed. Zemach
lifted himself up on his elbows and spoke in a whisper, but

clearly. "There's six thousand nine hundred pounds in my account at Barclay's Bank, the money that Stella left me. Even if I remain alive I won't be able to use that money. If I had known Stella and the way she thought perhaps I would know what to do with it."

Lippa stopped him. "Stella loved you. She wanted you to have the money to do as you pleased with."

"I want to transfer the whole sum to England in Stella's mother's name," continued Zemach without taking any notice of Lippa's interruption. "They were very attached to each other. I had the impression that Stella missed her very much. Write her a letter and explain all this to her. She'll try to do something with the money in honor of Stella's memory, or give it to some synagogue in Liverpool. Hint that I think it would be best to give it to some children's home over here, but don't insist on it—the money's hers. Go straight to my office and tell the articled clerk to go to the bank and bring all the documents necessary for the transfer and I'll sign them. He knows what to do."

Lippa left for the office and Zemach immediately fell into a deep sleep. There was no rise in his temperature during the night and in the morning it dropped still lower. He had pulled through the second crisis. A week later he could already get out of bed. Old Benton, despite his feebleness, came to visit him and found him sitting on the verandah and watching the white clouds sailing past in the sky. They sat side by side for a long time without talking. At last Zemach said, "You know what I'm thinking about? I'm thinking about myself and Stella. Once I thought I married her for her money, and perhaps that was true when I married her. Maybe I would even have gone on thinking so if she were still alive, but because she's dead I've come to realize that it wasn't so. She was one of the silent souls who weave their lives in secret, whereas I've always needed to display my wonder to the world. You see those light clouds in the sky? If Stella were sitting here and watching them, she would look at them with her big wondering eyes and drown their beauty inside her and keep quiet, but me—I feel immediately that I want to paint them, for my own sake and the sake of others." He fell silent, and then added, "I should have painted her portrait."

"Why don't you start painting again?" asked Benton.

Zemach moved in his chair and a faint blush appeared on his pale cheeks. "I myself," he said with a shamefaced smile, "wonder why. Perhaps I haven't got the necessary courage; perhaps I'm a coward. I avoid going to exhibitions and whenever I see a good painting it literally hurts me. When I was at Bezalel I used to feel depressed and elated by turns. Sometimes I felt there were great powers latent in me and I was going to be a genius, and sometimes I felt I had absolutely nothing in me and the most I could hope for was to be a miserable imitator of the great. I was afraid most of all of wasting my life trying to be an artist only to realize my mistake when I was an old man. It's a cruel game and only the lucky, chosen few can hope to win it; a few more die before winning, and the vast majority lose altogether. I was always impatient and eager for quick prizes, and when they didn't materialize I gave up in despair. As far as I know the poet hasn't yet been born to sing the anonymous thousands in basements and attics, in Jerusalem and Paris and New York, who seek and don't find, and don't give up, and die one after the other with their paintbrushes in their hands, without having tasted the fruits of life in this world and without gaining immortality either."

Zemach recovered from his illness with surprising speed. Within a month he was quite fit again, and back to his former weight, but not at his former occupations. He lost all interest

in communal affairs and did not return to his post in the civil
service. He didn't spend much time in his own office either.
He made his clerk a partner in the business and the latter
quickly succeeded in taking control of the whole office. Zemach devoted some time to writing a long essay on the need for
abolishing capital punishment, but his enthusiasm waned during the examination of sources and he never reached the final
stages of composition. He had no regrets though. He often
came to visit us at home, and spent a lot of time talking to my
mother about all kinds of little things, such as what she was
making for lunch, and what sort of dress she intended sewing
for my little sister. On several occasions he helped her with
the shopping and once he even put on an apron and helped
her peel potatoes.

Those were my last days at school. When I came home on
the last day with my graduation certificate in my hand and a
strange feeling of satisfaction mingled with disappointment
in my heart, I found Zemach sitting at the table talking to my
mother. He was wearing a checked tweed jacket with a slit
behind it in the English style and was overflowing with vitality as usual. I was always a little scared of Zemach. I imagined that he penetrated to the very depths of my being with
his alert, piercing look and discovered things I had no cause
to be proud of hidden there.

"The boy's getting more like me every day," said Zemach
triumphantly to my mother. Mother looked at me, shook her
head, and said, "Yes, yes, there is a certain resemblance."
From the tone of her voice it was clear that she was not overjoyed by the likeness. "Listen," he said turning to me, "why
don't you come and spend your long vacation with me, and if
you're a good boy we'll go for a trip around the country." I
looked at him and saw a mischievous glint in his eye, and
made up my mind on the spot to go with him. We went into

a shop which sold writing materials and Zemach bought rough drawing paper, charcoal pencils, and two boxes of water colors. We walked about the street for a whole hour until we reached the empty space between King George Street and Nachlat Shivah. Municipal laborers were busy preparing the ground for a park. They were digging trenches around the ancient olive trees with their twisted bodies and clearing stones away for flower beds. In the middle of the area wooden benches had already been placed and mothers were playing with their children under the trees.

We sat down on a rock and Zemach gave me paper and charcoal and started teaching me to draw. I drew the Arab house standing alone among the rocks and the olive trees. In its time it had been used as a prison for women and heavy iron bars still surrounded all its windows.

"Don't draw a small house in the corner of the page," he said. "Draw the house on the whole page." He took the paper and slashed across it ruthlessly with heavy black lines. He drew and went on speaking at the same time. "You must draw the house the way you see it, not the way you think a house should look. You see," he said, pointing to the corner of the building, "those two windows are smaller than the others and they don't look like windows at all, but like two black blocks." He gave me a new page and I started to draw according to his instructions.

"Don't be afraid of the charcoal," he said. "Hold it firmly in your fingers and get the feel of it." At first his instructions weighed heavily on me, but gradually I began to understand what he was getting at, and I became absorbed in my drawing. I felt a shudder of joy at my mastery of the piece of charcoal, which began to draw lines according to my bidding. I drew the arched entrance with the big stones dovetailing into each other. Zemach glanced happily at my drawing and cried,

"Good, good! You're not exaggerating and that's the main thing."

While I was drawing I sensed that someone was standing behind me and watching me. I turned around and saw an attractive woman wearing a brightly colored scarf on her head, with slightly slanting eyes and a pair of rosy cheeks. She was standing and smiling. Perhaps she wasn't really smiling, but the shape of her eyes and her mouth gave her a smiling look. I tried to continue, but I was too embarrassed. I could hardly draw in Zemach's presence, let alone that of a strange woman. Zemach was so absorbed in his own drawing that he wouldn't have taken any notice if a bomb had gone off close by.

"Mummy, Mummy," cried a little girl and ran up to the woman. Other children began leaving the benches and trees and running up to see the show. The little girl put her hand into her mother's and pointed to us with the other. "What are they doing, Mummy?" she asked. I was blushing all over and wanted to get up and run away. "They're drawing the house over there," said the mother. Her voice was like Stella's, only stronger. Zemach lifted his head and his face paled. The paper fell off his lap. I had never seen him so agitated.

The woman looked at him for some moments and then clapped her hands and cried joyfully, "Zemach, it's you. Good Lord, it's Zemach." Zemach took a handkerchief out of his pocket and wiped away the beads of sweat which had broken out at the roots of his hair and on his forehead. "Esther," he said. "Your name's Esther, isn't it? And what was your surname—don't tell me, let me remember—Edelman. Esther Edelman."

"Don't tell me becoming an important man has made you forget my name," she said, threatening him with an upraised finger as if he were a naughty child.

Zemach got up in great excitement, grasped her shoulder,

and said in a trembling voice, "I swear to you, Esther, during the past months I've thought of you very often, only I couldn't remember your name. Strange, very strange. My wife's name was Stella, and I suppose that if she'd translated it into Hebrew, she would have been called Esther."

The smile never left her face, but she looked embarrassed. "Zemach," she said, "you haven't changed. You were always theatrical."

Both of them began speaking excitedly and interrupting each other. He asked her when she had married, who her husband was, what he did, and how many children she had. She said that she had a son of about my age and asked him if I were his son. He took the little girl on his knees and started asking her silly questions, and she gave him silly answers, and in an overflowing of happiness he kissed her twice on both cheeks and promised to give her a big doll and a pram, and two puppies for baksheesh. He begged Esther to come and visit him and she gave him her address and asked him to come and visit her, and said that her husband would be very glad to meet him. It transpired that her husband read all the newspapers and went to all the public meetings and heard all the important speakers, and that he had also heard Zemach speak during the period of his public activities. Suddenly she remembered that she had to hurry home to make lunch.

Before she went Zemach took her hand and said, "Esther, do you remember that once I slandered you and said I saw you kissing a British officer? You cried."

She burst out laughing. "Maybe," she said. "Maybe I did cry. In any case when I was a young girl I was in love with an officer in the British police who lived with his wife in my aunt's house, and he never even noticed my existence. What wouldn't I have given then for one kiss from him!"

Zemach looked after her until she disappeared from view

and then he sank into melancholy. When we started drawing
again he stopped giving me instructions about how to draw
and started lecturing me about law and morality. "Talking to
that woman has taught me a lot of important things," he said,
"and one of them is that the extent of sin is the extent of the
sense of sin, and the extent of the sense of sin is the extent of
the suffering caused by self-accusation; and I'm afraid that
some people are persecuted by the suffering of self-accusation
until they go down to their graves." I nodded my head without understanding a word and without being able to see the
connection between the smiling woman and his philosophy.
He went on philosophizing and finding morals and object lessons in everything, and I listened patiently and felt that he
himself knew quite clearly what he was talking about. He
taught me many things, among them things my mother was
not supposed to know about. He taught me to look and to see
and to draw, and he taught me chess. He taught me to use
the big, ancient German revolver he kept in the attic, and he
taught me to play cards. He taught me English love songs and
he taught me to say in French, "I love you, my darling." He
grew more and more like his brother Lippa, only where every
small event reminded Lippa of a joke, every small event taught
Zemach a great truth.

Translated by Dalya Bilu

3

THE LITTLE DOCTOR

TONIGHT I DREAMED that I was in the army camp next to Jerusalem again. There was a party going on in the big mess hall, with pictures pasted on the walls, green branches standing in the corners, and chains of colored paper festooning the ceiling. Blue and red and yellow lights shone through the paper streamers and the Air Force Band played dance music, but nobody was dancing. Everybody was too busy stampeding the buffet, grabbing and eating everything he could lay his hands on. A big fat man in civilian clothes and a red bow tie elbowed his way through the crowd to reach the girl soldier serving behind the buffet. He seized her with both hands, opened his mouth wide and gave her such a ferocious kiss on her nose that I was afraid it would be left behind in his mouth. But instead of screaming aloud in horror, the girl seemed perfectly content with her lot. From the expression on her face it was quite clear that she was glad to be in his arms, that desire was flooding her limbs, and that this coarse creature was about to devour her down to the last curl and earring and high-heeled shoe. Suddenly a very small captain jumped onto the civilian's back and began hitting and kicking him, but he went on sucking the soldier girl's nose lustfully without taking any notice of the blows and kicks raining down on him. All of a sudden the captain whistled shrilly, jumped down to the ground and began dancing and spinning about in the middle of the room to the strains of the music. The girl went on melting in her brutal lover's arms, the soldiers went on eating voraciously, and nobody paid any attention to the capering captain but me. He was tiny, more like a child than a grown man, but his uniform was still too short and too tight for him. He leaped high in the air with great agility, shook his head and arms in time to the drum, and once he even executed a full somersault in the air. I watched him anxiously, afraid he might fall on his head and break into pieces like a china doll, but he succeeded in landing on his feet like an acrobat, winking at me as if he were an old friend alluding to some secret known only to the two of us. I had a strange feeling that I had known him for many years, but that something about him had changed and I couldn't remember his name. I wanted to join him in his dance and whisper an important secret in his ear, and then I woke up and the sun was already beating fiercely on the windowpane.

During the morning the dream receded from my thoughts, but toward afternoon the image of the little captain rose up before my eyes again and for some reason I felt that I owed him something. In my dream no one had paid any attention to him. His blows and kicks and his ridiculous dance had not even given rise to derisive laughter. I felt that I should have grabbed people by the scruff of their necks and shouted in their ears, "Look! The man who seeks truth and pursues justice is dancing in front of you!" I don't know what truth and justice had to do with it. In the dream, at any rate, everything made sense and seemed logical enough. All through luncheon I racked my brains about the little captain, and when I rose from the table with my mind made up not to think about him anymore, an ambulance passed by the door and I remembered that the captain was none other than the little doctor from Abyssinian Road, who had appeared in my dream wearing an officer's uniform.

The little doctor from Abyssinian Road was my uncle Lippa's boyhood friend. Their friendship began in 1915, when both of them entered the Hebrew teachers' seminary founded by the Ezra Society. As you may remember, my uncle Lippa was a little strange. His friends were a little strange too, and my mother was always slightly apprehensive when Lippa arrived at our house with a new friend. Once, I remember, he brought Levi the drunken Georgian porter. Having spent all his life among Ashkenazi Jews, the only language Levi knew was Yiddish, but he had never once succeeded in pronouncing a single sentence of this language correctly. Whenever I tried to speak Yiddish to my grandmother she laughed and said that I spoke Yiddish like Levi the porter.

The little doctor was Lippa's best and oldest friend, and the most popular with the family. He was popular with us even before he became a doctor, and the affection we all felt for him had nothing to do with his medical degree. I remember him from the days when he was still a teacher called, naturally enough, the little teacher. He is linked with my earliest memories because he was like one of the family then, in and out of our house all day long. His name was Baruch Mordechai Fielding. Although the name Fielding is typically English, there is no reason to suppose that any of his forefathers had ever set foot on the soil of Albion, nor, needless to say, was there any connection between him and the famous English writer of the same name. In any case, the matter of his name may safely be left to the genealogists, who are well versed in the curious metamorphoses of Jewish family names.

To this day a photograph of Baruch Mordechai in the days when he was still a student at the teachers' seminary hangs in our house. In the picture the young student is seen sitting at a desk of imposing dimensions with ornamental carvings and legs in the shape of Corinthian pillars. Behind this desk, which was the most precious possession of Boroshkin, the doyen of Jerusalem photographers, all the seminarians and Zionists and socialists and other heretics who lived in Jerusalem between the years of 1913 and 1920 had their photographs taken. On the desk are three books, two of them on the subject's left, next to the large inkwell in the shape of a kneeling wooden camel (the work of an anonymous student at the Bezalel School of Art), and the third lying open in front of him. He is gazing into space and looks as if he has just this moment lifted his eyes from the book. With one hand he supports his head, heavy with thought, and the other holds a quill and is stretched out before him on the desk top, ready to take down inspired lines of poetry or philosophical reflections at a moment's notice. As a rule, the image created by these remarkable portraits is one of a man of letters par excellence, who is at the same time a man of action. The portrait of the young seminarian Baruch Mordechai Fielding, however, conveys no such impression. He does not look like a scholar pausing in his reading to ponder the deeper significance of what he has just read, and he does not look at all like a banker with the power to decide the fate of nations by a stroke of his pen. He looks like a little boy dressed up as a detective from Scotland Yard—and all because of the Homburg hat on his head, under whose broad brim his eyes peer out with a serious smile as if to say, "I'm not really a detective, I'm Motke the seminarian in my Homburg hat."

He had a weakness for broad-brimmed, high-crowned hats, and they caused him not a little trouble. Every passing breeze would blow his hat right off his head and roll it all the way down the street, to the delight of the passers-by. And another troublesome tendency exhibited by all his hats was that they invariably got caught on nails and shelves or any other kind of jutting or protruding object. On entering our house he would remove his hat, look about him, and finally put it down on the sofa, where he kept glancing at it both for the pleasure it gave him to see it and for the fear that I might thoughtlessly sit down on it, as had indeed once happened when I was three years old. (I shall never forget the profound sorrow reflected in his eyes when he held the squashed hat in his hands and silently attempted to push the felt back into shape with his fingers.)

As an enlightened and progressive man he had a liking for the innovations of science and technology, and he was the first inhabitant of Jerusalem north of Jaffa Street and east of the Schneller Orphanage to acquire a radio and an electric iron and other such inventions of the twentieth century. The price he paid for these innovations, however, was high—not only in terms of money but also in terms of health—for everything connected with industry and technology, and in general anything demanding manual skill, was his enemy. His mind was sharp and clear, as befitting a descendant of the greatest rabbi in Israel in his time, but his hands refused to obey him, and the simplest operations, such as opening a tin of sardines or removing a nail from his shoe, placed his life in danger. Whenever he tried to use his electric iron, there was an accident. If he didn't get a shock which was enough to put him out of action for the rest of the day even before starting to iron, he was sure to burn his trousers, or the blanket on which he was ironing his trousers, or himself. But all the troubles which beset him as a result of the work of his hands could not dampen his ardor for manual labor. The most important event imprinted on my memory from the time before he went to France to study medicine was the repairing of the dog kennel in our yard. In the corner of the yard there still stood, by some miracle, an ancient dog kennel dating from the days of Abu Saud Effendi, the father of Saud Effendi, from whom my grandfather had purchased the house. Possibly it wasn't a kennel at all, but some kind of granary or storehouse, but as far as I was concerned it was a kennel. In this kennel, whose walls were cracked and riddled with holes and half of whose roof had already disappeared in Saud's time, I would sit and daydream. The hero of my dreams, in addition to myself, was a brave and clever dog called Abner. Abner was my best and most devoted friend, the loyal companion of all my adventures. One day I decided to repair the kennel and live in it with Abner, and I started collecting bricks from all the neighboring yards. While I was busy collecting the bricks the little teacher came into the yard and observed my labors with great interest. At last he approached me and asked me what I was doing. I told him that I was going to fix the dog's kennel. He opened his eyes wide in surprise, looked about him, and finally asked, "What kennel? I can't see any kennel here!"

"This kennel," I said, pointing to it.

"So that's what it is," he exclaimed, "and here was I thinking all this time that it was an oven the Arabs used to bake their pitta in! And what will you do with it when you've finished fixing it?"

"Abner will live in it," I said. I was ashamed to tell him that I intended living in the kennel with the dog. The little teacher looked at me for a while in silence and then remarked, "And I never knew until now that you had a friend called Abner."

"Abner's a dog," I told him, "but he's cleverer than a lot of people."

This last remark of mine was so much to his liking that he decided to help me with the work. Inside the kennel there were tins of whitewash and paint and cement. He rolled up his sleeves and I saw that he had small, smooth, white hands. With his small white hands he poured cement and whitewash and water into a tin and mixed them all together with a stick.

He went inside and plastered the walls and afterward I handed him bricks and he repaired the roof with them. This work caused him so much satisfaction that he burst into song. If I hadn't been so tired from carrying the bricks, no doubt I would have joined him. I stood outside the kennel and he stood inside with the words of his song ringing in my ears:

> *Let's have the bricks,*
> *There's no time to spare.*
> *Build, builders, build,*
> *Away with sorrow and care.*
> *We'll all sing the song of building our land.*

When he had almost finished repairing the roof and there was only a small gap of about five or six bricks left, his voice died down and was heard no more. The patriotic song of redemption and revival issuing from the kennel was replaced by the sound of my mother's voice calling from the house. When I didn't answer she came outside to look for me. Suddenly she stopped in her tracks, looked at the kennel in horror, and turned pale green.

"What's that?" she asked. I looked and saw the little teacher's white hand sticking out of the hole in the roof.

"It's Motke Fielding's hand."

"But what's he doing there?"

"Helping me to fix the kennel."

We worked for a whole hour, Mother and I, before we succeeded in getting him out of the kennel. We were afraid to break the bricks with a hammer in case one of them should fall on his head. When he emerged his face was as white as the whitewash splashed on his hair, and the first thing he asked for was a glass of water. Afterward he remarked that while he was sitting in the kennel a number of things he had read about the lives of coal miners in England had become clear to him.

He was then a teacher of Hebrew, Bible, and Mishnah in the Tachkemoni school, and all the children of Jerusalem knew the little teacher. I think that he was no taller than most of his pupils, who were all, without exception, taller than he when they left the elementary school at the age of fourteen. Thanks to the tremendous pedagogical powers stored up inside him, however, he succeeded not only in controlling his pupils, but also in winning their affection. This little man had a rich, strong voice which he cultivated for many years and which was his great pride. He was also a talented raconteur and actor, and his Bible lessons were famed throughout the town. His lessons were models of their kind. And yet, I don't think that he had much love for his pupils. He was weak. Weaker than all the other children when he was a child, and weaker than all the other men when he grew to manhood; he hated all manifestations of physical strength, which had always been associated in his experience with manifestations of cruelty. He taught the top classes in elementary school and his pupils were at the age when children revel in the strength of their bodies and bully those weaker than themselves. I think that in his heart of hearts he hated even those of his pupils lucky enough to be enjoying a happy childhood—those with healthy minds in healthy bodies who, whether they know it or not, are the lords of creation.

The little teacher was a teacher for nine years, from the age of twenty to the age of twenty-nine. He was an extremely hard-working man, and he was always studying something. During his second year of teaching, a new teacher came to the school, an elderly German Jew who gave singing lessons and taught the children to play the flute. His name was Ernst Cohen and he had a piano in his house. The little teacher, who had never seen a note of music in his life, began taking piano lessons. He applied himself to the study of music in the same way that he had applied himself to the rest of his studies —with extraordinary enthusiasm and devotion. He had an excellent ear and a soul sensitive to sounds, and after eight years of constant study he played the piano like a professional. When he was thirty years old he decided to go abroad to study medicine.

When Baruch Mordechai Fielding went to France to study medicine, all his friends, except Lippa, were married men with grown children, whereas he had remained an eternal student. At the age of thirty he would still argue about philosophical problems with all the ardor of a boy of eighteen before he sinks under the cares of making a living. He was not interested in philosophical systems for their own sake, or even in casuistry and logic-chopping. He wanted an answer to the questions that troubled him, and to these questions he could find no answers in books. He wasn't interested in money or power, or even in schemes for reforming society and bringing salvation to the masses. What he was looking for was meaning in the world around him and in his own life. When he went to study medicine, he hoped that it would bring him closer to an understanding of the mystery of human life. It was by way of being an attempt to take hold of something concrete and particular on a road which was always leading him toward the abstract and the general. He always tried to hang on to life in this world with all his might, and extract from it all the pleasure it could possibly afford. He was always palpitating with an eager readiness to laugh and be happy and enjoy himself. He was always keen to see good films and new plays and go to parties, but at the end of every party the same little mosquito would start buzzing in his head and asking like Ecclesiastes, "Mirth, what doeth it?"

When he went to France to study medicine he had just

enough money to pay for his passage on a freight ship and a month's stay at the cheapest hotel in Paris. We accompanied him to the railway station—my uncle Lippa and my mother and I—and he was very excited and smiled and told jokes in his usual manner and his small white hands trembled. In the throng of British policemen and Arab porters crowding the station platform he shrank to infinitesimal proportions, and I had a funny feeling that he was in danger of disappearing altogether in the train from Jerusalem to Haifa. To sustain him on his journey he took a tin of pickled olives and a basket of sandwiches, which he intended to last him until he reached Marseille. My uncle Lippa, who had recently returned from his travels in America, gave him a steady stream of good advice on how to conduct himself in the great cities of the Diaspora, and he nodded his head without hearing a word, he was so excited. We all helped him to climb onto the train, because he had succumbed to an attack of weakness and couldn't manage the ascent by himself, thus barring the way to an Arab peasant from Batir with a sack of carrots on his back. "These Jews," shouted the Arab, "fill up the whole country until there's no room to move," and here he added several rude and energetic curses. Before we could take leave of the little teacher properly, the engine whistled and the coaches groaned and moved off. A month after he set out we received a postcard from Marseille, and a month after that a postcard from Paris, and from then on we heard nothing at all from him for fifteen years.

Dr. Fielding came back to the country at the end of the War of Independence and worked for about six months in various military hospitals. Many well-known doctors, most of them Jews, visited the country at this time. They came to tend the severely wounded, and after their work was done most of them returned to the countries from which they had come. The newspapers would announce their arrival and sing their praises, and among the rest the name of Dr. Fielding, the famous French Jewish heart specialist, was mentioned. I don't know if Dr. Fielding had really made a name for himself as a heart specialist or if this was simply a fabrication of the newspaper reporters who wrote about him. Perhaps he came by his publicity in the newspapers because he arrived in the same airplane as a great American brain surgeon, and the reporters who descended on the latter at Lydda airport thought that there was some connection between him and the little doctor from France. In any event I do know that the little doctor was a competent and highly conscientious member of his profession. The head medical officer of the Israel Defence Forces asked him to stay on at the Ramat Hatsofim hospital, but he refused because he wanted to live in Jerusalem. He spent some time living in various hotels in the capital until he finally found an apartment after his own heart in Abyssinian Road. He liked the quiet of the twisting lane, and the high stone walls and the pine trees and cypresses peeping over them, and the red-tiled roofs showing through the trees, reminding him of a small French town in Provence. His apartment had a spacious hall and two big rooms and his furniture consisted mainly of his large library, a piano, and two big reproductions of Toulouse-Lautrec. During one of my visits he jokingly remarked that he liked and understood this French painter because both of them always saw every woman they met from the bottom up.

I met him by chance on King George Street in Jerusalem about two months before I was due to be demobilized from the army. Although I had read about the arrival in Israel of the French Jewish heart specialist, the information had not made any impression on me. The little teacher who had gone to France in the days of my childhood had been effaced from my heart by the passage of the years. It was twilight on a short and rainy Friday and I was hurrying from the army truck which had brought me to town for the weekend to the home of a friend where I intended spending my leave. The shops were already shut and the last buses were driving empty down the streets to the depot. I met him on the corner of Ben Yehuda Street. He was walking with rapid steps and both hands deep in his coat pockets and he looked lost in thought as he hurried on his way. If it hadn't been for the hat on his head I might not have recognized him at all. During the fifteen years he had spent in France he had not overcome his weakness for high-crowned, broad-brimmed hats. At the sight of the little man in the Homburg hat my heart contracted and childhood memories welled up and overflowed in me. At first I was overcome with a desire to run up to him and embrace him and lift him up in my arms, but I stopped myself and walked a few steps behind him. Perhaps I was mistaken; perhaps my imagination was playing tricks on me; perhaps he had changed over the years and would no longer take any particular interest in me. After I had made sure that it was indeed he, I stopped him and said: "Shalom, Doctor Fielding. Do you remember me?"

I felt too tall and horribly clumsy next to him. He stood looking at me for a few moments without recognizing me. I told him my name, and then his eyes lit up and he gave me a long, kind look, and put his little hand in mine, and finally said in his rich fatherly voice, "Bend your head, you great ruffian, and let me give you a kiss on your forehead."

I felt my face burning and blushing but I did as he bade me, and it was only a queer sense of shame that prevented me from kissing him back. He urged me to come home with him and I complied willingly, and all the way we talked without stopping. He asked me many questions about what had happened at home and in the family and the country during the long years of his absence, and I answered him briefly and precisely, and he kept up a steady stream of surprised and joyful exclamations, just like an excited Frenchman. And then I plucked up the courage to ask him some questions about France and Paris and his studies and so on. "Listen to me, my young friend," he said, "there are twenty-three different tribes in this country, each one worse than the next, and the tribe of doctors is the worst of the lot. So please do me a favor and don't call me doctor."

We both laughed, but I couldn't stop myself. What should I have called him then? Mordechai, or Motke, or Mr. Little Doctor? I asked him questions about all sorts of profound and weighty matters, but the question which was most important to him I failed to ask. It simply never occurred to me to ask if he was still a bachelor or if by any chance he had found himself a wife. He talked and talked and in the end he couldn't restrain himself any longer and told me without being asked: "Yes, and I'm a married man now you know . . ."

"Is that so?" I cried in great astonishment. He didn't seem to me like a married man, the husband of a wife. "If that's the case then you're to be congratulated. I congratulate you from the bottom of my heart."

I gave him my hand and I saw that he was beaming with happiness. He told me about his wife with much love that burgeoned and burst forth unintentionally between his joking words. He told me that he had met her in Paris and that she was the daughter of a famous family of rabbis and that for some time she had been an opera singer. He also hinted that she was a very beautiful woman. While he was revealing the secrets of his heart to me I experienced an extraordinary sensation. In the distant past I had been a child and he a man, and now he was talking to me like a friend, equal in degree and age and experience of life.

To me it seemed strange, for some reason, to hear a man of forty-five speak with such enthusiasm about a woman he had married at the age of forty. And not just any man, but a doctor, a specialist in heart diseases. Up to now I had come into contact with doctors only when I was ill, and they had all seemed stern, pedantic men who would never have succumbed to the follies of the heart; men who expressed their opinions with profound gravity and who stood on their dignity more than other people. Dr. Fielding, however, was innocent of the trappings of greatness. He had not acquired the habits of an important man and spoke to me quite simply and frankly. He told me how his heart had contracted inside him the first time he set eyes on her, and how he had wooed her, and how she had responded. After one month and one week they were married. This is not to say that until the age of forty he had never fallen in love or wooed a woman before. He had tried his luck many times and been defeated many times, but he had never given up. He had not lost heart even in the hour of his bitterest disappointment, and his sense of humor, so far from deserting him, had emerged stronger and subtler than ever. But now that he had won a wife whom he loved, he was like a man with a loaf in his basket, he was truly overflowing with joy and kindness. The thread of cynical bitterness running through his manner of speaking and his view of the world had faded, and his philosophical yearnings and cravings for absolute solutions had been buried under the foundations of his new life. As a middle-aged doctor he was absorbed in concrete cases and specific problems, and he was too busy in his work and his private life as a married man to search for the general significance of the great and wonderful phenomenon called Baruch Mordechai Fielding.

When we reached his house it was already a quarter to six,

and the silence of the Sabbath had fallen on the whole town.

On the threshold he wiped his feet several times on the mat with scrupulous care, like a man preparing himself to enter a holy shrine. His anxiety infected me too, and I tried to remove the last particle of mud adhering to my nailed boots, whose clatter in this atmosphere of calm seclusion seemed crude and uncalled for. On the door was a small brass tablet and on it was written: DR. B. M. FIELDING. And in smaller letters below: Heart Specialist.

He rang the bell and gave me a smile which was both encouraging and bashful. He even appeared a little tense. He was like a man about to reveal his most sacred and precious belonging. After a few moments, which seemed to me a very long time, we heard the sound of a woman's slippered footsteps. The door opened and his wife appeared before us in full force, like an unexpected gust of wind. She was a big, broad-boned woman with smooth abundant hair framing her face and flowing down her back. Her face was white with the kind of whiteness glistening from the faces of actors seen from the first rows of a theater. Her eyes were big and blue and they too glittered like light blue beads. Her mouth was full and wide and very red, and when she smiled her teeth were exposed. They were white and there was a gap separating the two front teeth from each other. Perhaps she was beautiful, but it was difficult for me to tell because of the shining white of her face and the redness of her lips and the blueness of her eyes, which would have looked fine in the stage lights of a dark hall, but gave her a somewhat sickly appearance in the ordinary light of day. Her face was big and all of her looked big in the red dressing gown which fell about her like a curtain draping a statue.

"Monsieur le docteur!" she greeted him with a glad cry in a strong, slightly hoarse voice. She embraced him with both arms and gave him a resounding kiss, and he held her face in his two little hands and kissed her and said, "Nicole my child, please make the acquaintance of my young friend. This big brave captain is Lippa's nephew. I have known him literally since the day he came into the world. I knew him even before he knew himself."

"I'm not a captain," I stammered in embarrassment in broken French, searching in the recesses of my memory for whatever was left of the French lessons of bygone years. "I'm only a second lieutenant." Nicole held out her warm hand with exceptional cordiality and fixed me with her glittering blue eyes in a look which held a lot of motherliness and a little feminine seductiveness too.

"Well, well," she said, "I've always had a weakness for officers." Here her tongue began to twist around a flow of French so rapid that I couldn't understand a word of what she was saying.

"Parlez lentement, s'il vous plaît," I said when she reached her first pause for breath. We all laughed and went inside. The doctor went to wash his hands and she helped me to remove my greatcoat and hang it up on the rack.

"You don't speak Hebrew yet?" I asked her.

"Yes," she said. "I know how to say 'Shalom' and 'Don't push—there's a queue.'"

When we sat down to dinner there were two candles on the table in high silver candlesticks, and the Sabbath loaf was covered with a cloth embroidered with the words, "If I forget thee O Jerusalem let my right hand forget its cunning." The setting of the table affected me with the same spirit of festivity which had pervaded our house on Friday evenings when my grandfather was still alive.

"Are you Orthodox?" I asked her.

"No," she replied, "but I observe tradition."

"Didn't I tell you she was a rebbitzin? She's the daughter

of a well-known rabbi from Bialystock," said Dr. Fielding, who was in gay and playful spirits all this time.

I don't know whether Nicole received this compliment in the same enthusiastic spirit in which it was paid, but in any case she burst into throaty laughter and from then on we began to speak in fluent Yiddish. She told a lot of jokes in Yiddish and laughed a lot, and gradually the picture of a Jewish girl, daughter of a so-called rabbi who had emigrated from eastern Europe and landed up in Paris, of all cities, took shape in my mind. Her mother tongue was Yiddish. She had learned Yiddish at her mother's knee, spoke it and thought in it, and yet nothing had clung to her of all the great culture born in this language on the bedrock of the Bible and the Talmud and nurtured in the dark of the long exile. Even Shalom Aleichem was foreign to her. She may have had Jewish vulgarity in her makeup, but no Jewish folklore. She had grown up in Paris and spoke French like a native born and bred, but she wasn't a real Frenchwoman either.

Throughout the meal I tried to discover in her qualities which might justify the great and deep love which the little doctor felt for her, but to no avail. There was only one moment, when she was serving the soup and not looking at us, when her face was pale and serious, and her eyes were sad and full of longing for the unattainable.

After supper we sat on low stools by the piano. Dr. Fielding took off his jacket and went to prepare Turkish coffee. All his life he had boasted of his expertise in the preparation of this excellent drink, and he had even acquired a special electric kettle for the purpose. The Turkish coffee reminded him of the days of Turkish rule and he took off into those distant times and came back to regale us with several marvelous stories from the days when Jamal Pasha ruled Jerusalem with a strong arm.

After the coffee I decided that the time had come for me to

take my leave of them, but the little doctor wouldn't hear of my going. Nicole too protested. She was standing by the piano and leafing through the musical scores lying on it, and the idea of asking her to sing suddenly flashed through my mind. She was ready and willing to comply with my request, and the little doctor too didn't wait for a second invitation but sat down at the piano immediately and played a few chords with an assurance and a dexterity which seemed wonderful in fingers that generally failed at much simpler tasks.

Nicole stood by the piano with one hand resting on it and her other hand, which held a handkerchief, clasped to her bosom, and began to sing. Her loud voice filled the whole apartment. While she sang she looked straight at me and smiled as if I was part of the audience in an opera hall.

For some reason I couldn't face her eyes and evaded them by looking sideways. Suddenly she came to a stop without there having been any hint in her singing of the approaching end. I lifted my eyes and she made me a little curtsy and I applauded enthusiastically. She sang several other arias from various operas. Her voice, which was very powerful, seemed to me too prosaic, and I found it not at all to my liking. When she had finished singing she sat down next to me, and I saw that she was extremely excited and encouraged by my applause, and I was suddenly flooded with pity for her and for the little doctor, who was also overjoyed by the success of the concert. I felt myself to be boorish and contemptible for disliking her singing in the secret of my heart.

"Can you sing any Hebrew songs?" I asked.

"I know the song 'Hey, the Jeep!'" she answered. "Your cruel radio plays it all the time and I can't get away from it. I hum it to myself in the kitchen and the grocery shop and everywhere. However much I hate it, it makes no difference, I can't get it out of my head."

"Let's sing the 'Jeep,'" cried the doctor and ran to the piano. We all sang "Hey the jeep, hey the jeep, what a night to be alive" at the top of our voices, and after that we sang "The Granny in the Negev" and "A Horse and Cart." I myself knew only the first verse of all these songs, and they scarcely knew the first two lines of the first verse, but we managed to stretch out the words we knew to cover the whole tune.

The small apartment filled up with cigarette smoke and the thumping on the piano and the sound of our singing, and the inhabitants of the Moulin Rouge peered at us from the paintings of the great, sad artist in the joyful melody of color which can only be purchased at the price of pain and suffering.

"And now to the wine, gentlemen, to the wine," cried the doctor and Nicole rushed off to the kitchen and brought a bottle of Toquay wine. I drank a glass and asked for another, and saw that the time was already half past twelve.

"I must go," I said to them. "My dear friends, I thank you very much."

"Mais, mon capitaine," protested the doctor, "tomorrow is Saturday and you can sleep as late as you like."

"Stay with us a little longer," said Nicole, and started singing an American song in a heavy French accent. The song said that you could sleep late on Sunday morning.

"What are you doing on Saturday night?" the doctor suddenly asked me.

"There's a soldiers' party at the base," I replied.

"Ah, what a pity," said the doctor and continued strumming the tune of "The Granny in the Negev" on the piano with one hand. "You see, on Saturday night I'm on duty at the hospital. I would be extremely grateful to you if you could take Nicole out to the cinema. She has no friends in Jerusalem and on the nights when I'm working she has to stay at home alone."

"I would be glad to take her with me to the party," I said, and the moment the words were out of my mouth I regretted my hasty offer and hoped that they wouldn't take it up.

For some time I had been having fantasies about winning at this party the heart of a certain girl from the signal corps whom I had met at battalion headquarters. My first sight of her had set a chord vibrating in my heart and subsequent chance meetings had left me feeling deeply mortified because I was sure that I had behaved like a complete idiot in her presence. At this party, I said to myself, I'll take her by storm. In my mind's eye I saw the way things would go at the party down to the last detail. I knew exactly in which corner of the hall I would meet her, I knew what I would say to her and what she would reply. I knew what the first dance we would dance together would be and I knew that all the following dances would be mine. "To a party, why that's wonderful," cried the doctor.

"Oh, wonderful," said Nicole and executed a pirouette like a ballerina preparing herself for the decisive leap of the ballet. "And what shall I wear to the party?" She hurried to the wardrobe to find a suitable dress.

There's no way out, I thought in despair, I'm lost.

"There's no need for anything special," I said with a miserable smile and an awful fear in my heart that she would appear at a soldiers' party wearing operatic fancy dress.

"On the contrary," she responded with a triumphant cry and her glittering eyes glittered more than ever. "Perhaps you think that I'll come to the party dressed with the vulgar lack of taste of the women here in Israel? I shall certainly wear something special, something stunning in its simplicity."

An hour after midnight I emerged into the cold Jerusalem night. The hearty welcome I had received at the little doctor's home had suffused me with a melting sensation of modest, homely joy. I was grateful to them and wished them well. My happiness was mixed with a little pride at being able to give them pleasure by the invitation to the party. It was a way of repaying them for their kindness to me, but at the same time I couldn't help wishing that I hadn't been so hasty.

As the hour of the party drew closer my apprehensions increased, and while I was getting ready to go to Dr. Fielding's house to fetch Nicole I was overcome by actual panic. I imagined her in a purple dress with her hair piled high on her head. I appear with her at my side in the big mess hall in the camp where the party is being held and everyone turns to stare at us in amazement. Everyone is astonished by this strange creature and they all imagine for some reason that she is my wife. A scornful smile appears on the faces of all who behold her. Suddenly she gets up onto the table and starts singing in a loud hoarse voice and I am overcome by one great wish—for the earth to open its mouth and swallow me alive. The audience laughs; screams of laughter greet her and I see her in all her terrible humiliation and my heart curdles inside me. She is a poor creature deserving of great pity and the audience is cruel as a pack of murderers, and rage boils up in me and I want to pour out my wrath on them.

When Nicole opened the door of her house a weight was lifted from my mind. She looked sweet and pretty. She was wearing a blue dress, the color of her blue eyes, and her hair was neither piled up in a tower nor even tied back in a ponytail, but flowed smoothly down her back as it had yesterday.

"How do I look?" she asked me.

"You look lovely," I answered.

She smiled and let me in. "Shall we have something to drink before we go?"

"With pleasure."

We drank coffee. After we had finished Nicole repaired her lipstick and put on a silver fur coat with my assistance. On the way my fears and doubts returned.

"There's transport waiting for us at the corner of Jaffa Street and Melissanda Street," I said, "but it's not a taxi and not even a bus. It's an army truck and you'll have to show a sporting spirit and climb up onto it like a veteran soldier."

She laughed. "If the worst comes to the worst you'll help me, mon capitaine," she said. I had already given up pointing out her mistake to her and had come to the conclusion that French people call all soldiers "capitaine." "There's only one thing I'm afraid of," she added. "I'm afraid I might tear my nylon stockings."

When we reached the truck there were already some people seated inside it, and others were standing outside. To my great relief I saw that several soldiers had brought girls who were decked out in elaborate party dresses, and even some of the soldier girls were wearing civilian clothes. Nicole climbed onto the truck without any mishaps. I sat down beside her in the darkness of the tarpaulin with my heart full of mixed feelings. When we arrived at the camp and entered the hall I blinked my eyes against the light which flooded us after the dark of the journey. The hall was crowded with people. Nearly all the soldiers were in uniform and most of the girls were wearing civilian dresses. "Dear soldiers," murmered Nicole. "Look, Jewish soldiers. Brave Jewish soldiers. Isn't it wonderful, they're just like the gentile boys at home." I saw that she was proud and moved, and I changed my mind about her at once.

We sat down at one of the tables and prepared ourselves to listen to the words of the camp commander, who availed himself of every opportunity to make a speech. The people at our table sent veiled or open glances in Nicole's direction, and she was fully aware of them. It appeared that these glances were not burdensome or embarrassing to Nicole; on the contrary, they encouraged her. She felt quite at home and her behavior was free and friendly. Motke the Ginger, who arrived late, as usual, couldn't find anywhere to sit and came and stood behind us. He called me aside on the pretext of having some important confidential information to convey to me and asked me who the mysterious beauty sitting next to me was.

"She's the wife of the famous doctor, Doctor Fielding," I said, adding offhandedly, with hidden pride, "You must have read about him in the papers."

"You should know by now that I never read the newspaper," he said. "Anyway, what's she like?"

"She's a Frenchwoman, from Paris."

"Is that so?" he called out loud and his eyes lit up. "A Frenchwoman from Paris! That's really something! I saw at once that she wasn't an Arab peasant woman from Umlabbes. And how old is she, if I may ask?"

This question took me by surprise. Up to now it had never occurred to me to speculate about her age.

"She's twenty-five," I answered with assurance.

"That's what she says." He brushed this aside with contempt, fixed her with the appraising eye of a connoisseur looking at a painting, and passed sentence with an authority which brooked no question. "She's thirty-one exactly."

At this moment my eyes darkened and my heart sank inside me. In the corner of the hall next to the stage, stood the girl from the signal corps arm-in-arm with a mustachioed captain who kept giving her sideways glances like a man feasting his eyes on his own private property. She was talking to him animatedly without taking any notice of what was going on around her, and he nodded his head from time to time and gave her meaningful looks.

"Maybe," I said. "Maybe she is thirty-one. By the way, do you know the captain with the mustache standing over there in the corner with the girl from the signal corps?"

"Him? Sure I know him. That's Yoske Eizen, who was badly wounded when he got into a minefield that he'd sowed himself. He's going to marry the girl. They say she's got money." He went on chattering and delivering himself of witticisms to the best of his ability and I left him in the middle and returned to Nicole, and for the rest of the party I felt sick. My head was heavy and there was an oppressive feeling in my chest and I was altogether a broken man. A whitish, grayish fog separated me from everything that was going on in the hall. Of the whole of the party nothing remains in my memory but the end, when we climbed onto the truck and drove to town. It was half past two in the morning. The streets of the town were still wet from the rain and glittered in the light of the lamps, but the clouds had dispersed and the sky was clear and scattered with stars. A dry cold penetrated my bones and sent a shudder through my body. Nicole leaned on my arm and walked beside me in silence. When we arrived at the entrance to her house she thanked me and suddenly asked, "Tell me, mon capitaine, what made you so depressed tonight?"

This question cut me like a knife. I felt that I could bear it no longer and I told her everything. I began from the first day when my heart had contracted at the sight of the girl from the signal corps. She listened attentively and heard me out to the end without saying a word, and then she said, "One thing is clear. You don't love this girl because you don't know her at all. Her looks attract you, and no more. I can console you only by promising you that you will forget her very soon and that all this will be nothing more than a passing episode." So saying she pressed a hasty kiss on my lips and went inside.

A week after the party the girl from the signal corps married the captain with the mustache and I never saw her again. I myself was about to be demobilized in just under two months, and I was in a strange and volatile mood. A wild and rather reckless happiness at the prospect of my discharge was tinged with an oppressive feeling which sometimes turned into a gray depression and sometimes into a nervous fear of the future. There were moments when army life seemed to me the best life possible, and there were moments when it filled me with such disgust that I wanted to beat my head against the walls of the barracks hut. In a moment of great sadness and ancient melancholy which rose up in me like the sea tide on a moonlit night, I found myself walking the Jerusalem streets and my feet were carrying me to Abyssinian Road. A longing awoke in me for the warmth of home and the security of stone walls and domed ceilings and kind, simple words and heartfelt laughter. It was dusk and there were no lights yet in the windows. When I reached their house it suddenly occurred to me that there might be nobody at home. I rang the bell and there was no reply. I went on ringing for a long time like a man calling for help.

Nicole opened the door. She was wearing the red dressing gown and her hair was disordered. She looked as if she had just woken from a dream. "My God in heaven," she exclaimed. "You frightened me out of my wits. I was lying and reading a poem by Edgar Allan Poe about the shrieking of alarm bells when I heard your wild ringing. Come in quickly and close the door. I may still die here in your hot country of the cold and the drafts."

For some reason I suddenly felt cold too. She went out to fix her hair and I sat down and leafed through the book of French translations of the works of the American poet, which was lying on the sofa. When she returned she fixed me with her glittering eyes and asked why I was so pale. "Perhaps

you've got a temperature?" She placed her hand on my forehead and her touch sent shivers through my whole body.
"I'll make you a cup of hot cocoa with milk. Do you like
cocoa? I like it better than any other drink in the world."

While she was preparing the cocoa I knew that I should
get up and make my escape, but I was too cold to move. After
drinking the cocoa I'll get out of here, I said to myself firmly.
But I was overcome with weakness and began having an intimate conversation with her instead. She told me of her
great loneliness since coming to Israel: twice a week Dr.
Fielding was out of town working in military hospitals and
during the rest of the week too he could not call his time his
own, and the people of Jerusalem were unsociable. She
talked on and on and the shivers which had taken hold of me
from the moment she opened the door increased until I felt
that my hands were trembling. I answered her with banali-
ties about the loneliness of all men. I told her of the feeling
of immeasurable solitude which overtakes soldiers in their
barracks. Because my tongue had been loosened and because
of my weakness I lost all restraint and dwelt upon my own
feelings of confusion and disorientation, and then suddenly I
sensed her head on my shoulder and her long smooth hair on
my cheek. I felt that if I didn't get up and run for my life
that very moment I would fall down at her feet. In a kind of
blackout I started embracing her ardently and showering her
with kisses, and all the time shivers ran up and down my body
and I couldn't speak.

The next day, when I was walking down Ben Yehuda
Street, I saw the little doctor getting out of a taxi that stopped
outside a travel bureau. He had a leather case in his hand
and he was hurrying home. At the sight of him my heart
turned over and I felt my face burning. I made a sharp turn
into a side street to avoid meeting him and all the way my

heart pounded like a sledgehammer. I knew that I would never be able to look him straight in the eyes again. This little man, hurrying home with his little steps to the wife he loved, was raised in my eyes at that moment to the rank of sainthood, and I wasn't fit to stand beside him, let alone enjoy the bounty of his great affection for me. Not only would I never dare to visit him again, but I doubted whether I would even be able to walk down the street he had chosen for his home without feeling apprehensive.

Three months after I had been demobilized from the army I found a job teaching in a night school. Although I would have preferred any other occupation under the sun, and teaching was the last alternative after all other hopes had failed, from the first moment I walked into the classroom I found myself deriving a good deal of satisfaction from it. My pupils were mostly adults who worked all day to earn a living for themselves and their families and came to study in the evenings out of their own free will, and my work was limited to teaching them what was on the syllabus without any problems of maintaining discipline and keeping order. I loved the pairs of tired eyes that followed me earnestly in an attempt to grasp what I was saying. Time and again I saw working men who came to class in their overalls fighting hard to keep their eyes open. I taught Hebrew and Bible and after some weeks the principal informed me that I would have to fill in for a teacher who had been taken ill and give lessons in Talmud and Mishnah as well. To my alarm I realized that I had forgotten what I knew of the Talmud, and the tractate of *Baba Metzia,* from which I had to teach a few pages, had disappeared from my house. That same evening I hurried to my grandmother's house to borrow the necessary volume. My late grandfather, may his soul rest in peace, had left a set of the Vilna edition of the Talmud behind him, and since the day of his death no one had looked at it.

When I arrived at my grandmother's, I found, to my surprise, the little doctor sitting at the table with a glass of tea in front of him, and Grandmother sitting up in bed and looking at him with her purblind eyes. During the past years her eyes had dimmed and she had to grope her way around like a blind person. He was speaking to her and she sat and nodded her head. "Grandmother's ill," I thought, "and I haven't been to visit her for over six months."

"Grandmother, are you ill?" The cry escaped me before I could collect myself sufficiently to greet the little doctor. My face was on fire and I didn't know how I would approach him and put my hand out in greeting.

"What makes you think that I'm ill?" asked Grandmother tremulously, taking fright at my cry. "I'm not ill, thank God. I'm well and whole. How are you? And why haven't you been to see me for such a long time?"

The little doctor sat in his chair looking at his glass with a distracted air, and pursing his lips in a bitter smile which sent a shiver down my spine. Suddenly I felt sure that he had found everything out and had come to tell my grandmother what kind of a grandson she had.

"Alors, c'est comme ça, mon capitaine," ejaculated the doctor in French, and there was so much bitterness in his voice and such profound dejection that I felt myself twitching like a worm cut in half with a razor blade. I dropped into a chair without saying a word.

"Why so silent, my young friend, why don't you ask me how I am and how Nicole is?" he continued in a voice which turned into a shout. "You think your grandmother's ill and I've been called here to treat her? Not at all. I wasn't called here, I came here, and I didn't come to ask her about her health but to tell her about myself, since she can't come to me. So let me tell you that Nicole is gone. She isn't dead, she's gone, she's run away."

The pendulum of the old clock hanging on the wall swung back and forth and cracks appeared in the plaster of the ceiling. A film of white covered Grandmother's eyes and her face was shriveled. Her false teeth were immersed in a glass of water on the chest of drawers and her mouth was pursed like a long thin crack in the hollow between the tip of her nose and the tip of her chin. She sat in her bed with her eyes fixed on the little doctor and her hands were laid in her lap and she soaked up his cries like a shock absorber. She said not a word and her face was ancient like the faces of mummies thousands of years old, and there was much suffering in it and much sorrow.

"Perhaps you'll have another glass of tea," said Grandmother suddenly to the little doctor. "There's a fresh brew in the pot."

He leaned back in his chair and his one hand was spread out in front of him on the table and his feet hardly touched the ground. He stared at the glass in front of him, and there was a bitter smile on his face. His high-crowned hat was lying on the sofa with his big leather bag beside it. He didn't take his eyes off the glass and the fingers of his hand lying on the table ceaselessly crumbled a piece of rusk. "When I came home once from Tel Aviv," said the doctor, "Nicole read me a poem of Edgar Allan Poe's about bells." He gave vent to a bitter snort of laughter and added, "You won't believe it, my young friend, but it's a fact that Nicole loved poetry. You hear—poetry could sometimes bring tears to her eyes. She had a poetic soul. She admired everything noble and exalted. She even wrote poetry—epigrams, occasional verses—in green ink she wrote them. I don't know what kind of ink other poets use, probably every poet has a special ink that he likes best. Nicole was only inspired by green ink. She tied all her poems in a bundle and took them with her, but she forgot to take the ink. She left the inkwell on the shelf and I threw it after her and it hit the picture on the wall and dyed it all green."

The doctor went on telling the tale of Nicole's flight until close on midnight. Grandmother fell asleep at nine o'clock and he sat on and told me all the details of the affair until grandmother woke up and said, "Baruch Mordechai, it's midnight and you must go home to sleep." Grandmother never needed a watch. She knew the exact time at every hour of the day and night. Once when she was sick and I was sleeping at her house, she woke up after midnight and asked for a glass of milk. I groped my way in the dark and she said, "The time is a quarter to three," and so it was.

On the way the little doctor went on with his story. I accompanied him home and he stopped at the door and told me in detail how Nicole hit him with the stick used for stirring the boiling washing. On this episode he dwelt especially, describing it at great length also when he repeated it to my mother. For a whole month he went around knocking on the doors of all his friends and acquaintances, telling the tale of Nicole's flight. She ran away three days after their fifth wedding anniversary. In the morning, after putting on his white coat in the corridor of the internal medicine ward, he went into the head nurse's room to look at the register, and he saw that it was the day of their wedding anniversary. He hurried to the office and asked another doctor to take his place. He rummaged in his pockets and saw that he had only two pounds, and returned to the hospital and borrowed ten pounds and went to buy a present for Nicole. He bought the collected poems of Alfred de Musset and worked out that the change would be enough for them to eat at a good hotel.

When he reached home it was half past nine. He guessed that Nicole would still be lying in bed, reading the newspaper or daydreaming. He opened the door and the smell of cigarette smoke filled his nostrils, but he was not surprised. Nicole let out a scream and sat up in bed and her breasts were exposed and their nipples were erect and bright red. The boy, who was tall and thin, was standing by the table pouring water from the kettle into two glasses. He was very pale, white as a sheet, and the water went on pouring out of the kettle. The little doctor was not surprised. He was quite crushed by the terrible pain inside him, but he was not surprised. The book of translations of Edgar Allan Poe's poems was lying on the floor, next to the bed, and the little doctor bent down and picked it up and closed it and put it on the piano. And the tall boy went on holding the kettle. Nicole stretched out her hand for her red dressing gown and covered her shoulders and the little doctor went out of the house and shut the door behind him and ran down the street until he came to a public lavatory. He went into a cubicle and tore the volume of Alfred de Musset's poetry to pieces, dropping the pages one by one into the lavatory bowl until the water washed them all away. Then he sat down with his head in his hands and cried until his strength was exhausted. He ached and cried but he wasn't surprised. After the well of his tears had dried up he went outside into the street and felt a great hunger. He went into a restaurant and ate voraciously and suddenly got up and hurried home. Nicole was still sitting in bed with the red dressing gown over her shoulders. A mirror was propped up against her knees and she was combing her hair. The two glasses were standing on the table and there was nothing in them but coffee dregs. The doctor went down on his knees and wanted to kiss her hands, but she pulled them angrily away and went on combing her hair. "Don't leave me, Nicole," whispered the doctor. "Please, please stay with me. Don't go away from me. He's fifteen years younger than you are, he'll get sick of you and shake you off like dust from old clothes, and go and find a woman of his own age. It won't last more than six months."

"I don't care what happens after six months," said Nicole in a weary voice, as if she were tired of repeating the same thing over and over again. "I want to live my life now, as long as I'm still able to enjoy it."

The doctor went on begging her and she got up and went into the kitchen and he followed her and implored her to stay with him and she went into the bathroom and he went in after her until she took up the stick and hit him. She hit him and he tried to catch hold of the stick and kiss it, and she grew wild with anger and started kicking him and biting him until she fell helplessly into the bath. That whole month the little doctor came knocking on our door and showing us the blue marks and bruises that had blossomed on his body, and telling us that he would be ready to take a beating every day if only Nicole would stay with him. And then he fell ill and spent the next six weeks in the internal medicine ward of the hospital where he worked. He spent a lot of time reading during those six weeks, especially fiction of a humorous nature. He read Shalom Aleichem and Mendele Mocher Sefarim and Mark Twain and Cervantes and Dickens several times over. I went to visit him often. At the beginning he was dreadfully pale and wasted, but with the passing of the days he regained his strength. He never mentioned Nicole at all and spoke only of the books he was reading and the men who wrote them. He spoke of creators and their works with an enthusiasm which occasionally bordered on joy. "You know," he said to me once in a moment of exaltation, "during the past few days I've come to certain conclusions about matters that perplexed me when I was a young man. All my life, I searched for the purpose of things, but all my studies led me only to their causes. It seems to me that there is a certain purpose, and that purpose is creation. Happy the man born with creative powers, and happy the creator who experiences a lot of suffering in his life. It seems to me that a certain amount of suffering is good for all of us. Otherwise we would never be able to enjoy great works of art to the full."

Translated by Dalya Bilu

4

THE PHARMACIST AND THE
SALVATION OF THE WORLD

WHEN I WAS NINE years old and my brother Danny was fourteen, a new pharmacist moved into our neighborhood. On my way home from school one day I saw to my surprise that there was a new pharmacy next door to Menachem's kiosk, and it closed down again as suddenly as it had opened up. Two or three months later, when I glanced at the pharmacy on my way to school, I saw that the door was locked and the shutters down and on the shuttered window was a notice saying, SHOP TO LET.

This pharmacist, despite the shortness of his stay in our neighborhood, caused a great stir in it, and long after all traces of him had disappeared people were still discussing him and recounting his exploits.

His most momentous deed, which gave rise to a scandal the like of which had not been seen since the day Rochele, the daughter of Menachem the kiosk owner, ran away to Nablus and married an Arab government official from the Dejani family, was the battle he waged against Dr. Simon, the neighborhood doctor. Once when Dr. Simon went into the pharmacy to make a telephone call, the pharmacist fell on him shouting, "Get out of here you murderer," and began beating him up. Dr. Simon didn't keep his hands in his pockets either, but gave back as good as he got. At the end of this battle, Dr. Simon was thrown out of the pharmacy to the strains of loud applause from the drivers who were crowding around the doorway to see what a fight between a pharmacist and a doctor looked like.

There were some who said that the pharmacist was nothing but a missionary, and if not he himself—then at least his friend. The pharmacist had a friend and they both slept in the laboratory at the back of the pharmacy. Others gave it as their opinion that they were both members of British Intelligence. Another theory was that they were communists. All this, however, became known to me long after the pharmacy had closed down. I myself only succeeded in seeing and speaking to the pharmacist once, and this is the way it came about.

One morning, when I was going to school with my brother Danny, I looked at him and was overcome with pity. He seemed to me in a very sorry state. In contrast to his face, which was shrinking and growing smaller, his nose was growing bigger, and as an added embellishment several pimples had appeared on his forehead and chin. I must have stared at him wide-eyed in dismay, for he suddenly turned on me and demanded, "What are you staring at me like an idiot for?"

That was Danny all over. It was always impossible to get on with him. "Idiot yourself," I replied. "But why have you got so many pimples on your face all of a sudden?"

"Good morning!" said Danny. "Have you just woken up?"

"Yes," I said, "I've just woken up."

When we got home from school Danny went straight to the mirror and never moved from it all afternoon. He stood squeezing his pimples devoutly and making strange faces at the mirror. After three hours his pimples stuck out like red and purple flames.

"Danny, stop squeezing your pimples," I said to him. "You'll get blood poisoning."

In those days Danny was vice-president of the Health League at school and he was always going to hear lectures from Elikeren the nurse on the various kinds of germs and viruses. He was also well versed in the names of all the different diseases, but more than anything else in the world he was afraid of blood poisoning.

"Stop talking about blood poisoning," said Danny.

"Perhaps there's a cure for them," I said. "Go to the new pharmacist and ask him. You know there's a new pharmacy next door to Menachem's kiosk."

"Good morning," said Danny. "Have you just woken up?"

"Yes," I said. "I've just woken up."

"So you go and ask him."

"Why should I go?" I asked him. "I haven't got pimples on my face."

"That doesn't matter," said Danny. "You can still go and ask him if he's got a cure for pimples."

"I won't get blood poisoning," I said. "You're the one who'll suffer."

"If you don't stop talking about blood poisoning, you'll come to a bad end," shouted Danny.

"You won't get blood poisoning," I said and jumped for the door. When I reached it I turned around and added, "You've already got it."

"Bring me the bottle of alcohol," called Danny suddenly in a despairing voice. I brought him the bottle. "And now bring some absorbent cotton."

I would have brought him the cotton gladly if he had spoken to me like a human being, but he always liked giving me orders. "What do you think I am, your servant?" I asked him.

"Don't be so smart," yelled Danny in a rage. "My life's in danger and you stand there trying to be smart."

I looked at him and I saw that his life really was in danger.

His chin had swollen up and was as red as a tomato. I brought him absorbent cotton and he soaked it in alcohol, dabbed it gingerly on the tip of his chin, and immediately let out a yell.

"For God's sake," he said, "dab my face with alcohol."

Danny leaned against the wall and I gave the cotton another soaking in the alcohol until it was sopping, and then smeared it on his face with all my might while he stood writhing under my hands. At that moment a whistle was heard outside.

"It's for you, Danny," I said. "That's your whistle."

"Don't let anyone in now," begged Danny.

I went outside and saw Rina standing there with an exercise book in her hand. "Is Danny at home?" said Rina.

"What do you want Danny for?" I asked her.

"None of your business," said Rina. "Don't poke your nose into things that don't concern you."

"Danny's not at home," I said and went inside. Before I could shut the door Rina was upon me. Danny was standing in the room making faces at the mirror as usual. When he saw the two of us in the doorway he whirled rapidly round like a criminal caught red-handed. He looked about distractedly for help and when he realized that none was forthcoming, sank helplessly onto the divan.

"What's the matter?" asked Rina. You could see that she was really worried.

"Nothing," I said. "He's only got blood poisoning."

"Blood poisoning?" exclaimed Rina. She too was a member of the Health League. "What are you saying? We must call an ambulance. How on earth did you get blood poisoning, Danny?" Danny turned his face to the wall and said nothing.

"There's nothing to be surprised about," I said. "He's been standing in front of the mirror and squeezing his pimples for the past three hours."

"Loathsome, despicable liar," cried Danny and jumped up from the divan. Rina held him back and stared at his radiant chin. Danny was so red that it was impossible to tell if his pimples or his blushes were to blame.

"Believe me," he said, forcing a sort of smile to his lips, "I only squeezed one little pimple on my chin, and that for no more than three minutes."

"You're both fools," said Rina decisively, leaving no room for argument.

"It's not blood poisoning, it'll go away. Still, something should be done."

"Let him go to the new pharmacist and ask for some medicine," I said.

"How can I go outside with a chin like this?" inquired Danny in a voice of despair.

"Never mind," said Rina. "It's not the worst chin in the world."

"Let's go then," said Danny with the air of a man going to his doom, and they went out together with me following close on their heels.

"You stay where you are," ordered Danny with an angry glare in my direction. I stood on the verandah and watched the two of them walking toward the pharmacy. I stood still and waited for about three minutes and then I set out after them.

Danny was standing inside the pharmacy with his back to the door and Rina was leaning lightly against him. I looked at them and saw that Rina was really keen on Danny. Why she should have been keen on him, God alone knows. Lately he had grown so irritable that it was impossible to talk to him, and his way of speaking, too, had grown nervously hurried and disjointed. Sometimes he spoke so quickly that it was impossible to make out what he was saying.

They were both standing and listening to the pharmacist. I went inside and stood next to Rina. The pharmacist was the strangest pharmacist I had ever seen. He had no spectacles on his nose and no tie around his neck, and what amazed me most of all—he had no shoes on his feet. Underneath his khaki pants his bare toes peeped out between the straps of sandals. If it hadn't been for his white coat I would have taken him for a manual laborer. He was sitting perched on the edge of the table with one leg resting on the back of a chair and the other, on which he propped his elbow, dangling down and kicking rhythmically, and holding forth to Danny and Rina. When I entered the shop he stopped talking and gave me such a glare that I dropped my eyes and stared at the toes of my shoes. Suddenly he smiled and announced gaily, "The younger brother has arrived!"

"How do you know that I'm his brother?" I asked. I was thunderstruck.

"Ho, ho!" cried the pharmacist. "You're alike as two peas in a pod."

"That's not so!" I protested passionately. "I don't look like him."

I had never been so insulted in my life. Danny gave me an angry look and said, "What are you doing here?" I was standing in a safe place and had no fears on his score.

"And so,"—the pharmacist turned to Danny and continued with what he had been saying—"you live in the house across the road. Well I'll be damned! When I packed my bags twenty-five years ago and left for Paris to study the art of painting, the house you live in didn't exist. The whole street didn't exist. From Meah Shearim to the Schneller Wood there were only fields and rocks and olive trees. In order to reach the Alliance School I had to go through fields. Do you know why I went to the Alliance School?"

"To learn," said Danny.

"No!" shouted the pharmacist. "To be a Zionist! When I was your age I decided to be a Zionist. I ran away from the yeshiva, cut off my side-curls, and started going to the Alliance School. So you also want to be a Zionist?"

Danny looked at him and didn't know what to say. He was completely confused.

"No," I answered for him. "He doesn't want to be a Zionist. He wants to be a doctor. He's the vice president of the Health League."

"Well I'll be damned!" exclaimed the pharmacist and opened his eyes wide in amazement. "And you, young lady," he continued, turning to Rina, "are you also in the Health League?"

"Yes," said Rina, "I'm also in the Health League."

"And what do you do in the Health League?" asked the pharmacist.

Rina looked at Danny and waited for him to answer. Danny looked at Rina and waited for her to answer.

"They meet in the afternoon and hear lectures from Elikeren the nurse on germs and diseases and blood poisoning," I said to the pharmacist. "And they also look after the health of the pupils and inspect their fingernails."

"Well I'll be damned!" shouted the pharmacist and pounded the table with his fist.

"Wonder of wonders!" He got off the table, raised himself to his full height, and waved his hand in the air. "Young lady and gentlemen"—his voice became deep and solemn—"I stand before you in all my shame. I possess a Master's degree from the Sorbonne University. I studied the art of painting under the greatest artists in the world for six years, and I studied philosophy for two years, I'm a qualified pharmacist, and in spite of all this I know nothing about diseases, I've never

known how to look after my health, and my fingernails are
dirty to this very day."

With these words the door of the pharmacy opened and a
bespectacled gentleman with white hair and a red nose entered the pharmacy. He was holding a bundle of pamphlets
in his hand and he was very excited. "Jacques!" He addressed
himself directly to the pharmacist and stepped on Danny's
foot. He was so excited that he didn't even see us. He
started speaking French with a rapidity that held me spellbound, and presented the pharmacist with one of his pamphlets.

The pharmacist glanced at the pamphlet, laid his hand on
the gentleman's shoulder, and said to him in Hebrew, "Doctor Gamelin, allow me to present to you the three most important Zionists I have ever met. The persons who will determine
the future of the people of Israel and the whole of humanity."

The gentleman looked at us and smiled. He inclined his
head and said, "Pierre Gamelin."

"And this," said the pharmacist, turning to us, "is my good
friend Pierre Gamelin, Docteur en Theologie. A righteous
gentile. He taught me Hebrew grammar and he is about to
bring salvation to the world."

Pierre Gamelin took three pamphlets from the bundle in his
hand and gave one to Danny, one to Rina, and one to me. I
looked at the pamphlet and saw written on its cover in large
letters: THE ROAD TO THE SALVATION OF THE
WORLD.

"My young friends"—Pierre Gamelin addressed us in Hebrew—"know that on you yourselves, on each one of you,
the fate of the world depends. On you"—he thrust his finger
toward Danny with a vigorous movement of his hand, and
Danny retreated slightly; "and you"—he thrust the same finger toward Rina; "and you"—and he pointed at me. "And

you must know too"—here he raised his voice almost to a roar—"as you will discover by reading this book, that the way to save the world is simplicity itself. It is nothing else but the love of man. And now, my children, run along home and start work."

"What work?" I asked.

An irate expression crossed his face. "The work of saving the world," he replied.

"And how do you do that?" I asked.

This question exasperated him to such a degree that for a moment I thought he was going to attack me physically. "By love," he yelled, "by the love of man."

I wanted to ask him how to love man, but I was afraid to.

That night, before I went to sleep, I asked Danny what the pharmacist had given him for his pimples.

"He didn't give me anything," said Danny. "He said that fortunately for me, medicine had not yet discovered a cure for pimples."

I tried to fall asleep with no success. I kept thinking about the pharmacist and his friend. I tried to imagine what Jerusalem had looked like before our house had existed and before the whole street had come into being. I thought about the fields and the rocks and the olive trees. I thought about the strange pharmacist who had gone to Paris to study the art of painting and studied philosophy and returned and opened a pharmacy. I thought about his friend and I wondered how a French gentile could teach a man born in Jerusalem Hebrew grammar. I thought about the words of Pierre Gamelin, and I couldn't understand how a boy like Danny and a girl like Rina and a boy like me could bring salvation to the world. I thought about the love of man and how it was possible to love man. How it was possible to love every single man. I thought about Rina and came to the conclusion that she was the only one of us who had it in her to save the world. If she could love Danny, then she could love every man alive.

"Danny," I called suddenly, "are you asleep?"

"Yes, I'm asleep," said Danny.

"How is it possible for a pharmacist not to know anything about diseases and how to look after his own health?"

"That's how it is in Paris," said Danny. "Over there the students bribe the professors."

"You know, Danny," I said, sitting up in bed, "I think the pharmacist's not quite right in the head, and his friend seems mixed up too."

"Good morning," said Danny. "Have you just woken up?"

"Yes," I said, "I've just woken up."

A few weeks later the pharmacist disappeared and I never saw him again. Many years have passed since then and still, whenever I pass by the old neighborhood or step into a pharmacy, my heart quickens with the hope that I shall meet the sandaled pharmacist again, or his French friend who was an expert on Hebrew grammar and wanted to bring salvation to the world.

Translated by Dalya Bilu

5

THE WOMAN WITH
THE FAMILIAR SPIRIT

IN THOSE DAYS a man died and was no more. Except that
it wasn't really a question of days, it was simply a way of looking at things. Today I know that only the dead bury their
dead. And to the dead the prophet Jeremiah said, *"it shall no
more be called Tophet, nor the Valley of the Son of Hinnom,
but the valley of slaughter: for they shall bury in Tophet till
there be no place."*
Tophet only became an abomination, a tophet, when the
people they wanted to bury there were alive. It was here, in
this place, on the way to Ein Rogel, that Jeremiah stood looking down on the Valley of the Son of Hinnom and the Tophet
and the waters of Gihon and the causeway to the Fullers'
Field. Exactly here, on this hill, was the border between the
territories of Judah and Benjamin: *"And the border went up
to the top of the mountain that lieth before the valley of Hinnom westward, which is at the end of the valley of Rephaïm
northward."*
On the causeway to the Fullers' Field the Moslem women
beat the washing of the red-faced, yellow-bearded king of
Jerusalem who is not the priest of the most high God. I am
the priest of the most high God, and here I stand wearing the
robes of the Knights Templar, writing the chronicle of the
king. Standing and writing. How can I be standing and
writing? I who like writing in as much comfort as possible,

with both my elbows resting on a broad table, a real table with decent proportions. This isn't a big table, it isn't a table at all. It's a kind of lectern in a church. I'm standing leaning over it and writing. The page rustles in the wind and when I pass the palm of my hand over it to smooth away the creases, Gothic characters jump at my eyes. I leaf through the pages of a German magazine in a café garden. It's morning. The time is half past nine.

This is the first time I've had an attack of this sort in broad daylight and in the open air. Up to now this sort of thing has only happened to me at night and in closed rooms. Never in the streets and alleys, the courtyards and squares of Jerusalem under the dome of the night sky. The night has a fear of its own in the alleys of the town and its courtyards and squares and the mountains surrounding it, and who knows it as I do, face to face? But this fear, which includes an agreeable frisson at the awful grandeur perceived by the eyes of the flesh, is nothing at all compared to the terror of closed rooms, which is the terror of the other dimension of the soul when the attack comes. I call it an "attack" for lack of any apter word, and also because the term attack seems in keeping with the approach of the professional soul doctors of our day to phenomena of this kind. Moreover, it has about it, this word, the encouragement that comes from the crossing of swords. The moment that the soul of a man is attacked, he has the right and the duty to fight for it, for his soul, to strike the attacker and chase the invader out of his territory. Heaven is my witness that this is exactly what I did. I fought for my soul—for what seemed to me then to be my "soul"—night after night for weeks on end. I asked help of no one, for I knew that no one could save me, not even those dearest to me who were sleeping in the room next door. Their kind of closeness was useless to me now.

This is the way it begins—in silence. The silence of the room at night. In the knowledge that it is about to appear, I concentrate on my work—correcting examination papers. What were the reasons for Saul's defeat on Mount Gilboa? Peretz Ben-Lulu answers thus: "King Saul fought with the uncircumcised Philistines on Mount Gilboa and lost the war because he went to the woman with the familiar spirit and she was a witch woman who opens fortunes with cards and coffee and sticks ghosts onto a person and King Saul went to her after it was written that all the witches had to be killed and he himself killed all the witches and the wizards and my uncle Shiko also went to a witch who opens fortunes and she told him that he would win thirty thousand pounds on the State Lottery and so he went to buy a ticket and so a five-ton Mack diesel ran him over and so they took him to the new hospital and so he died the in night . . ." Fail, or just pass? Here it is behind my back. It stands still and I know it not. Silence—and I hear a voice. My hand freezes between "just" and "pass" and a spiraling ferment runs up my spine toward the nape of my neck and disappears into the depths of my head. The ferment dies away into a thin cold film of fear. If I don't turn my head around and confront it face to face, I'll turn into a pillar of salt fear. I stop breathing so that my breath won't turn into a scream, and with an effort above and beyond the strength of my body I turn my head around to confront him face to face. A thin film of dust covers Churchill's *History of the Second World War*. I get up to blow the dust off with my imprisoned breath and sit down again to the fate of Peretz Ben-Lulu's uncle Shiko who, too, like King Saul in his day, was tempted to go to the witch who "opens fortunes." What's the origin of this expression "opens fortunes"? I've heard it from Saul the shoemaker, too. "She'll open your fortune for half a pound." This means that they see it as a question of "opening." The witch, in their opinion, opens a double doorway for you—into the future in the form of good or bad news, and into the past in the form of the spirits of the dead.

The door of the verandah is open and the blind is down almost to the sill. The focus of my attention is fixed on Peretz's fortune teller, but its circumference discerns the body of darkness standing like a pillar through the slit in the blind. And the spiraling ferment starts again and crystallizes into a thin cold film of fear. If I don't go and confront it face to face I'll turn into a pillar of salt fear. I push back the chair, propel myself toward the door, and peep through the slit in the blind. The plants are silent in their pots. I don't return to the table, but walk up and down the room with tense, jerky steps before sitting down in an armchair. Now it fills the whole room. The tension in the air is freezing the room into a motionless silence. All solid substances are solid only because of a supreme tension. The floor of the room and its ceiling, the walls and the bookshelves and the books themselves and the table and chairs and copper utensils are solid and firmly fixed in their places only by virtue of this supreme tension. If it should slacken even for a second they would all melt and begin to drip and soon evaporate in whitish tongues of steam. I must fight to the end. If I allow it to reveal itself I'll be sucked out of this solid substantiality like water swallowed into a pipe or air sucked up into the mouth of a pump. This confronting it face to face, this fixing it with the eyes of the flesh, is what ensures its disappearance, for the senses of the flesh were created to perceive the sensual nature which stands like a barrier between men and the spirit which is the father. The world of the senses is the mother of all life, hiding with her very substantiality the spirit which sowed the seed of her substance in her. Before the sensual substance melts I burst into the baby's room. I bend over the bars of his cot. I see myself bending over the bars of his cot. I see the whole room, the pictures on the walls, the toys arranged on the shelves, the paper he scribbled black and red before going to sleep, and myself bending down and stroking his head. I see all this as if with the eye of a fly whose vision spans a circumference of 360 degrees, located in the lampshade suspended from the ceiling. The light is out, the whole room is plunged in darkness, and I found my way to the baby's bed by the reflection of the light shining in the bathroom. But now like a fly surveying the room from the heights of the ceiling, I see everything clearly in a uniform mauvish gray light, including the sleeves of my sweater where they have worn away at the elbows and the edge of my wallet sticking out of my back trouser pocket. I put my hand behind my back and push the wallet down and close the pocket button. "The strange thing about all this," I say to myself in a whisper, "is that I'm not at all surprised by the fact that I can see myself from behind, as if I were standing behind my own back." This whisper echoes in my ears as if it were coming out of a long copper tube, and the spiraling ferment running up my spine toward the nape of my neck grows more intense. This means that the time has come for Tikun Hatzoth, the Midnight Vigil.

The Midnight Vigil is a midnight walk through the streets of Jerusalem and its alleyways and courtyards. From the terror of rooms closed like prisons I flee to the open spaces of the Jerusalem night, which hits me in the face with a pure smell of mountains and the cold sparkle of stars in its deep skies and the resinous scent of pines and the mustiness of ancient stones. Night in Jerusalem in the midnight of its streets is the perpetual vision, the refuge into which I escape like someone going into a cinema after the film has already started and the lights have gone out. The permanent reassuring decor of an old, familiar play into which a man sinks in order to exorcise

his own being. The moment I'm out in the open the fear
leaves me. Only its memory persists for a little longer, like
the memory of a forgotten dream. I am like a man who has
just woken up into the reality of the outside world penetrating
him through all the gates of his senses and remembers for an
instant that he has just had a dream, but cannot for the life of
him remember what he saw in his dream. I have just this
moment completed the circuit of the Little Triangle—Jaffa
Road, King George Street, and Ben Yehuda Street. (The
Big Triangle consists of King George Street to the corner of
the windmill overlooking the walls of the Old City and back
along St. Julien Street, now called King David Road, to Jaffa
Road.) I turn off Jaffa Road and descend narrow steps into
one of the alleys of Nachalat Shiva. An even narrower cob-
bled lane branches off this alley. Saul Haimjan used to live
in the fourth house on the left when we were both in the
sixth grade and sat on the same bench in the municipal boys'
school. After that we never sat on the same bench any more
because he left school and went to be an apprentice to a
plumber.

He was the strongest boy in the whole school and he grew
up to be the strongest man I know. He was the man who
broke out of the old prison in Jerusalem and escaped with the
other four members of the Irgun Zvai Leumi who were caught
with him. On the very night that he was arrested he dismantled the iron bed in his cell, broke the locks of the door
with a bar from one of its posts, and escaped. The British
refused to believe that any man was capable of performing
such a feat with his bare hands. Now he is a plumbing con-
tractor living with his wife and his three children in Rehaviah,
and he is still strong enough to bend iron bars with his bare
hands. I don't know who lives here in this old house of his
in Nachalat Shiva now. I go into the inner courtyard and
see the mouth of the cistern in the corner and the row of

rusty tins used for geranium pots. I don't know why I am always so moved by the sight of flowerpots in slums. Tattered washing hanging on a line stretched right across the court-yard, a torn mattress vomiting its pissed-on straw out of a basement window, and in the middle of all this the geranium blossoms, peeping out in a kind of innocence that tugs at your heart.

He was sixteen and I was fourteen when we stood looking together into the mouth of the cistern and he told me about his adventures with a prostitute called Agnes in Melissanda Street. Those of us who had gone on to high school would never have dared to go to a prostitute. The soft deep waters of the cistern exuded a musty coolness, and he told me that she asked for twenty grush, two days' wages for a good ap-prentice like him. She asked for twenty grush, but she never took the stockings off her legs or the dress off her body. She only pulled it up. "What's this?" he asked her. "Aren't you going to take your stockings off?" She was dumbfounded. "What?" she demanded scandalized. "Aren't you ashamed of yourself?" And for some reason he really was ashamed. In the end, however, she agreed to make this shameful sacri-fice for him in return for another five grush. She lay flat on her back, opened her legs, crossed her hands behind her neck, and looked at the ceiling while indifferently chewing a piece of gum. Saul Haimjan shut the lid of the cistern with a dull metallic thud. "You know," he said, "it's as if she's not inside her body. As if her soul's outside her body. As if her soul doesn't care what her body does; her soul doesn't care what I do with her body."

A baby's wail suddenly rends the courtyard. I stand stock-still like a thief caught red-handed. "Sleep, sleep, my dar-ling," a woman's voice murmurs hoarsely from inside the house.

This new life in the old house doesn't know its former life.

Saul Haimjan himself hasn't been here since he went to live in Rehaviah. In his new house he has a high-fidelity radio-phonograph and an electric refrigerator and a washing machine and a mixer and a blender and he is about to buy himself an almost new Volkswagen. He works hard, from six in the morning to seven at night, and sometimes later. He works for all the building contractors in the town and they all know him. At least, that's what they think. That's what his new neighbors think, too, the neighbors who are a little frightened of this big-bodied artisan with his loud resonant voice and his strange laugh. "But the truth is," he confided in me, "that even my wife doesn't know me. Even my children don't."

Even a wife and children are only next of kin. If you're lucky they're also dear to your heart, close to you with the closeness of the three-dimensional soul—and that's the most that any man can hope for unless a window to the fourth dimension has been torn open in his eyes. I myself didn't know him until the attacks came upon me and he took me to the woman with the familiar spirit. And in this world of ours, the world of the three-dimensional soul whose tools and concepts and language and conventions I am compelled to use to tell my story, the credit must go to Agnes the prostitute—of good and blessed memory to me at any rate. I know that forcing things belonging to the fourth dimension into the confines of the three-dimensional world is liable to distort them to such an extent that they may end up by seeming ridiculous, but this slight risk of appearing ridiculous, or even grotesque, is one which faces any man who looks at his reflection in a narrow, distant mirror.

As for the story itself—I was sitting, as is my wont on mornings free from the nuisance of teaching, on a wicker chair in the shade of an ancient pine in the garden of the Café Peter in the Street of the Valley of Rephaim.* In this valley—so

* *Rephaim* in Hebrew means giants or ghosts.

I learn from experts on the topography of the Bible—the Rephaim dwelt in the days of Abraham the Patriarch and it was here too that King David defeated the Philistines. But all this is ancient history. The only traces recognizable here today are those of a much more recent past—that of not even a hundred years ago. These houses surrounding me were built about eighty years ago by German Christians, members of the Society of Templars, who actually gave the quarter the name Rephaim and in their language called it Templer Kolonie Rephaim. They also surrounded their houses with these stone walls and planted these trees. I don't know if there is any connection between these Templars of eighty years ago and the order of the famous warrior monks in the days of the Crusader Kingdom of Jerusalem. During the days of the Second World War the Mandate authorities removed the Germans from their homes and replaced them with British soldiers and officials. In the evening hours the café is usually full of Hungarian Jews of the café owner's acquaintance, who fill the place with their loud, penultimately accented syllables, their cigarette smoke, and the fervor of the card games in which they are sometimes joined, oddly enough, by Iraqui Jews. During the day the place is empty because of its distance from the center of town and its lack of an espresso machine or any other modern amenity capable of attracting men firmly anchored in the world of progress. Ancient pine trees in a secluded garden, a high stone wall overgrown with moss, and creaking wicker chairs are capable of attracting only those stricken with longings for a different reality, another substantiality to which they can attach themselves only in intimate seclusion, anonymity, and self-effacement. It is these few who make their way here in the mornings, trembling with tension, for hasty, breathless, extramatrimonial encounters. Thus, for example, on every Tuesday morning, the third day, of which it is twice said, "and God saw that it was good,"

I am assured of seeing the famous head of the Internal Medicine Department at the hospital pushing open the gates to the café garden. Not, to be sure, with his habitual self-esteem and authoritative bearing, but with a hurried, furtive air, casting anxious glances to his left and right. He selects the most secluded bench, in the corner behind the angle in the fence, and once seated, sinks into a profound meditation behind the pages of whatever paper he finds lying close to hand. The trouble is that she, the woman for whose sake he has been trying so desperately to efface, and even to obliterate himself entirely, she rushes gaily up to him from the taxi which brings her here three quarters of an hour late with a clatter of high heels and a waving of bare arms in a magnificent and uninhibited salute, and before he has time to defend himself snatches the newspaper out of his hands so that it won't interfere with her embraces. I avert my face discreetly and see the sturdy neck of Saul Haimjan, who is walking calmly down the street with his erect bearing and the slight familiar tremor in his left knee. Before I can call out to him he sees me and stops. I wave to him and he greets me with the usual salaams, and we begin talking about all these things. I tell him, as if it were a matter of course, that only last night, at midnight, I walked around the Little Triangle, as we used to do every Saturday when we were boys, and also went into the yard of his old house. But it was not a matter of course for me to have suddenly departed from the lighthearted tone of our exchanges on all the chance meetings of the past ten years, and I sent him a hint from the world of the attacks in these words: "Do you remember, Saul, how we stood next to the mouth of the cistern in your yard and you told me about your first time with Agnes the prostitute? Last night, when I was standing in the yard and I saw the cistern mouth, I remembered what you said then."

As I speak I can sense my voice sinking lower and lower

under the pressure of his eyes until it drops to a dead whisper. "Believe me or not," I continue in this spookish manner, only my lips moving and my voice inaudible, "I felt exactly like her, I felt that my soul was outside my body, that I was standing behind my body and seeing myself from behind."

In contrast to my ghostly whisper he bursts into loud laughter as if he has just heard a great joke—a strange laugh like the blowing of staccato notes on a ram's horn which is enough to unnerve his business acquaintances and his learned neighbors and, needless to say, his wife during one of the constant quarrels between them. This laugh upsets the order in the café garden and throws it into an uproar. The famous doctor's face contracts in a grimace of pain, and the lady of the clear voice and the radiant face turns toward us in astonishment strewn with the light of an inner joy. "Is this thy voice, my son David?" King Saul asked David on the rocks of the wild goats after coming out of the cave. And she too would have cried, "Is this thy voice, my dear Saul?" If only her powers of speech had equaled the strength of her feelings, and if only her knowledge of Hebrew had been equal to the occasion. However, since her powers of expression were meager in the best of circumstances, and in the Hebrew language in particular, all that came out of her mouth was the cry, "Mr. Jan!" She probably meant to say "Mr. Haimjan," or perhaps she thought his first name was Haim and his surname Jan. In any case she reinforced her cry with an inviting wave of her hand and he rose and went over to her. "This is Mr. Jan," she explained to the famous doctor, who had somewhat belatedly realized that he had not been found worthy of the miracle granted Korach and his followers whom the earth had opened up to swallow, and unwillingly resigned himself to the fact that he was exposed to every eye—"who did the plumbing in my new house."

"Dr. Pascalowitz doesn't remember me," said Saul Haim-jan, "but we've already met. The doctor was our medical officer when we occupied the Valley of Rephaim and the whole area from here to Bet Zafafa."

"Yes, yes, of course," said the doctor, without specifying exactly what was a matter of course—that is to say, whether it was a matter of course that Haimjan remembered him, or whether it was a matter of course that he did not remember Haimjan—and his outstretched hand was swallowed up in Saul's.

"Sigmund will excuse us for a moment," said the lady with a smile in the doctor's direction, rising from her seat. She took hold of Saul's elbow and piloted him toward the pine tree, in whose shade they stood and spoke together until the doctor finished smoking the cigarette in his hand and lit another one.

Saul returned and sat down at the table by my side with a soft and somewhat distant expression on his face. At this moment it became clear to me that the woman was Agnes, and I found myself becoming strangely garrulous. "This isn't the way I imagined her at all. I thought she was much older. Why, it's fifteen years since you went to her. Still it isn't really so surprising. It's quite possible that she herself was only twenty then, or even less. Which means that she could easily be no more than thirty-five today."

Her excitement at seeing him wasn't at all compatible with the words of the youth of fifteen years ago—"her soul doesn't care what her body does; her soul doesn't care what I do with her body." And hadn't she moreover just explained to her companion that ". . . this is Mr. Jan who did the plumbing in my new house." Which meant that their relationship had over the years transcended the commercial ties of the flesh and moved into the sphere of the art of building and creation.

And another conclusion to be drawn from this same short sentence was that she was a householder in Israel. A new house in Jerusalem the Rebuilt. A capable woman, what's more, who conducted her affairs with intelligence and good taste, to judge from the way in which she kept the passionate Dr. Pascalowitz languishing in suspense. These and similar fragmentary reflections clouded the horizons of my thoughts until they completely eclipsed the obvious question, namely: whence came this clear and certain knowledge that the woman before me was indeed Agnes, she and no other? The knowledge leaped out of my innermost self and crashed through the windows of my consciousness like a bullet fired from the muzzle of a gun, and the presence of Saul was only the finger which pressed the trigger.

"And so," continued Saul with the same soft and somewhat distant expression on his face, returning to what I had been saying to him before he had uttered the strange laugh which had caused Agnes to become aware of his presence, and which had been cut off in his encounter with her. "You felt exactly like her. You felt that your soul was outside your body. Well, well. I see, my learned friend, that you too will end up by paying a visit to Miss Clarissa Oberlander."

"Is it worth it?"

"It's nothing really. Just a way to pass the time. No tricks, even . . ."

And in this way I too ended up by paying a visit to Miss Clarissa Oberlander, Agnes's old friend.

After the relationship between Saul and Agnes had deepened beyond the flesh to the spiritual bone beneath, Agnes took Saul to the séances conducted by Clarissa, her friend in the revealed world who had opened a way into the occult world for her. As for me, I did not go to see the woman with the familiar spirit until the second attack came upon me in broad daylight, and by then the relations between Agnes and Clarissa had deteriorated to such an extent that Agnes had stopped attending the spiritualist séances of her friend with the familiar spirit altogether, which goes to show that familiarity with the spirit world is no protection against the troubles that plague human relations in this world. Because of these troubles I didn't see Agnes at the séance which I attended, but I did see her in the dimension of the second attack which overtook me in broad daylight, the same attack which caused me to ask Saul to take me with him to one of the séances.

The second attack was on the same continuum as the first, like a recurrent dream which follows its predecessor and forms a sequel to it. I am standing bent over a lectern in a church and writing the chronicle of the red-faced, yellow-bearded king of Jerusalem. The king has raised me to the dignity of exalted office, and he has also entrusted me with the writing of the history of the kingdom and the education of the nine-year-old son who was born of his union with Agnes of the clear voice and the radiant face. I go over to the arched church window and see the Moslem slave girls beating the washing on the causeway to the Fullers' Field. They stop their work and fall on their faces at the sight of the king riding down the path leading to the Valley of Rephaim, where the cavalry are gathering for the holy war against the infidel. The columns of riders fill all the paths—from the Ophel and the Mount of Olives and Gethsemane and the Valley of Jehosophat and the Kidron and Ein Rogel, they weave through the Valley of the Son of Hinnom and assemble in the Valley of Rephaim. From there they will ride along the bed of the Sorek Stream until they reach the plain. The whole people, men and women, graybeards and babes in arms, have ascended the rooftops and climbed the towers and perched on the battlements in order to acclaim the King and his army. I alone have remained here, in the church. The knights of the military order of the Temple are passing by the window now. A big red cross is sewn onto their white robes and I am one of them. The last knight, the one bringing up the rear, turns toward me the face of Saul Haimjan and waves his sword at me in greeting, and I bless him with the sign of the cross. I bless their going to war, too, arming them with faith and inspiring them with courage to triumph over the infidel, and promise them that they will inherit the kingdom of heaven. But I myself am not accompanying them into battle, because I have risen to greatness and high office. The king has placed his trust in me and made me responsible for educating his son and writing the history of his kingdom, for the benefit of the generations hidden in the bowels of the future.

The knight pulls the reins and the horse's mouth drips saliva. He stamps his feet and stops. The head of the horse and that of his rider fill the window like a picture in a frame. This knight is not a nobleman by birth, but he is my good friend. His father was not a knight nor his mother a lady, nor were they even of the respectable burgher class. He springs from the humblest of the common people, but still he has a dauntless spirit. He is valiant in arms, honest and righteous in his deeds, and wise in his words—although he was never taught to read and write in his youth. It was I who raised him from the rank of arms-bearer and knighted him after he had saved my life from the hands of Moslems plotting to kill me when we were climbing to Jerusalem, the capital city of the kingdom.

His face in the window frame is swarthy, like the faces of the poorest of the townsfolk, bearing witness to the mixing of Moslem blood over the generations in the veins of those who had borne them. His expression is soft and somewhat distant. "My learned friend," he says to me, "give me your blessing before I die." "Do not sin with your lips," I say to him. "You will return from the battle crowned with glory, and many great deeds of heroism are still before you."

"No, for I shall surely die," he answers me, and the expression on his face is soft and distant. "Evil thoughts are in my heart, and the man who thinks them will not live. Evil thoughts, heretical thoughts have come upon me. I doubt one of the basic tenets of our church and faith. I doubt the resurrection of the dead."

"What troubles you, my son?" I ask him and prepare myself to receive his confession from the other side of the window.

"Tell me, Father," he asks, and his eyes are troubled, "tell me, I pray you, is there any way of proving by reliable and authoritative evidence that there is a future resurrection? Is there any way of proving this outside the doctrine which I believe, the teaching of Christ our Savior and the holy men who followed him?"

"The teaching of our Lord and Redeemer is sufficient," I answer him, "for in many passages of the Gospel he plainly teaches the future resurrection of the body. He promises that he will come as judge to judge the quick and the dead and the world with fire. To the elect he says that he will give a kingdom prepared from the foundation of the world; but the wicked shall be consigned to the eternal fire which is prepared for the devil and his angels. The pious declaration of the Holy Apostles and the Patriarchs of the Old Testament suffices."

"I firmly believe all this," he responds, "but I seek a reason whereby this can be proved to one who doubts these things and does not accept the doctrine of Christ and believe in a future resurrection and another life after this death."

I answer him in these words: "Put yourself then in the place of a man so afflicted and let us try to ascertain something about this matter. You acknowledge that God is just?"

He answers, "I acknowledge that nothing is more true."

Then I continue: "Is it also just that good be repaid for good and evil for evil?"

He replies, "That is true."

"In this life," I go on, "that does not often happen. For some good people suffer nothing but troubles and adversity in this world, while many evil persons rejoice in continual happiness, as the evidence of daily life teaches us."

Again he answers, "It is so."

"If so," I say, "there will be another life and a resurrection of this flesh, when all who have merited either good or evil in this life must receive their reward."

To this he responds, "This seems to me to be true and good beyond measure. Your words have been as refreshing to my spirit as a shower of rain on dry grass. You have wrested all doubt from my heart and saved my soul from the tophet prepared for heretics. It is not for me, a poor and ignorant man, to laud and praise your name but you have merited much. Here we are setting forth for the Holy War against the Moslems in defense of our souls and lives and faith, and I know well how hard it is for you to remain behind, and how great is the temptation in the heart of a man to prove himself in the battle and win a hero's laurels! But even I, the last and least of the knights, am well aware that your work here is more important for the future of us all than victory in the battle. The king did well in choosing you to tend to the soul of his small son. The soul of the heir to the throne lies in your hands like clay in the hands of the potter. His pure and innocent soul is tied to yours, and he looks up to you as to his father and mother, if not more so. For the king has spent his life on the field of battle, and forgotten gentle manners and even moral principles; more than once the child has been removed from the dining hall to spare him the sight of his father's drunkenness and shame. The king is only the father of his flesh, but you are the father of his soul. May the blessing of God be upon you all the days of your life. Amen, amen."

The Knights of the Temple have already crossed the Valley of Hinnom and only the last of the riders can be seen on the other side. The knight spurs his horse to overtake them, and the whole populace bursts from the gates of the city in their wake: from the Zion Gate and the Dung Gate, Herod's Gate and the Lions' Gate, the crowds of people pour to take their leave of the departing warriors. The church bells are all ringing, the bells of the Church of the Holy Sepulcher and of the Church of the Mother of God, the bells of the Church of Lazarus of the Resurrection and those of St. John the Almoner. The thunder of the bells fills the temple nave until there is no room left to breathe and I, alone here, kneel beneath its weight and bow to the ground. There is something good and pure and precious and holy that I have to do but I don't remember what it is. I have an urgent duty to perform, but its memory has escaped me and only the urgency remains. I know that it is here, here in this place, but I don't know who or what it is. The domed ceiling, full to the depths of its height with the clamor of the bells, leans on my head and presses down like the weight of the world. If I don't escape in time I'll be crushed like a beetle under the hoof of a war horse. I retire to the vestry to seek what I have lost. My hand pushes the heavy wooden door open and I bend down and enter. Her hands grasp the bars, her face is to the window and her back to me; it is Agnes, the mother of the heir to the throne. I go up to her and lean over her shoulder to see what is happening outside. The window overlooks the inner court and there is nothing to be seen but the high stone walls of the fence. Agnes does not turn her face to me. I take hold of her shoulders with both my arms and rub my face in her hair. I kiss the nape of her neck for a long time. She turns her face up and sighs.

"Why did you stay so long?" she asks me.

And I say, "I was fortifying Saul's spirit before he goes into battle."

Agnes answers, "He is more important to you than I am, and I believed in your love."

She falls face down on the sofa and I crouch over her. "Show yourself to me," I whisper into her ear, "for the sight of your body surpasses the imaginings of desire. Take off your headband and your ribbons and your ornaments, for the glory of your flesh is better by far than the bravery of tinkling anklets and crescents and rings. All your finery is worthless compared to the quivering nipples of your breasts and the bountiful curves of your thighs, and all the balm of Gilead and the perfumes of Damascus are as nothing compared to the rose of your mouth and the desire of your blood-red lips."

"Please don't stop," she murmurs. "Please let me hear your voice going on, and on and on. You speak to me and your words arouse my desire. You water my furrows with your words and melt me like rain falling on mown grass, like a shower of raindrops at the full moon. Go on, I beg you, and don't stop . . ." I pull her girdle and tear it open and the robe falls to the ground. Agnes crouches on the sofa in all her nakedness. I lean over her and the sound of the swift steps of the nine-year-old boy running with all his might down the length of the nave in search of me echoes in my ears like the thunder of the bells which preceded it. Here he is behind the vestry wall. Here he is, the child, the heir to the throne, and I still haven't the strength to pull my shuddering body away from Agnes's clinging, sucking flesh. The child's shadow blackens his mother's white flesh. He stands in the doorway, his satchel in his left hand, and in his right the rosary I dropped when I was confessing the knight Saul at the window. He picked it up and has hurried to return it to me, full of happiness at his find. He stands looking at us, still breathing heavily from his joyful, skipping run. He looks at us in silence. His thin legs begin to tremble. The trembling increases until he is shaking all over and the coral beads of the rosary dangling from his hand swing to and fro. His legs give way and he sits down on the threshold steps, without letting go of either the satchel or the rosary. His bony knees are close together and they keep knocking into each other. A kind of moaning shudders between his lips as if he is feverish.

"The child is ill," I say to the Moslem doctor who was summoned from Damascus after the court doctor had admitted that he, like the other physicians of the West, was ignorant of the diseases of the East. "White spots have appeared on his feet, his ankles, and his shins," I explain to the Moslem, drawing back the sheet to expose the child's legs. The child is lying on his back on the church altar, which serves as his bed. The doctor takes a needle from the pouch in his belt and begins to prick the sick child's legs with it. His legs don't move and there is no change in his expression. The needle penetrates deeper into the flesh, and there is no visible reaction. It is clear that he has no feeling in his afflicted legs. In the vestry the doctor delivers his verdict without hesitation. The child has leprosy. Gradually, over a period of many years, his limbs will rot and disintegrate. First he will lose the feeling in his hands and feet, then he will lose the light of his eyes and go blind, and in the end the rot will afflict his brain. Who knows whether he will live to see the light of day on his eighteenth birthday, and who knows whether it would not be better for him to return his soul to the Creator, extolled be His name, long before. I kneel down before the child and pray. "My Lord the Grand Vizier," says the Moslem doctor, for I have

indeed been appointed by the queen mother and the council
of nobles to the office of chancellor of the kingdom and guard-
ian of the heir to the throne, until he attains his majority—an
appointment which took effect from the moment we received
the news of the death in battle of the red-faced, yellow-bearded
king of blessed memory, who fought like a lion to his last
breath, as befitting one who bore the cross of our Lord Jesus
Christ. "My Lord who is elevated and exalted over all this
kingdom! It is related (but God alone is all-knowing, as well
as all-wise and all-powerful and all-bountiful) that there are
ancient holy men, hermits dwelling in the mountains and the
deserts, who read the hidden thoughts of men and see into
their hearts. These men possess the secret of the healing of
souls and by this means they can cure too all the afflictions of
the flesh and its evil maladies. But I, the humblest of your
slaves and the least of the doctors of the flesh, I possess nothing but what my eyes behold and what my bag contains in the
way of soothing balms and potions and drugs, and in none of
these is a cure for leprosy to be found. Nothing remains but
for us to pray to the Merciful, the Compassionate, and hope
for the best."

And I pray. For many years now I have been praying to the
God of mercy and compassion to remove the leprosy from the
child and transfer it to my flesh. I pray to the Mother of God
not to postpone my punishment to the world to come. I pray
to Jesus Christ in the greatness of his mercy to afflict me at
once with the child's leprosy and with festering sores of every
kind, and not to postpone my just deserts to the day of judgment. I implore him in the fullness of his grace to cure the
boy now, this very moment, and infect my body with his illness. I pray and pray and know that I am unworthy of this
grace. The child's big brown eyes, fixed in a wide-open stare,
have been blind for centuries; his face disintegrated long ago,

and only the two blind eyes fixed in the face of the clock are left. The clock has stopped and a spiraling ferment runs up my spine toward the nape of my neck and disappears into the depths of my head. The ferment melts away into a thin cold film of fear. If I don't turn my head around, I'll turn into a pillar of salt fear. I stop breathing so that my breath won't turn into a scream and with an effort over and above the strength of my body I turn my head around to confront it face to face. I see the famous doctor pushing the iron gates of the café garden open with a hurried, furtive air, casting anxious glances to his right and left. Which means that it is Tuesday, the third day, of which it is said twice, "and God said that it was good," that the time is ten o'clock in the morning and that Lady Agnes is due to appear within the hour. I make haste to remove myself before she arrives, and hurry to Saul Haimjan's workshop to ask him to take me at last to one of Miss Clarissa Oberlander's spiritualist séances.

We arrived at her house on Monday evening at five to nine. On the corner of the street my eye fell for the first time on a sign reading: "Clarissa Oberlander. Psychotherapy. Sundays, 5–6 P.M." I often pass this sign, whenever I visit the cinema on the corner, and yet I've never noticed it before. In the street itself I used to play in the days of my childhood many years ago—a quarter of a century and more. In the place where the sign now hangs there used to be a high-class café—or so it seemed to me then because of the round pillars supporting its ceiling—whose main business came from the British soldiers and policemen. Here my father was in the habit of sitting in his free hours, and sometimes he used to take me with him. I remember how strange and pointless the whole business of sitting in cafés seemed to me then. What was there in this boring pastime of just sitting about, all crowded together, that made it so attractive to grown-ups? Once Father wanted to show off my talents to his companions and asked his friend, the limping café owner, for some sheets of paper. He said to me, "And now, David, draw something for us." I was glad— not so much because I wanted the approval and admiration of the grownups surrounding me with their cigarette-smoke smell, but because I had found an interesting occupation to dispel the boredom of enforced idleness. I drew and drew and was carried away and filled all the sheets of paper and asked for more. To this day there sometimes rises in me, embarrassed and ashamed and painful, like the memory of the neighbor's daughter standing in the melancholy pool of light from the street lamp and waiting for us in vain because our eyes had gone whoring after the tapping high heels of girls in other streets, the old passion of my youth for filling rough pages of paper with colors and forms, and, as is my wont, I appease it with the vain promise that "when I have the time, one Saturday morning, I'll go out to the fields and draw." Why precisely to the fields I don't know. Opposite Miss Clarissa Oberlander's house is the shoemaker's shop where I used to go to mend the soles of my shoes, which wore out once every two or three weeks. I would sit and wait for the soles to be repaired with my eyes fixed on the picture hanging behind the shoemaker's back.

Once I found myself sitting on the tree in the picture, and it was a picture of horses and hunters in red coats. Only the voice of the shoemaker, who had finished mending my shoes, dislodged me from it. When Saul Haimjan rang the bell on the iron door, an ancient memory tugged at my heart—not from the days of my childhood, but from a dream I dreamed in the days of my childhood. I leave the shoemaker's shop and get into a gray car. I drive it. I know how to drive it, but I don't know where the brakes are or how to stop it. I hold the steering wheel and drive the car in a mood of exhilaration tinged with an exciting frisson of fear. The car picks up speed until it is flying so fast that it no longer obeys the steering wheel. The steering wheel obeys it. I abandon myself to the acceleration of the flight and my whole being shudders with a horrifying gaiety.

Saul Haimjan rang the bell with his right hand; in his left he was holding a bottle of orange squash. On the way he had explained to me that each participant in the séance brought some light refreshment with him because of the sensitivity of the woman with the familiar spirit. Belonging as she did to a family of property, she was always on her guard against those people who were less eager to contact the spirit world than they were to enjoy the delicacies of her table free, gratis, and for nothing. It seems hardly necessary to point out that even in its palmiest days, when the people living on it were re-garded, according to the notions of those times, as holding high and privileged positions in society (that is to say, primary school teachers and petty officials in the national institutions), the street had never set eyes on a man of property. Let alone now, when the only people left in it were the poorest of the shoemaker's customers, those who weren't ashamed even now of going to the cinema with patches on their shoes. This being the case, what was she doing here? A woman of property, who was furthermore a healer of souls (as it said on the sign, Sun-days from 5 to 6 P.M.), and, as if this wasn't enough, also a woman (as her more intimate friends, those admitted to her confidence, were well aware) with a familiar spirit, learned in occult wisdom? To this day I don't know the answer to this question, and from the little that Saul Haimjan told me, it seems that her family have not yet found a satisfactory explan-ation either. It appears that she belongs to a family of ship-builders from Germany who, when Hitler rose to power, fled to England, where they are known today by the name of

Oberlander and Co., Shipbuilders. Until I met her, I had always assumed that shipbuilding as a family occupation had died out among the children of Israel in the distant days of Deborah the prophetess, who was puzzled even then by the tribes which followed this outlandish calling, as we learn from her great question, "And why did Dan remain in ships?" One thing, at any rate, was clear and might as well be stated here: these shipbuilding Oberlanders of Liverpool, whether they were descended from the tribes of Dan, Asher, and Zebulun or not, were obviously quite content to remain in ships in the West—as long as Clarissa remained in the East.

Clarissa herself opened the door to us. She had a pair of enormous breasts overflowing from the low neck of her tight blue dress, and short white socks turned down over the tops of her heavy shoes—the kind of white socks which used to adorn girls' ankles in the days when blue skirts and Russian sarafands were in fashion. The munificence of her bosom was counterbalanced by the blight which had devastated her head, and her sparse gray hairs—a surviving remnant of the glory of bygone days—refused to submit to the discipline of her fingers, which were constantly returning to smooth them down. Nevertheless, traces of a distant charm could still be discerned in her broad face with its high cheekbones, short nose, and small, slightly squinting eyes, which twinkled with a sort of smile as if ready and willing for a mischievous wink. This woman, who seemed to be somewhere between her fiftieth and sixtieth year, had about her the aura characteristic of well brought up girls from the beginning of the century—an aura which always touches my heart with a bitter compassion, like all fond hopes which have been shockingly mutilated by reality. It wouldn't have surprised me in the least if Saul Haimjan had informed me that she had been a socialist preaching conscientious objection during the First World War and a communist fighting in the ranks of the International Brigade during the civil war in Spain; just as I felt no surprise at seeing Sigmund Freud, left hand on his hip and right hand holding a smoking cigar, looking out of a big picture hanging opposite the door of the room which we entered, after passing in Indian file through a long dark corridor between two rows of various artistic postcards, both framed and unframed. This was the order in which we walked down the corridor: at the head marched Miss Clarissa Oberlander with a nonchalant hum which changed into a shrill staccato whistle, and behind her, sturdy and broad-shouldered in his narrow-fitting Sabbath clothes and the tie knotted tightly around his massive neck, stepped Saul with the hand holding the bottle of orange squash thrust forward in a military salute. Behind him I groped my way with caution after an accident with the row of paraffin tins standing at the entrance to the corridor.

The room was smothered in threadbare furniture. A tap fixed for some mysterious reason below the portrait of Freud was dripping into a cracked enamel basin. Dusty bookshelves bent under their heavy load of books, Botticelli's Venus rose from the water under the penetrating gaze of Freud, a Persian carpet lay beneath a three-legged table and a plush armchair, and the whole place was charged with an ill-boding, spooky tension. There were two people sitting at the table. One was a thin and very red-faced Jew who had a turban wound around his head like an Indian and went by the name of "the Hindu." After spending thirty years in India he had attained the exalted degree, for which he was famed throughout Jerusalem, of being able to deliver a lecture in the Y.M.C.A. while maintaining the lotus position for three hours on end. The other was a good-looking young man with a long narrow mustache, who was an electronics instructor in a vocational school. He was holding some kind of camera in his hands and it was

this which had brought down the wrath of the Hindu and of
Miss Clarissa Oberlander on his head. It appeared that he
was resolved upon photographing the spirits of the dead who
would take part in the evening's séance with infrared rays.
The Hindu opposed this project on two grounds, both meta-
physical and moral, while the woman with the familiar spirit
without going into these subtleties commanded him to "stop
this nonsense at once." The young man accordingly took his
camera and left. The Hindu too got up to leave soon afterward, because he had suddenly remembered his little girl who
was waiting for him. This rather endeared him to me, his
being the father of a little girl and his remembering her.

After the two of them had gone, Saul Haimjan and I were
left alone with Clarissa, who was still smarting with annoy-
ance at the impertinence of the electrician, and with nothing
to do but wait for Temmes so that the séance could begin.
Because of the disagreement between herself and Clarissa
which I have already referred to, Agnes did not come, nor did
we expect her. As for Temmes, he came more than a quarter
of an hour late because his fifth alarm clock had failed to go
off. The five alarm clocks standing in a row on the table by
his bed were always set to go off at one-minute intervals,
otherwise he would never have woken up. According to him
this marvelous capacity for sleep was not an inherited talent,
but simply a function of the difficult conditions of his life.
For the past thirteen years he had been working harder than
could be expected of any normal man. At night he worked
as a proofreader on the Hungarian newspaper, and during
the day he was to be found in the biology laboratories of the
university, where he had been preparing himself all these
years to qualify for the degree of Master of Science. Twice
during the past five years he had attempted to take the final
examinations, and on both occasions he had been forced to

withdraw at the very last minute, when he was already sitting in the examination hall with the question papers before him, because of the drowsiness that suddenly overcame him; he felt that his head wasn't clear enough to reveal its hidden treasures, and it would have been unseemly for him, Temmes, to receive mediocre or maybe even lower marks in his final examinations after so many years of study and research. His perseverance in his studies was thus no less than his profound capacity for sleep and his figure was accordingly a familiar one—the figure of a man in his forties with a big face, eyes looking out wearily from behind dark glasses, a balding head, and fat hairy legs emerging from khaki shorts—to all the generations of students who had passed through the laboratories of the Department of Biology during the last decade. However, since the students and their teachers were strangers to the world of spiritual reality, they were familiar only with Temmes's material aspect, and he himself was careful to keep any hint of the occult world, in which he had attained a higher degree than Saul Haimjan and the others, from their ears. He was closer to Miss Clarissa Oberlander than they were, and even met her outside the hours of the séances. Recently their relationship had penetrated to a level of profound intimacy, and she had started to consult him on matters pertaining to the question of marriage. From Saul I learned that it was Temmes who had inserted Clarissa's brief and pointed advertisements for a suitable husband in the "Personal" columns of the German-language newspaper and the *Jerusalem Post*. They ran as follows: "Cultivated, well-educated, middle-aged woman of independent means requires middle-aged man. *Requisite* qualities: nobility of spirit, broad-mindedness, love of art, psychological understanding of the feminine heart. *Desirable* qualities: ability to earn his own living, aesthetic appearance, tall stature. *N.B.* Those over the age of sixty-five are definitely requested *not* to apply." Temmes brought a packet of biscuits with him to the séance and handed them over to Clarissa. After apologizing for his lateness due to the break-down of the fifth alarm clock, he gave me his hand in greeting and said, "You look familiar to me. We've already met some-where."

"Very likely," I said. "It's difficult for one old Jerusalemite to meet another without having run into him somewhere be-fore, in the army or in the university corridors . . ." His face too seemed familiar to me from long ago.

"Perhaps from the biology laboratories?"

"No," I said, "I was never a biology student. From the Café Peter probably, in the German Colony. You sometimes play cards there in the evenings . . ."

A vein started to throb in his temple and he blinked his eyes with the air of a man whose feelings have been hurt. "I work at night," he said. "I haven't any time for cafés."

"Maybe in the morning then." I hurried to repair the pain-ful impression created by my remark about playing cards at night in cafés. "I usually sit there on the days when I don't teach. On Tuesdays usually, and also on holidays . . . In the mornings I'm always at the University, in the biochemistry laboratory."

This blundering and fruitless exchange did nothing to im-prove the ill humor and sulky looks of Clarissa, who was still upset by the obstinate persistence of the young technician in his impertinent plan to photograph her invisible guests with-out even obtaining her permission. If the politeness customary between strangers imposed a certain constraint on her manner toward me, the intimate relationship between herself and Temmes allowed her to order him to sit down in these words: "Stop talking nonsense already, Mischa, and sit down. Isn't it enough that you came so late? And stop drumming on the table with your fingers. It makes me nervous. Well, why are we standing? Let's sit down." And we all sat down around the table.

"In what language shall we conduct the séance?" Clarissa asked rhetorically, and Saul gave the expected, in fact the only possible answer, which was "English" since Clarissa herself knew no Hebrew and Saul and I spoke no German. It must be said in praise of all those present that none of them tried to dazzle the others with the polished phrases of Englishmen born and bred, old boys of Harrow and Oxford Univeristy, but each spoke as his heart bade him—Clarissa in an English that sounded like a German dialect and Temmes with a pure Hungarian accent. As for Saul Haimjan, I expected him to sound like the announcer on Radio Ramalla in one of its English-language broadcasts, but he surprised me by sounding exactly like a Russian, perhaps because his ancestors came from the Caucasian mountains.

In any event, there were no hitches due to misunderstandings, and we all obeyed Clarissa's instructions. She ordered us to open the séance with a silent prayer. "Each of us," she said, "will close his eyes and pray to the good Lord to remove all alien thoughts and sinful desires from his heart. May He light our way in the darkness and make us worthy to meet superior beings and pure spirits and the souls of the dear departed." I accordingly closed my eyes. Through their lids I succeeded in making out a diamond brooch in the shape of a rose pinned to the bodice of Clarissa's blue dress. "This diamond brooch," I said to myself, "is the only sign so far of our hostess's wealthy family."

Hardly had I expelled this trivial reflection from my mind when Clarissa jumped up from her place and exclaimed, "Oh, I forgot! We must put out the lights and play some music. Music always helps. So what shall we play tonight?

I think we would all like to hear something by Bach." She
went to put out the light and the room immediately sank
into darkness. Only Clarissa's diamond brooch glittered in
the night-light standing on the table. She fumbled with
the buttons on the phonograph, on whose turntable the Bach
recording already reposed, and it erupted into a series of
rasping noises from the scratching of the blunt needle on
the sensitive surface of the record. She stopped it at once
and returned to her place at the table with the remark, "I
think we will do without music this time. I forgot that the
phonograph needle was spoiled. I seem to remember asking
you several times to buy me a new packet of phonograph
needles, but you always forget what I say to you. Mischa,
Mischa! Stop being so scatterbrained and learn to concentrate."

Michael Temmes, to whom the last words were addressed,
shook his head sadly, and we all returned to our silent prayers
without the assistance of music. This time I distinguished between the lids of my half-closed eyes a string of amber beads
hanging on the wall not far from the basin, of the kind the
Arabs feel between their fingers when sitting on café stools
or walking in the street. These beads bothered me. Instead of
sinking into silent prayer I started worrying about where I
knew Temmes's face from. Maybe we had served together in
the army?

"No, no. This time it isn't going to work," said Clarissa at
the end of the prayer. She glanced around the room and said
to Temmes, "Mischa, you try to be the medium this time."
Mischa protested quietly but firmly. He was too tired for the
tremendous concentration required of a medium.

"Try clairvoyance," said Saul Haimjan. "We'll help you."

"They will refuse me this time," said Clarissa. "The boy
with the camera made me too cross, and the Hindu was not
in order either."

Temmes reached for the top of the bookshelf on his right and drew forth a rectangular wooden board with the letters of the Latin alphabet written all around its margins. "Let's try the planchette," he said, and placed it on the table. In the meantime Saul whispered into my ear in Hebrew, "I felt at once that it would be a flop. The night's lost."

"Not everything is lost," I replied for some reason.

"Mischa, Mischa," shouted Clarissa, jumping up again from her armchair, "you know very well that I hate the planchette. I can't stand the sight of it!" And she seized the board and flung it in the direction of her bed. The planchette sank into the bedspread, whose belly swollen with pillows and eiderdowns reached almost to Venus emerging from the water. By now Clarissa was breathing heavily from anger.

"We'll have to be satisfied with meditation then," said Saul, and folded his hands in his lap.

"Right, right. Quite right!" cried Clarissa and sat down again.

"The best way to meditate," she said, turning to me, "is to sit straight up in your chair, and not to sink back into it. Don't stretch your legs out in front of you, but try to bend your knees at an angle of ninety degrees. Fold your hands in your lap, hold your head well back, and close your eyes. Try to concentrate all your thoughts on one thing, say a flower . . ." Her small, slightly squinting eyes, always ready for a mischievous smile and hinting at the charm of a distant youth, stared into mine and something faraway and offbeat looked at me from their depths. "In the course of time," she added, "you will learn to distinguish what comes from within you from what flows into you from without."

Once again the four of us sat around the round table, on which Saul Haimjan's bottle of orange squash stood side by side with the packet of biscuits brought by Michael Temmes, and closed our eyes in preparation for meditation. I tried my best to follow her instructions and invited a yellow rose to appear before my mind's eye. The rose appeared, full blown and on the verge of fading, and stationed itself before me, but my thoughts refused to concentrate on this flower and returned instead to the nagging question of Temmes's face, and where I had seen it before. I was fighting as hard as I could against this distraction, when the sound of a thin snore reached my ears. I opened a slit in my eye and glanced toward Temmes, who was already deep in the sleep of the just.

"Mischa, you've fallen asleep again," cried Clarissa, who had become aware of Temmes's snoring at the same time as myself, and slapped his hand which was resting on the table.

He opened his eyes and said slowly, "I wasn't sleeping. My nose is slightly blocked by a cold, and so my breathing sounds to you like snoring." Saul Haimjan, who was apparently accustomed to these little contretemps, continued sitting erect in his chair with his eyes closed.

"And you too." She turned to me. "What's bothering you? Why aren't you concentrating? Here, this will help." And she dexterously removed the amber beads from the wall and threw them into my lap. "Close your eyes and feel the beads with your fingers."

I adjusted my posture according to her instructions, closed my eyes, and felt one of the beads with my fingers. The moment I felt the cool smooth touch of the greenish brown beads on my palm, the Moslem doctor turned the face of Michael Temmes toward me and said, "It is related (but God alone is all-knowing, as well as all-wise and all-powerful and all-bountiful) that there are ancient holy men, hermits dwelling in the mountains and deserts, who read the hidden thoughts of men and see into their hearts. These men possess the secret of the healing of souls, and by this means they can cure too all the afflictions of the flesh and its evil maladies. But I, the humblest of your slaves and the least of the doctors of the flesh, I possess nothing but what my eyes behold and what my bag contains in the way of soothing balms and potions and drugs, and in none of these is a cure for leprosy to be found."

"Good," said Clarissa, "that will be enough for tonight." She brought glasses and plates from the kitchen, and poured the orange squash into the glasses and put the biscuits on the plates. She herself contributed a packet of Black Cat cigarettes, which she pulled out of the carton she had brought back with her from her last visit to her family on the shores of the North Sea.

"Let us hope that the next séance will be better," said Temmes.

"Yes," said Clarissa, "nine o'clock on Monday evening in two weeks' time. Try not to be late as usual." When we were already at the door, she turned to me and said with a mischievous smile in her squinting eye, "And you—don't forget to bring something of your own with you!"

Translated by Dalya Bilu

6

MOSES AND THE NEGRESS *

I LOST many years ago my joy on waking, the joy that summer when we moved to the house of Mr. Gabriel Luria and I first saw his father, the old Turkish Bey, and his mother with her dreaming eyes. Joy on waking endures only in memory, and in my silly hope of its return.

One summer day, a strange and important one in my life, Gabriel Luria returned from Paris, but I'd heard about him, since his mother had let us a flat in their Prophets Street house several weeks before he got back, and I knew the house where he had been born, and his mother also, before he himself was displayed to me with his mustache square as a die, and his cane and Panama hat. But I can't say I knew the old man, I hadn't seen him more than at most two or three times. Yehuda Prosper Luria, Gabriel's father, that old Sephardi Jew, was in several ways unusual: quite apart from the occasional mistress, he had two wives, and in this resembled our fathers in that golden time when the Children of Israel still lived in tune with their nature. One wife, Hannah, belonged to the Pardos, an aristocratic old Sephardi family, and everyone said she was unusually kind and gentle. They lived together in his Jaffa house, where the three sons and the two daughters of his marriage grew up. Gabriel's mother, the second wife, belonged to a very poor Ashkenazi family from the Old City. The old

* from the novel *The Palace of Shattered Vessels*

man installed her in his Jerusalem house in Prophets Street, and every now and then he'd stay there a week or so. In the last years of his life, he'd stay there only once every three or four months. In addition to his two wives, the old man had another distinction: the title Bey, conferred on him by the sultan. Moslems and the Jews of the old *Yishuv* continued to address him by his Turkish title Bey, even after the sultan was deposed and his entire empire dissolved. I don't know whether he was given that title because of his office or that office because he was a Spanish national in Jaffa with a Turkish title; in either case he was the Spanish consul in Jaffa till the arrival of the British, and Europeans used to call him Monsieur le Consul. He died several weeks before the return of Gabriel, his youngest son.

In regard to the age of "the old Spaniard"—that's what his Jerusalem Ashkenazi wife would call him, but when she flared up she called him "the old Turkish bed-hopper"—in this as in everything there were differences of opinion between her and her rival the first wife. His Jaffa wife said—and Gabriel believed *her*— that the old man was eighty-nine when he died, but his Jerusalem wife, Gabriel's mother, maintained he'd achieved his century two or three years before he deserted this world. Gabriel himself didn't know the precise age of his father and he told me years later his mother had always had a tendency to exaggerate the number of years marking her off from her husband, and one could safely assume the years she had subtracted from her own age she had added to her husband's. With time she widened the chasm of the years between them till, on his death, it was clear to herself and her audience that fifty years separated her from "that old Turkish devil," who seduced her into marriage when she was "an innocent girl of fifteen" and he "an old lecher of sixty-five." Her son calculated twenty years at most separated her from her husband, and Yehuda Prosper Bey was fifty-five years old at the time of the birth of his youngest son Gabriel.

The old Bey still held himself straight, on those few occasions I saw him in the last year of his life, but an old man's stiffness had been poured into his joints. His head, under its hat, was shaved as his cheeks, except for a thick mustache overhanging each side of his mouth and black as his thick eyebrows. His quivering belly preceded him, and at his side, tall, thin, and a little bent, disposing his camel-like legs here and there, walked Señor Moïse his friend, who, it emerged, shaved him every day and dyed his mustache and eyebrows when that need arose. I didn't know, then, that the brave black color of the mustache and eyebrows of the old Bey was one of Señor Moïse's achievements. He was an artist in barbering and hair dyeing, secret and anonymous as the nameless great, retaining their anonymity because they thought of their art and not their name. I assumed that Señor Moïse's real function was to fend off the attacks of his Jerusalem wife on the consul.

Once he had taken off his hat and overcoat, the old Bey would seat himself on the porch in the red plush armchair Señor Moïse had fetched up from the cellar, tell his beads, and hum away drearily, while his wife, with the gentle look and dreaming eyes, in increasing anger, from the doorway hurled her sharp complaints at him, in a Spanish laced with Yiddish curses, or a Yiddish decorated with Spanish insults. Señor Moïse would interpose himself, calming her down with soft words and gestures, begging her pardon but it's not right, it doesn't reflect well on your husband or yourself. During all this time he was waiting for that moment when the verbal attack would end, to be followed by the bombardment of the clothes, which he caught with the agility of long service, and in order of flight: first the hat of the old man, next his scarf, and, last, his coat. His hat, for some reason, was a favorite target, and she would crush it in her hands and work it over with her feet. In the first bombardment I witnessed, she managed to snatch his hat from the old man's head just as he was going out the door, and to hurl it over the balcony and the stone wall into the street. But the hat had a stony strength and endured all the woman's inquisitions. After Señor Moïse had retrieved it, brushed it with a small brush he took out of his inside jacket pocket—where it seems it was kept for any eventuality—and with his long hands smoothed away every wrinkle, as innocent and undamaged as before, that hat returned to the shaven head like a washed pumpkin of Yehuda Bey. Her real anger, it is said, had its source in the tarboosh her husband wore in Turkish times, and with the transition from the Ottoman to the British Empire, there was a "transference," as the psychologists would put it, in her feelings from the red column with the black tassel to the black pot with the brim. Long-legged Moïse—so she told me—had only a few years back been raised to the dignity of a "Señor," since that time when he'd managed—according to her—with his cunning and his stratagems to snare her husband's soul and to subdue it to his own will; for "the old Turk" doesn't lift a finger till compelled to by that "slave who reigns" over the soul, body, and money of his former master. Even those few miserable coins the old man throws her from time to time—"as one throws a bone to a cur"—and this only after the waters have overwhelmed her soul, after rows and threats that if he doesn't pay her the alimony due her she'll sue him, she'll reveal to the judge and the entire world "his concealed virtues"—even those worn coins paid for with her heart's blood aren't given her personally by her husband, they're passed onto her through Long-legs, who all his life was a base domestic. He had been an orphan in Turkish times and died of hunger three times daily till the consul felt sorry for him, took him in, and when he grew up made him his kawass. The servant of a dignitary was called a kawass in Turkish times. When the consul went out, his uniformed kawass preceded him, and cleared a way for him with his staff.

Our landlady's stories were the only source of information about the old Bey and his friend Señor Moïse, so it is interesting that all her name-calling did not diminish him for me, just as her stories about "Señor Moïse's intrigues and cunning," through which "he acquired control of the body, soul, and money of the old Turk," did not prevent my observing the elements of respect, gentleness, and love in Señor Moïse's service. The attack repelled, and with no further need to defend the Bey from his wife, Señor Moïse would sit at his master's side on a stool, and together they would watch the setting sun. I once overheard snatches of conversation they had about the greatness of Moses. "Our master Moses"—so the old man said —"had the power to breathe the breath of life into dumb things. He cast his rod on the ground and it became a serpent; he told Aaron, 'Take thy rod, and cast it before Pharaoh, and it shall become a serpent,' and it became a serpent. You see, Señor Moïse, only God can breathe the breath of life into dumb things, and God conferred a little of his power on our master Moses the man of God."

"But Prosper Bey," Moïse answered, the effort at deep thought corrugating his brow, "the Egyptian magicians also had the power to breathe the breath of life into a rod, for it's written, 'now the magicians of Egypt, they also did in like manner with their enchantments. For they cast down every man his rod, and they became serpents.' "

"Of course, you're right,"—the Bey sat up, and with an enormous red handkerchief wiped away sweat beads giving off sparks from his well-shaved head in the setting sun—"the

Egyptian magicians got their power from their gods, and our master Moses his from our God, so there was war between their gods and our God, but the Lord our God overcame the Egyptian gods in that war, for it's written: 'But Aaron's rod swallowed up their rods.' "

"Just listen to His Holiness," his wife shouted from the doorway, "you'd think he spends his whole life doing good and Bible-reading. All he can think about is Moses, Moses." She held an old checked scarf in her hand, and she crossed the porch to wrap it around her husband's neck. "Tuck it in carefully," she said. "All I need now is for you to get pneumonia. You should know there's a freezing wind in Jerusalem in the evening. You look like some street-boy in your open-necked shirt." That was the last time I saw him. Several weeks later we heard of his death in his Jaffa house, and in my memory he still sat there on the porch of our house in the checked scarf his Jerusalem wife wrapped around his neck, his hoarse old voice, in impotent rage, repeating, "our master Moses, our master Moses," and sweat beads on his shaved head shooting fireworks at the sunset.

But I saw Gabriel's mother almost every day, over the years we lived in the house she inherited from her husband. Into that tangled inheritance I cannot enter, if only because she herself and the old judge alone knew its details. Years later Gabriel told me his mother had defrauded her enemy who, according to the old man's will, was the legal heir to all his property. The old man left all his property to his Jaffa wife and his children by her, and nothing to Gabriel's mother save the tenancy of his Prophets Street house for the remainder of her life, and the income from its rent. He didn't mention Gabriel in his will, which was not inadvertent, though Gabriel had the impression, when he last saw his father just before going abroad, that he didn't remember him, and that in the old man's muzzy brain Gabriel had been confused with his father's brother David. Yehuda Prosper's older brother had been called David, and when they were still children Yehuda followed him around like a shadow till David suddenly died on the day of his bar mitzvah. His father would unexpectedly hug Gabriel when he was a boy, saying, "You're exactly like my brother David, God bless him, you've his face and movements. He didn't live long enough to be your uncle, he died suddenly on his bar mitzvah." The old man was in a blur when Gabriel said goodbye before going off to Europe. He plucked at his black mustache, his black eyebrows reared like two crests of one somber wave, and in a hoarse old voice he growled, "David, I've told you already you're not to go to Bethlehem." He cleared his throat, hawked, his face got very red. "On the way you can go to Rachel's Tomb, but don't stay long, or you'll have to sleep there overnight." Gabriel was not struck out of the will, I've already said, from inadvertence. It was because of Gabriel's behavior, or rather because of the way he squandered his father's money in Europe, for years neglecting his medical studies, despite his father's letters threatening to stop his allowance and disinherit him if he kept up his prodigality. So if Gabriel had a roof over his head when he got back penniless, it wasn't because of the father he so much loved—and Gabriel never loved anyone more than he loved him—it was because of the chicanery of his mother.

I would see her, as I said, nearly every day when we lived there, especially during the long school holiday, since I spent most of it on our porch. There weren't very many children's summer camps at that time, and we would play in the yard and change our books at the Bnei Brit Library, which I believe still survives, in the same building in an alley off Prophets Street. I would read on the porch, and she would interrupt me at some crisis in the story. She would ask me to take the folding bed down to the cellar, or fetch it up from the cellar, or to shift the commode so she could get at some remote corner with her broom, and then shift it back once she'd swept that corner. She would confer on me errands not requiring over-much skill, for instance, buying matches or a can of olive oil or clothespins or some other article not likely to decay or rot, and independent of that perishable scale of values with its innumerable rungs of good and evil. It was for this reason I was never sent to buy a loaf of bread, or a *rotel* or *oquia* of tomatoes, which demand an innate talent for fine distinctions in addition to the requisite experience, though it was in this connection I received from her a protracted and well thought out lesson: a bread must be well baked, for there's nothing worse for the digestion than underbaked dough, which shouldn't be overbaked, either, because then it infringes on the zone of the burnt. And she'd known loaves whose dough hadn't been properly kneaded or leavened, whose crust was burnt and whose insides were soggy. Then how is a man to do right, that is to say, to choose from all the loaves the properly kneaded, leavened, and baked loaf? He must first have sharp senses, then exercise them, and hone them with life experi-ence. He needs an eye for the glow of the right loaf, a nose for its warm smell, a hand to probe the tension of the crust covering the soft flesh of the bread, and an ear alert to the tiny crackling voices of the bread's guts pressed against its skin. Even she, with all her experience and her fastidious senses, sometimes had to go back to the shop and change her bread. And at the end of all these lessons, enlivened by demonstra-tions of the color, smell, touch, and crackling voices of the right loaf, chosen by her, she would send me out to buy a cake of laundry soap, or of carbolic, thereby deepening the insult that in her view I was not equipped to buy a loaf of bread. Years later, when I laughingly told Gabriel his mother had slighted my matured senses, he told me I'd no idea how grateful I should have been to her for not sending me on those errands, which were the nightmare of his childhood—that nightmare of returning rotten tomatoes, burnt bread, rancid butter, wormy rice, kerosene-smelly cheese.

"Gabby," she would say, "take this rancid butter back right away to Red Ear." This was her name for the grocer; she had a good eye for the distinguishing peculiarities in a man, for his general look and his specific defects. And his right ear *was* red, even when he paled. Nobody saw it till the Old Bey's wife took a hard look and delivered that verdict, which stuck to him the rest of his life. Something trivial, hidden, entirely unremarked became a focus, a point of reference. Everyone interrogated by her eye—shopkeepers, domestics, friends of her husband—was awarded a nickname, and not only that but an impersonation also, for she was a natural mime. When she told, for example, the story of her quarrel with the Black Cockscomb, that is to say, Dinah the Persian washerwoman, awarded that name for her general look and particular hairdo, she would give you not only what Dinah said but her way of saying it, gestures, voice, intonation.

Sometimes, inspired, she would imitate her interlocutor in the actual course of their conversation: she would adopt a Yemenite accent when talking to the Yemenite plasterer, and with Red Ear, a Galician Jew, she would have a pronounced Galician intonation, which gave her the twofold pleasure of satisfying her innate craving for drama and for imitation of a man of two unusual qualities: he was both a shopkeeper and a Galician. She considered all shopkeepers thieves, all of them anxious to unload the shoddiest goods at the highest prices. All Galicians were born crooks. "You're a foolish boy," she would tell Gabby when he winced away from returning some purchase. "What stops you giving Red Ear back his rancid

butter? A Galician shopkeeper isn't ashamed to cheat a child—
he palmed off on you last week's butter—yet you're ashamed
to return it. What kind of world are we living in? You're
ashamed to tell him he cheated you. Well, of course, it's nice
for a shopkeeper when a fool falls into his shop."

In defense of the Bey's wife, I must say she did not send
merely her son back with shoddy goods, or her husband to
change the present he had made her. Like all perfectionists
she was stricter with herself than others, and spent a lot of
time returning purchases that displeased her, or about which
she had changed her mind. She was a perfectionist also in her
cooking. But because she was so fastidious her meals came
into the world rather late, which is why her husband, when
they still lived together, complained he never got his food at
the right time, and there was no sequence to the dishes.
Really to enjoy one of his wife's masterpieces, the old man
said, one had to devote the day to it: the salad was prepared in
the morning, the main dish at noon, the soup arrived at Minha
and at Ma'ariv the dessert. Of course he was exaggerating but
he did convey some notion of his Jerusalem wife's life rhythm.
She suffered, like all perfectionists, from the flawed reality
around her, and in her good times even, when she had the
whole house to herself and a Moslem maid, she would complain. Then how much more so at the end of her life, when
she rented the house to us and descended to live in the basement. She was then a woman of over sixty, with astonishing
changes of expression that kept pace with her moods. She
had been dark and delicate when young; it was her delicacy
and gazelle-brown eyes (for oddly enough Gabriel inherited
his blue eyes from his Sephardi father, not from his Ashkenazi
mother), her graceful movements and laughter which cap-
tured the heart of the Spanish consul when he paid a cere-
monial call at the Evelyn de Rothschild Girls' School, where

she was about to complete her studies. It was she who presented him with flowers on behalf of the graduating class. After many years of marriage, he still thought himself physically and spiritually gross in comparison with her. Gabriel was thirteen before he heard his father, in one of their quarrels, call his mother a delicate viper; the Mishnaic caution against the law students, he commented to Señor Moïse, referred really to the Jerusalem wife, who bites like a fox, stings like a scorpion, hisses like a snake, and whose words are like live coals. She kept that delicate look in old age, though now she was bent and slow and stiff. Usually she seemed immersed in a distinct and distant world, even when making her rounds of the market; her movements were slow, and she had a tendency to sink into long, remote thoughts and reveries, so she never had time enough even for her routine needs. She was always occupied cooking, mending, cleaning, though she lived entirely on her own and did not keep up connections after her husband's death, till a late friendship sprang up between her and her sister Pnina.

She would sit for hours outside her door on the porch, with an abstracted look polishing rice in a *siniyeh,* a flat copper dish. Sometimes she would sing softly and pleasantly, and it always surprised me that those songs and the hysterical abuse of her husband issued from the same mouth. The ancient, animal sound of her abuse gave me gooseflesh. No one who heard her singing could have guessed at the wild beast inside this delicate, gentle woman, just as no observer of the deep friendship that developed between her and her sister Pnina, after the death of the old Bey, could ever have imagined the atrocious war she waged on her sister thirty years back, on discovering she was the mistress of her husband, Yehuda Prosper Bey. It belonged to Gabriel's saddest and most shaming childhood memories. His adoring and attentive mother became a tigress. "Mother, please, I can't bear any more."

She didn't listen. In the rush to finish off her sister who claws back but retreats, her blind anger can bring down her son. She held on like a wildcat, all nails, to her sister Pnina's hair, her neck veins bulged, she shrieked, "Madonna! Who ran after the fat prick of the Turkish adulterer? You shrinking spinster, I'll scratch your eyes out." Her scream didn't have a human sound, it was more of a hiss. Pnina was her elder sister, a pious spinster who had never left home but lingered there for years after the disgraceful marriage of the younger sister to that "Turkish adulterer." In the sisterly quarrels preceding the discovery of her affair, Pnina held her sister responsible for her spinsterhood, that infidel sister who was the slave of "the fat prick of the Turkish adulterer" and became his "concubine." And what God-fearing Jew would marry a woman whose sister was the concubine of a Turkish adulterer? This is what Pnina said in her prolonged spinsterhood for as long as the affair continued in secret with that same Turkish adulterer. But when the affair came to an end following its discovery, of course it was a God-fearing Jew she found itching to marry her. After the death of the old Bey, his widow grandly allowed herself to be reconciled to Pnina, who became a kind of lady's companion, especially when her sister's bouts of headache and her mysterious backache began. She would lie back in bed, swathed in a turban to prevent dizziness, and permit her elder sister to fuss over her, even send her sister on errands. Pnina may have got a scolding from time to time; occasionally she became an object of teasing, but in general the sisters enjoyed a good gossip.

She would sit hours at the door, peeling ba'miah, and sing children's songs to herself in a soft, clear voice at sunset, or tell me stories about Gabriel if I asked. I would ask, and she would respond, but of herself she would not volunteer anything, for I knew her at the end of her life, and her reverie was given to herself, her aches and pains; her feelings to her

own childhood and adolescence. That is why I heard the first
time of his childhood studies, of the period when he still attended the tiny yeshiva of Rabbi Avremale in the Old City,
not from his mother but queerly enough from Yitzhak the son
of Red Ear, when I went to the grocer for half a rotel of gran-
ulated sugar and a dozen clothespins. Gabriel was sent first
to the cheder and then the yeshiva of Rabbi Avremale, and
from there he went on to Kol Yisrael Chaverim, the Alliance
school. After graduating he joined the Teachers' Seminary
established by the German-Jewish society, Ezra. Of all people
it was his father, the Sephardi Jew with the Turkish title,
who decided he should begin his studies at an Ashkenazi
cheder. He wanted his son, he said, "to strike roots in the inheritance of his fathers," and he preferred the Ashkenazi
cheder to the Sephardi Talmud Torah because "the Ashkena-
zis are more exacting than the Sephardis."

When he had sent his long roots down into his fathers' inheritance (as interpreted by Rabbi Avremale, whose yeshiva
later on fostered generations of Netorei Karta *), his son Gabriel—the Spanish consul thought—could offer his branches
to any wind without risking his soul.

Reb Yitzhak, Red Ear's son, who after the establishment of
the State became one of the supports of Netorei Karta, appeared to me a prematurely old Jew, though he couldn't have
been forty, since he went to the same cheder as Gabriel. Red
Ear's own name for his son was not Yitzhak but Reb Yitzhok.
Reb Yitzhok was a big man, and he had an enormous beard
blown every which way like a horse's tail at a gallop, but his
sidelocks exerted the principal charm. I have never seen sidelocks as grandly long as his among any Jews I've encountered
in Meah Shearim market or the Hungarian Quarter. There
are dandies who braid their sidelocks but he let them grow as

* The most bigoted and fanatical of Jewish religious sects.

they liked, so they streamed into his beard like two frothing rivers into the sea. On an errand of my landlady to his shop, I would address him in Hebrew but he would answer in Yiddish. Of course he knew Hebrew but he thought it was talked only by atheists, who had drunk from the waters of "that troubler of Israel, Eliezer Ben-Yehuda, may his name and memory be wiped out." I told him to charge the half rotel of sugar and the dozen clothespins to the account of Mrs. Luria. He looked severe. When he had noted down the purchase, he asked me, with lowered eyes, whether her son Gabriel had got back from abroad. "He's clever," he said, "but wicked. He has a pagan soul. You don't often find such a soul even among the goyim. They've suppressed their cults. He was still at cheder when he set up his cult."

When a man was called a renegade, or a goy, by a religious Jew, or a woman a whore, I had never thought of that man as a real goy, or attributed the actions of a whore to that woman. Passing through Meah Shearim without a hat, I had several times been called such a goy, and my sister had been called a whore because of her light summer frock. Such terms don't carry any private weight, and I took them for what they were, as a general designation for anyone not religious.

So if after all I was impressed by Reb Yitzhok, it was because both words and tone implied unusual wickedness in Gabriel, a kind of savagery marking him off from the usual run of atheists and even from goyim; but such phrases as "the soul of a pagan" and "the work of star-worshipers" didn't give me a clear notion of what he had actually done. Even Gabriel's mother would not explain that when I got back with the half rotel of sugar and the dozen clothespins, and recounted part of what Red Ear's son had said about her son. Of course I would only repeat what was least likely to offend her, phrases like "working the sun and stars." "What did Reb Yitzhok mean," I asked her inquisitively, "saying Gabriel worked the Zodiac when he was a boy?"

"He can go to hell," she said calmly, quite unruffled by what he'd said, and I was amazed an old man with such a beard and sidelocks could be consigned to hell. "Like father like son. A Galician thief. Look what dirty sugar he gave you."

She poured the sugar into a bowl, put the clothespins into a drawer of the commode, then went out onto the terrace to cut choorfesh—that's the Arabic name for this vegetable, and that's my name for it as I don't know its Hebrew name even today. In France it has a domesticated cousin, the artichoke. As she seemed occupied with the choorfesh, I thought she hadn't heard my question about the strange cults of her son in his childhood, so I cast around for a way of getting back to the subject. Talking as if to herself, she anticipated me.

"So Gabby did 'foreign' work as a child. Any kind of work is foreign to those schnorrers. He was full of fantasy when he was a boy, like the old man; you know the old man is Oriental, all Orientals are dreamers. He was soaked in their fantasies, especially about Moses, anything about Moses. Now what did Moses really do? He took over a rabble, sons of slaves, and made a great nation out of them. Why did he drag them around with him forty years, where a decent man wouldn't show his face? I say he did it because he was ashamed to appear in public with them; he couldn't be seen among decent people together with that mob of slaves with their first-day-out look. That old Turk never stopped thinking about Moses; I think if he'd had a Negress he'd have become a Moses. And Gabby is flesh of his flesh. He got his strong body from his father, his strong body and his imagination also. Every day he'd get back from cheder with a new story about something wonderful happening to him on the way. He daydreamed so much I began to worry about his health. He had such pictures in his mind. You know, there should be a limit to everything, you can hurt yourself carrying things too far. Dreamers stumble, they get lost. And look what happened to Gabby. He was talented. He was never short of money. His yeshiva head, his teachers at the Lemmel School and the Alliance, they all said he had a good grasp of everything. He had a sharp mind. And we gave him everything. The Jerusalem poor in their wildest dreams never saw what we gave him. And none of his friends went off to Paris like him, sent off like a prince to finish his studies. If he'd returned when he should, he'd be the biggest doctor in the country. He'd be bigger than Doctor Ticho, Doctor Mazia, and Doctor Wallach all squeezed into one. And what did he do there? I ask you, what did he do there, all that time in Paris? What's he doing now? Wandering around like a tramp. He squandered his father's money. It's all because of his fantasies. I can't sleep at night, thinking about him. He gave his life to his fantasies; he got them from his father. I told you he's flesh of his flesh."

Her thoughts reverted to Yehuda Bey, and in discoursing on her late husband she forgot about her son. The more she expatiated, the more impatient I became, and I felt saddened by the knowledge I would get nothing out of her to give me a clear picture of the pagan cult of Gabriel's childhood— what she called his Oriental fantasies. Her reveries revolved around herself; she was full of the story of her life with the old Bey. Her dead husband had the real claim on her thought; she left her living son only a place in the margin. I tried several times to direct her back to the "Oriental" fantasies of the young Gabriel, but she had nothing to add, she would only emphasize they were a kind of Oriental sickness contracted from his father. Her old woman's talk annoyed me; it flowed along such a different riverbed from the one I had had in mind, but echoed peculiarly in my soul, not by day but at night, in a recurrent childhood dream which coiled itself around the conversation, just before his death, of the old Bey and long-legged Señor Moïse. Old Red Ear sits dozing as always at the door of his shop, his son Reb Yitzhok stands with wild sidelocks in front of the balance, and directs an angry look at the scales. It isn't the grocery shop, it's our porch, and old Red Ear is Pharaoh. I'm surprised that Pharaoh, exalted over all the kings of the earth, builder of the pyramids, of Pithom and Ramsese, in fact is merely the Galician grocer, that helpless old man. I'm disappointed, saddened by this gray small old helpless reality. The chief magician, that is to say, Reb Yitzhok, whispers in the red ear of Pharaoh, "Wake up, open your eyes, sit up straight. Here he comes. Stop snoring." I learn from his whisper that this uninterrupted snoring sending out ripples over the world originates in the nostrils of the red-eared Pharaoh now compelled to wake up because Moses the man of God advances along the terrace in his black London bowler hat and carrying his cane, breathless and puffing from the steep climb. Señor Moïse supports him under the arms, stands at his side, disposes his legs here and there, scouts around with his eyes, alert to any ambush. And at that moment the old woman emerges from the basement, makes for the old man, snatches the hat from his head, and works over it with her feet. The head magician is surrounded by a crowd of Hassidim energetically praying. Their eyes are closed in intense concentration, their mouths are wide open, but no one can hear them because of the snoring of Pharaoh who has relapsed into deep sleep. "Don't believe him," the old woman cries to the magicians, and she's pointing at the old Bey. "They're only Oriental fantasies, he's not Moses, he's not Moses. He doesn't have a Negress." Señor Moïse interposes himself, calming her down with soft words and gestures, begging her pardon but it's not right, it doesn't reflect well on her husband or herself. The old man, who's now sitting in a red armchair, wipes the sweat beads shining in the sunset from his skull, calls Señor Moïse over, and whispers something in his ear. The excitement among the magicians increases. They stand on tiptoe, rock to and fro on their heels, violently tremble. They beat their chests with their fists. The weight on my chest disappears, I feel refreshed. On waking I have the joy of knowing clearly beforehand that Aaron's rod, cast down at the command of Moses, will soon swallow the old woman and overcome Pharaoh's magicians and every windmill.

Translated by the author and Dennis Silk

7

THE KING'S EYE *

I SAW GABRIEL JONATHAN LURIA for the first time on a great and strange day in my life, the day on which my eyes plainly beheld, on the other side of the street, the King of Kings Haile Selassie, elect of God, conquering Lion of the tribe of Judah, the Emperor of Ethiopia. It was the middle of summer in the year 1936, and I was then a child ten years old, carrying water from the cistern onto the broad front verandah of our house, overlooking the Street of the Prophets. In front of me I saw the Emperor, stepping briskly up to the Ethiopian Consulate opposite the house, and then when I turned to face the other way, I discovered a man sitting on the wicker chair next to the verandah table, regarding me and the scene before me with smiling eyes. On that very day Mr. Luria had returned from Paris to his late father's house— for our house was, in fact, his father's house, and the well we drank from was his childhood well.

It was his mother who had rented their house to us, leaving nothing to herself but the room we called the "stair room" because it was built under the stairway leading up to the house, with its ceiling serving as the front verandah's floor. Although there was no connection between this underground room and the water cistern, which was located under the paving stones of the back yard, with the house itself separat-

* from the novel *The Palace of Shattered Vessels*

ing them, his mother complained that a chilly dampness from
the cistern was seeping steadily into her room and was bound
to give her rheumatism in the end. It was thanks to her mis-
fortune and the straitened circumstances which obliged her
to live off the rent from the house that I was lucky enough to
spend my childhood years in the very same house, at the bottom of the Street of the Prophets, in which Gabriel Jonathan
had been born in the first year of the twentieth century—
twenty-six years before I myself was born—and in which his
own childhood had been spent. A round window, like an eye
opening to the East, peeped out beneath the red-tiled roof,
and the other windows of the house were arched. The win-
dowpanes at the front of the house, opposite the main entrance in the Street of the Prophets, were made of colored
glass which I loved to look at from outside in the nighttime,
when the thick, opaque stone walls were soaked in darkness,
and the light stored up in the house filtered out in a kind of
calm desire through the rose of lights in each of the windows.
Around the paved courtyard standing on the water cistern was
a plot of land intended for a garden, but in the days of my
childhood no flowers were grown there and there was nothing
on it but an ancient olive tree whose trunk was so scarred,
fissured, and cleft that its heart had been torn out, leaving an
empty hollow in its place, and a row of pines and cypresses
standing along the high stone wall which surrounded the
house on all four sides. On the summer afternoons I would
stretch out full length on the round windowsill—the walls
were so thick—and look out toward Tur Malka at the top of
the Mount of Olives and the section of the Old City walls
facing the crowded square in front of the Damascus Gate.
Horse-drawn carriages stood side by side with the Arab company buses to Ramalla and Jericho, and a few taxicabs as well,
and throngs of Arabs in long robes and keffiyeh's and tar-

booshes milled and jostled between them. Fragments of Arab tunes floated up to my window on Arab-smelling breezes. The first wireless sets had just started appearing here and there in Jerusalem and the first sounds from them to reach my ears were these tunes, endlessly spiraling in the long-winded cycle, quaking with longings, of Arab love songs. The circle of Arab life which was revealed to me through the tele-scope in whose tube I lay—the tumultuous life swarming against the background of the Mount of Olives and the tower of Tur Malka, with its haggling and shouting and singing and smells, and its whole being which was dipped in a dream despite all its uproar—was like a direct continuation of every-thing I had learned in the Bible about the lives of our fore-fathers in Eretz Israel; it was in some sense a materialization of those lives, awakening ancient chords like those of a long-forgotten melody in my heart. But this materialization, de-spite its being a direct continuation, was not a natural con-tinuation, for it was I who was the scion of the stock of Abra-ham, Isaac, and Jacob, the natural and lawful heir of King David's dynasty here in David's city. Sometime, somewhere, something had gone wrong, as if a prince and a beggar had changed clothes in a masquerade; the beggar in the prince's clothes had settled in the king's palace, while the prince had taken up the beggar's staff and set out on a long journey whose vicissitudes had transformed him beyond recognition.

In the cellar of the house, where the rags of all the years lay piled in rotting heaps and their junk lay rusting, I found new treasures every time I went down with the landlady to help her carry the folding wooden bed, which she would bring up and take down at regular intervals for mysterious reasons known only to herself. Once I found a music box, which despite its hoary antiquity played, to the accompani-ment of groaning and creaking from its rusted metal and frozen cogs, the "Marseillaise" when I turned its twisted handle, and another time I discovered a Turkish shoub'ria in its sheath underneath a pile of sacks.

A little farther down the Street of the Prophets, on the other side of the road, was the building which housed the Consulate of Ethiopia. Above its entrance, inlaid in a skillful mosaic design, was an angry-faced lion holding a scepter and wearing a crown on his head. Next to the lion was written— so I was informed, in impeccable Hebrew, by one of the monks belonging to the Ethiopian community of Jerusalem— in Ethiopian letters: "Menelik the Second, Emperor of Ethiopia, descendant of the Lion of Judah." This Menelik preceded Haile Selassie on the throne of Ethiopia. When the Italians invaded Ethiopia and conquered it the Emperor went into exile, and during his sojourn in Jerusalem he stayed in the Ethiopian Consulate opposite our house. From the verandah I saw the members of the Ethiopian community waiting for their king, and standing at their head were the tall monks, whose black faces fused with the black of their robes and the black of the cylindrical hats which added inches to their height making them look like black poles come to life. A number of British policemen were keeping order, as usual, and a little throng of passersby had collected about them, Arabs and Jews, including several scholars with sidelocks and beards from nearby Meah Shearim on their way to the Old City.

When the Emperor emerged from his car my face burned and my whole being was buffeted by a wave of feeling in which shades of strange conflicting sensations whirled about like a kaleidoscope of shifting forms and colors spinning around very quickly on its axis. It was as a Negro dressed up as a British general in a comedy that the King of Ethiopia revealed himself to me for the first time—for the uniform he wore was the uniform of an English general in all its minutiae. From the insignia on the buttons to the leather strap slanting from the shoulder to the belt at the waist; from the two rows of medals on the chest to the decorations on the visor of the cap, not a detail was missing—except for the English general himself. The neck emerging from this general's attire was like the black polished marble whose gleam is grayish white, and so were the hands dangling from the general's sleeves. The erect slender body, supple and muscular, which ascended the steps with an agile grace was not distinguished by its height, and it seemed that every one of the monks—whose king was swallowed up by the building before they had time to kneel and bow down before him—was taller than he by the height of his hat. For one moment, before he turned into the doorway, I saw his profile in the shadow of the general's cap. It was adorned with a short pointed beard and an abundance of hair growing down his neck, and for all the delicacy of his features and the fine film of spirituality overlaying them like a varnish, the expression on his face was businesslike and brisk, as if he knew what needed to be done because he was firmly anchored in this world, and had no time to waste because he was in a hurry to implement all the schemes hatching under the general's visor thanks to which he would eventually overcome all the obstacles standing in his way.

The shade of his skin was actually far lighter than the skin of his subjects who were crowding about the gates of the Ethiopian Consulate, and had he been wearing a black robe like one of the Coptic monks he might even have seemed pale by their side. It was the light-colored British uniform that made his skin so dark, and it was this uniform too that was mainly to blame for the disappointment that played so prominent a part in the wave of mixed feelings that overpowered me. I had expected something altogether different: I was looking forward to a kind of radiance emanating from Divine Grace, which was specific to the being of a king to distinguish him from ordinary flesh and blood, and which would flow far out of him and be sensed by everyone, like the fragrance of orange blossom or the light of a lamp or the sound of a violin. The clothing of a king's body was suited to the splendid majesty of his soul, and if the king was Ethiopian, and the radiance of his kingliness flowed from the essence of the Negro soul, why then his clothing would be suited to this same essential Negro being, and in my imagination I could see no more fitting apparel for the Negus than a crimson cloak whose edges were trimmed with the fur of the silver fox, and on his head a crown of brightly-colored feathers from the wings of the rare birds which inhabit the thickets of virgin forests.

This British-officer fancy dress in which the Emperor of Ethiopia appeared, innocent of any mysterious kingly radiance, not only made him just like any common mortal, but more than that, and unexpectedly, it brought him excessively close to me, and this precisely with regard to the secret longings of the soul; for in the depths of my heart I too saw myself as a kind of British officer, noble and proud and strong and brave, granting favors to his friends and wreaking vengeance on his enemies, for his was the power and his was the glory. This emperor had realized what for me was still a secret dream: he wore the uniform of war and stood at the head of an army which took orders from him and fought his Italian enemies, and all that remained was for him to change his skin.

The crowd stood watching in respectful silence and the Coptic monks knelt and bowed and the British policemen stayed at attention and the sergeant at their head kept saluting until the Emperor disappeared into the door of the building. At this moment a slight mishap occurred. One of the policemen winked at his mate standing by his side. Whether this wink was directed at his Imperial Majesty or whether it alluded to the private affairs between one British policeman and another, I don't know. In either case it was taken up by Itzik the American Watchmaker who immediately raised his coarse and hairy hand in an insinuating gesture and called "Sambo" at the door closing behind the Emperor.

Itzik the American Watchmaker was neither an American nor a watchmaker. He was nothing but a bully of about twenty-five years old who worked as an assistant in the big fish shop on the corner of the alley turning into the Meah Shearim marketplace. In his childhood it had been his ambition to be a watchmaker, because he was fascinated by the watchmaker who wore on his eye the black tube of a magnifying glass which revealed a secret world to him, and held in his hands the delicate instruments which probed the innermost parts, hidden from the naked eye, of the smallest of ladies' watches. And indeed, as soon as he had failed for the second time to pass the fifth grade of the Tachkemoni school (at the time pupils of his sort could still spend two years and more in the same class even in primary schools) he found a job as an apprentice to a watchmaker, and from that day forth he declared himself to be a watchmaker, even though he only spent a few weeks cleaning the watchmaker's shop and flat and carrying heavy clocks from customers' houses to the shop and back to their owners again. He also liked announcing, with a triumphant expression on his face, that he was registered on the American passport of his father, who had once spent a number of years in America. Just as he had never succeeded in mending a watch, so he never succeeded in getting to America, but as he was a great success, on the other hand, at lifting heavy loads on his back and moving herring barrels around in the fish shop, his bosses lavished every form of hard labor in the shop and outside it upon him, even lending him to the owners of neighboring shops for the same purpose, which filled his heart with professional pride as a rare expert, unique and unrivaled in his field.

However, the essence of his greatness and the main reason for his fame with all the children of Jerusalem derived from the holy war he declared on cats. Without being ordered to do so by his boss, and without demanding payment for the performance of this godly deed, he called of his own free will, his own private initiative, for a war of extermination not only on the cats lying in wait outside the fish shop, but on every cat he came across, great and small, old, pregnant, or day-old kitten. In the course of these cat-battles he invented and perfected a number of tactical ploys, and I myself once saw him with my own eyes walking down the road to the Damascus Gate with a crate of fish on his head, when his practiced eye suddenly fell on a gray cat curled up on the fence of the Italian Hospital. Without putting down his burden, holding himself almost erect, he gradually bent his knees until his free hand reached the pavement and gropingly found a piece of broken brick, having taken firmly hold of which the American Watchmaker straightened up again and stood. With one hand supporting the load on his head, without deviating from his erect posture to increase the momentum of his free, throwing hand, he aimed the brick at the cat basking in the sun and hit him, and with the short, piercing, angry howl of pain which burst from the fleeing cat, the victorious warrior gave vent to a kind of gurgle of physical pleasure. He molested the Arab women coming to town to sell their wares too, upsetting a basket of eggs here or pulling a lock of hair there, but ever since the time he was locked up in the police station in St. Paul's Road (today its name has been changed to the Road of the Tribes of Israel and the building which once housed the police station now serves as a border emplacement next to the Mandelbaum Gate) and beaten up by the British sergeant for his pains, he was careful to conduct his operations in secret, which circumstances did not always permit.

Now, with the bawdy mocking sign he had made with his hand, and the cry of "Sambo" he had thrown at the exiled king's back, he fixed his eyes on the British policeman with a smile of mutual understanding in the expectation of gaining approval and further encouragement, but the latter shot him a look of angry contempt and moved off with the sergeant and the rest of the platoon in the direction of the police station. For a moment the hulking youth stood rooted to the spot with the smile congealing on his face, running his eyes back and forth over the Consulate windows as if considering whether it were incumbent on him to cast a stone at one of their panes. Then he extricated himself from his dilemma with two perfunctory cries of "Sambo" which he barked at a small child being towed after his mother who was walking toward the Ethiopian Church in the wake of the monks.

Together with the helpless rage and depression which flooded me, I suddenly experienced, terrible in its certainty, the sensation that I myself was being closely watched. "There is an eye that sees and an ear that hears and all your deeds are written in a book"—when I first came across these words two or three years later this same sensation rose up in me again together with the memory of the situation as a whole, how I had turned around and seen Gabriel Luria sitting on the wicker chair and watching me, the spectator of the play. He was sitting with his legs crossed, leaning back in the chair, his one hand holding a cigarette and his other hand resting on his silver-knobbed cane. He was regarding the whole situation like the spectator of a play in which I, like all the other actors, played an unwitting part. A good, reassuring calm radiated from him, and it was this, together with the engaging smile twinkling in his eye, which relieved me of the terror of the seeing eye whose regard was quite unique: it was very far away and very close at one and the same time. So far away that it turned me (and with me all the other participants in the play who were unaware of the seeing eye) into a little midget, a tiny dwarflike creature, and so close that every passing shade of thought and feeling and every slightest movement took on an extraordinary importance against the background of an ancient, hidden meaning.

Translated by Dalya Bilu

8

THE DOVE AND THE MOON *

OUR LANDLADY, Mrs. Luria, didn't like going into the pharmacy because of the pharmacist, Dr. Blum, who always—so she said—gave her either an oppressive feeling of guilt for having disturbed him at his important work, or else an unnatural sensation of strain, as if she were a little girl who didn't know the right questions or the right answers either. Her sensations on those rare occasions when he deliberately set out to be nice to her were twice as oppressive, strained, and annoying, and so she used to send me to him instead.

At the beginning I was of the opinion that he went about quite naked under his white coat, and that he had nothing on his skin but the spectacles pinching his nose, like a kind of scientific Gandhi, because nothing peeped out of the opening of this coat on top but the faded fair hair on his chest, and there was nothing to be seen below but his bluish white knees. Later on, however, I discovered that this initial impression was due to the fact that he wore no tie around his neck during working hours, and his trousers were khaki shorts—not the kind that everyone wore then, but the kind worn by the British officers and soldiers which were stiffer and more ironed. (Only now, while writing this story, does it occur to me that since the establishment of the State, short trousers have almost entirely disappeared from the country.) To complete

* from the novel *The Palace of Shattered Vessels*

the picture of this scientific Gandhi, he wore nothing on his feet while he worked but a pair of worn-out sandals, which had turned into slippers ever since the straps of their heels had fallen off and slapped the floor with his every step.

He was always busy transferring the contents of the Separanda and the Toxica departments from one cupboard to another, and rearranging the jars in each department. Since he had recently returned from the University of Beirut where he had qualified as a pharmacist, and his pharmacy was as new as his diploma on the wall, I supposed at first that he would bring this activity to an end as soon as the place of each bottle of medicine had been finally fixed. But days, weeks, and even months later—in fact for the whole of the period during which he served as a pharmacist—he continued to transfer the drugs from one place to another with the same expression—concentrated in its vacillations, brisk in its tortuousness, frowning and pursed—he wore when he paced back and forth in the cage of his laboratory, his face turned to the ceiling and his hands folded on his backside, holding the little book open at the place where he was supposed to be reading. When he was not trying to determine the right place for drugs, he was searching the heights of the ceiling for the meaning of the verses of the little book peeping through the fingers of his hands folded on his backside, and between the two he had to find time for the unavoidable nuisance of concocting eye drops for Mrs. Luria, his regular customer, who in spite of everything remained—through my good offices—the only one loyal to him to the end of the pharmacy's days.

"Ha, what does the younger generation say?" he would ask me twice a week without looking at me, since his eyes were busy examining the new Toxica department. "Who will save us?" Sometimes he would change the formula and ask, "Who will bring salvation to the world?" and once he said, "Who will save me?" Once he suddenly roused himself to look at me and ask, "And Gabriel, how is he? When did you see him last?"

"I've never seen him," I said. About an hour before, I had tried in vain to evoke some sort of picture of Gabriel in the days of his childhood from the words of Mrs. Luria, and I didn't know yet that I was to see him for myself in less than a month's time with his sudden return home.

"He must have gone abroad before you were born," he said. "That's the way of the world nowadays. A man doesn't see his brother."

"He's not my brother," I said, "and Mrs. Luria isn't my mother. She's our landlady." Apparently he didn't hear what I said, or else my words made no impression on him at all, for he fell to examining my face and said, "Yes, yes. You can see it at once. You're alike as two peas in a pod, except for the clothes. When we were children we studied Torah together in the Heder, and that Torah, that strong drug, is at the root of all his troubles. I told your mother so. 'Mrs. Luria,' I said to her, 'please give me your son Gabriel's address. I want to write him a letter. Do you know what is at the root of all your son's troubles? The Torah! Yes, yes—it was the Torah that poisoned his mind!' I tried to explain it to her, but she got up and ran away. She said she had no time for nonsense, and since then she's been afraid of coming in here. She's filled her mind with straw and chaff, there's no room in it for the things that are really important. Forgive me for talking like this about your mother, but there's no need for you to feel insulted—most mothers in our day, and in fact most human beings, are exactly the same. That's why they give the impression of people so busy with important affairs. She refused, naturally, to give me your brother Gabriel's address.

If you knew Gabriel's address, I would ask you to give it to me, but it's as clear as daylight to me that she's never disclosed it to you, just as she's certainly succeeded in keeping secret from you certain events that happened years before you were born, when Gabriel was still a child and used to go down to the Kidron valley on moonlit nights with his doves."

On moonlit nights with my doves, which I never had, to the Kidron valley I never went down, but once I went up to Mount Scopus on a night when the full moon floated up beyond the mountains of Moab, orange-veiled in a broad ancient silence charging the Judean desert night with the high tension of an existence beyond, lapping the pillars of the world with the waves of the mountain shoulders in a line of latitude from the peak of Nevo to Tur Malka, and afterward I dreamed a dream. In the recurring dream the moon would rise above the mountains of Moab and advance toward the Mount of Olives and grow bigger and purpler and suck up and absorb into itself the juice of the world, until I woke up terrified and throbbing with the awful knowledge that the soul of the squeezed-out world was about to expire. It was the terror of the other world that surrounds the manifest world as the sea envelopes the ship that dares to cleave with its prow the foam licking its bows, that great immeasurable sea whose primeval splendor can be enjoyed by the voyager only when he feels the deck firm beneath his feet and knows that his craft is in no danger of capsizing. It was the same terror that gripped me when I sensed the ghosts who filled the room in the dark of night, as I fell into the sleep which awakened me to their blood-curdling call, and when I mentioned it to Dr. Blum at our landlady's funeral, he told me something he had once read in a certain little book, whose name and author had both slipped his mind; namely, that it was always the way of the spirits of the dead to terrify us with their presence, unless we had loved the dead person when he was alive on earth. When it happened, not only did I not know whose spirit was terrifying me, I didn't even know if it were the spirit of anyone in particular. The very sensation that a being which filled the house existed, although it could not be grasped with the senses of time and place, was very terrible to me, like the terrible moon in the recurring dream which came back to me with the first allusion to the moonlit nights on which Gabriel had gone down to the Kidron valley with his doves. "Yes, yes," he added, looking steadily at the shrouded body of the landlady, who looked much smaller and more shriveled up in her death than in her life, "it's only after a person dies that we find out whether we really loved him."

I was suddenly unnerved by the thought peeping out of his eyes and his voice that it was her ghost that had come to haunt me on that night—a hasty and basically untenable conclusion on his part, since the night of terror had preceded the night of her death by seven weeks at least—but I was too experienced to try to argue with him, and went on listening in silence. Now, when it was undeniable that her soul had departed from her body, Dr. Blum felt himself at liberty to acquaint me with those details concerning the events in her son Gabriel's childhood which in his opinion she had deliberately kept secret from me, and which for the sake of the truth he himself should have proclaimed in season and out, but which he had repressed for her sake, not because she was worthy of it, but because he felt himself bound by some sort of elementary decency in human relations. Precisely at this point, and in spite of my experience, I tried to show him his mistake and prove to him that the landlady had made no attempt at all to keep the said events a secret, if only for the simple reason that she knew nothing about them, and to the little she did know she paid no attention at all, and to my questions

about the moonlit nights on which Gabriel had gone down
to the Kidron valley with his doves she had responded with
astonishment and said, "Ha? To the Kidron valley? With
his doves? The rascal must have been trying to sell them to
the Arabs of Silwan! Well really! So now at last, after all
these years, the great mystery of where our doves disappeared
to is solved! And to think that it never once occurred to me
to suspect him! Ha, ha, he was the one for mischief when he
was a boy . . ."—which shows that in her eyes it was nothing
but a childish prank of no importance at all, deserving of no
more than the forgiving smile she bestowed on it from a distance of thirty years.

"A childish prank of no importance at all!" The pharmacist
repeated the words of the landlady, transmitted to him by me
after a certain delay, and a bitter smile spread over his lips.
"Almighty God! I've always known that she stopped up her
mind with straw and chaff, but during all this time that I con-
cocted eye drops for her I never realized that she was so blind.
I tell you straight, I'm sorry for every drop of effort I wasted
on her during all these years. You know what the trouble
with me is? The trouble with me is that I know there's no
one to talk to, that I'm wasting my words on deaf ears, and
in spite of everything I go on trying to explain."

His anger seethed and grew with every word he uttered,
and when the funeral procession reached the cemetery, his
eyes behind their pince-nez spectacles were already misted
with helpless rage against the landlady, who so long as she
stayed in her bodily abode had allowed him to hope that if
only he could burst his way into one of the blocked-up open-
ings with his tireless knocking, he would reach her at last.
But from the moment she made up her mind to disappear
completely, she had robbed him of all hope of finding her,
even were he to succeed in tearing her deaf ears open with

his words and breaking into all the orifices of her untenanted
body; the landlady no longer peered through the weary eyes
or eavesdropped behind the curtains of the deaf ears, and as
he walked by the side of her abandoned house which was
returning to the dust and the stones from which it had been
taken, her address was more unknown to him than the address of her son Gabriel, which she had hidden from him,
although certain events of his childhood were hidden from
her, and the details known to her she had regarded merely
as a mischievous prank, deserving of no more, from a distance
of thirty years, than a forgiving smile.

As for me, I don't know whether the events deserve a forgiving smile or not. Because they reached me from the pharmacist's mouth and not from hers, and at a time when his
eyes were blurred with a mist of helpless rage at her demise,
I not only don't know what they deserve, but even how he
himself regarded them, he who was at least once an eye witness to them. But ever since they had fallen from his mouth
like fragments of ancient pottery, awakening with their muffled sound the memory of that other existence, existing beyond the oblivion which is born with our birth, I could never
see the new moon rise without there being born in me the
image of the boy Gabriel, who on his thirteenth birthday became bar mitzvah and therefore went down with his dove to
the Kidron valley, not at the new but at the full moon.

When he lay down on his bed the room filled with longing
and the window wide open to the east grew lighter from the
sill upward, and the wings of his dove fluttering outside
played on the string strung onto the moon, until she dropped
like a spark from on high and landed on the windowsill, a
silhouette against the moon floating up from below to be an
orange halo for her. He rose to the murmur of her call and
dressed himself and went out after her to the moon shedding

her reddish gold onto the mist surrounding the mountains of Moab and growing rounder and more silvery as she climbed higher. His foot did not stumble and his head did not smash into the abyss at the foot of the wall along whose battlements he sped from the tower of David above the valley of Hinnom and the Ophel and the Gihon spring and the Kidron stream toward the valley of Jehosophat; and no harm befell him, nor could it, so long as his soul, bound up with the life of the dove and beating between her wings, remained intact. When a stone from a catapult had once damaged her wing, he had fallen ill and only recovered when the wing had healed, and he knew too that with her death his soul would die, so that his only care as he raced above the ancient chasms was for the dove fluttering before him, until he jumped down at the corner of the Ophel and crossed it and turned aside into the bed of the creek following the course of the Kidron stream and passing between Zacharia's tomb and Absalom's tomb until he reached the rock altar which no iron instrument had hewn. The dove landed on the head of the rock in the direction of the invisible line beating inside her and extending from the Kidron stream through the valley of Jehosophat to bisect the point where the eastern slope of Mount Scopus hits the western slope of the Mount of Olives at the angle of the moon, and he lay on his belly with his arms at his sides and his legs pressed together, in line with the dove and the moon. On the fullness of the broad ancient silence, fragrant and merciful in its indifferent coolness, the moon strings vibrated in a trembling crescendo of desire and the longing of one world for another, until the pipeline of the spheres opened and the stream of abundance surged out of him and into the breath of the moon, inhaling the red of the high hills and exhaling the violet and silver effulgence in which he rose, and holding her pulsing and cooing above the altar, stretched forth his hand to slay his dove. No ram was caught by its horns in a thicket, and her blood gushed out and spilled onto the altar, bare of wood for the fire. From the corners of the altar the blood dripped blue in the light of the moon, drop after drop, and no fire took hold of the twitching corpse to offer it up as a sweet savor in the nostrils of the Lord, to please Him and revive His spirits with the gift of the soul which had perished with her sacrifice and did not forgive him.

"I'll never forgive myself for not getting Gabriel's address out of her," said the pharmacist on our way back from the landlady's funeral, removing the spectacles from his nose so as to polish away the vapors of his rage. Naked and bereft of their lenses, his eyes were sunk deep into their sockets and stared out helplessly at a world not theirs. "Now there's nothing left for it," he said with the same expression, concentrated in its vacillations, brisk in its tortuousness, frowning and pursed, which he wore when he was busy transferring drugs from one department to another, at the same time returning his spectacles to their usual place, clearly marked by the red groove running around the bridge of the nose, "but for me to try to study Torah at the University. Who knows? Maybe there they understand the law of the priests better than the rabbi who taught us Torah with Rashi at Heder when we were children. After all I'm no greenhorn any longer, and at my age I should see things with a calm mind and a tranquil spirit."

With this last point I fully agreed, but his biblical studies on Mount Scopus didn't bring him much tranquillity, this qualified pharmacist who, once he had removed his white coat and revealed to the world the trousers above his prominent bluish-white knees, looked more or less like any other civilized member of society, since in those days many respectable citizens were in the habit of wearing short trousers.

The helpless rage to which he had first succumbed at the landlady's funeral, and which had appeared to be connected —to use the language of calm minds and tranquil spirits— with a certain change which had taken place in her abode, and seemed likely to pass when he had adapted himself to this same change, not only did not disappear, but actually increased the more he attended lectures on the Torah on Mount Scopus and the more he discussed them with his teachers and his fellow students. In fact, he was no longer capable of stating his views—and not only in the matter of the Tabernacle and its appurtenances and the Tent of the Presence and the Ark of the Covenant, but about anything at all—without shouting and throwing his hands about in the void of the world like a man drowning in mighty waters and searching in vain for something to hold on to. His voice, which had once been clear and loud and pleasing to the ear (at least to my ear, sensitive to this day to the soft cadence peculiar to the speech of those who were born in this country and started speaking Hebrew in the days of the Turks), became hoarse from all his shouting, and like water streaming from a half-blocked pipe would sometimes spurt out thin and high, and sometimes splutter and bubble and cough, and it in itself was enough not only to alienate the teachers he put to shame in public, but to grate on the ears of anyone who was not hard of hearing. Even I avoided him several times in the street, pretending to be so busy with urgent affairs of my own that I was blind to what was going on around me. What exasperated him most about the Higher Academy of Sciences on Mount Scopus, infuriating him to such a degree that it ruined his voice, was the unfortunate resemblance he discovered between his professor, alive and kicking and propagating knowledge, and our landlady, may she rest in peace. "This terrible resemblance between them," he would say, "will drive me out of my mind one of these days." And like her too, this same professor was of the opinion that the whole business of the law of the priests and the Tent of the Presence and the Ark of the Covenant and the various sacrifices was a mere piece of childishness, deserving of no more, from a distance of three thousand years, than a forgiving smile. What could be forgiven her, however, a simple woman with no pretensions, could not be forgiven him, a man who wore a crown of academic honors and went forth to propagate knowledge in the name of unfettered science. From what he said, I understood that it was in the name of unfettered science, too, that the most serious of his disagreements with this same professor arose. In the opinion of the pharmacist the methodology employed by the professor was not sufficiently scientific, and it was this opinion of his—which he did not take the least trouble to conceal—which cut the Torah professor to the quick and decided him to get rid of his pharmacist-student, come what may.

Of the precise form taken by the termination of the pharmacist's studies on Mount Scopus I was ignorant at the time, since it coincided with the period during which I was avoiding him; but from what he told me later, at our last meeting in the Café Atara, I gathered that the two of them had conducted their farewell celebrations on a joint trip to the biology laboratory, which they had reached locked in a close embrace, to the sound of cheers from the male students and shrieks of laughter from the females. The biology laboratory itself was irrelevant to the expulsion of the pharmacist from the university, which had been decided upon long before they reached its precincts, and its involvement in the affair was due entirely to the insistence of the pharmacist, who needed it, by way of illustration only, in order to demonstrate what he meant by a scientific approach to the Torah. Anyone wishing to investigate the law of the priests on the basis of a truly scientific methodology must conduct as many exact experiments as possible—so he repeatedly insisted to the professor and the students and, in fact, to anyone who was willing to listen to him. In one of his classes he expressed the opinion that the Hebrew University should erect the Tent of the Presence and the Ark of the Covenant and the Tabernacle with all its appurtenances in all their minutiae, and that the professor and all his assistants and students should officiate as priests therein, offering up the sacrifices in strict accordance with all the rules laid down for them, and only then, after many years of exact experiments, would we have the right to express an opinion worth anything from a scientific point of view on the power of the rituals described in the Torah to make the God of Israel dwell amongst us, so that we would once again become His people and He would once again reveal Himself to us, and to the whole world, in all His miracles and prodigies, His mighty signs and portents.

While he was delivering himself of these remarks, his hoarseness dissolved and melted away, and the more he seemed to discern on the face of his professor an echo of agreement to what he was saying, so there returned and sounded again in his voice the pleasing cadence it had possessed in days gone by. The professor was not only nodding his head in agreement, he was actually beaming with joy. For a long time now he had been waiting only for a favorable opportunity to expel the pharmacist from his classes, and now that the right moment had arrived he was determined not to miss it. Congratulating himself heartily on the manner, at once elegant and entertaining, in which he was about to rid himself of his burden, the professor rose to his feet and solemnly announced that he had no objections at all to the methods employed by his colleagues in the Department of

Biology; on the contrary, he had nothing but the greatest respect for them, mingled with admiration for their heroic bravery. Only once had he himself ever dared set foot in the biology laboratory, and when he had seen with his own eyes a toad being dissected and skinned, he had fainted and only recovered after being treated with Valerian drops. Fortunately for him, they had not been busy sacrificing at the time, slaughtering the bull, for example, and sprinkling its blood, for then even Valerian drops would not have helped him. And now, since the esteemed student Dr. Blum had expressed the wish to offer up sacrifices experimentally, and since the sacrifices, as all those who had listened attentively to the words of the lecturer were well aware, came from the animal kingdom, and to be more precise from five species only—from cattle and sheep and goats and turtledoves and pigeons—and since the animal kingdom in all its species and subspecies, including the five species mentioned above, belonged exclusively to the Department of Biology, where his friends the biologists officiated with such praiseworthy courage, it was clearly incumbent on Dr. Blum to transfer himself to the Department of Biology forthwith, at once, and without a moment's delay.

The pharmacist, who was usually rather quick-witted, did not understand at first what this speech was leading up to, so moved and excited was he by the mistaken impression he had received while he himself was still speaking, that here, at long last, he had succeeded in opening the ears of the Torah professor, up to now as deaf as those of the landlady, Mrs. Luria. He even greeted with enthusiasm the idea of inviting other departments to participate in the great experiment. Only when all the students burst out laughing did the full significance of his status in the Department of Biblical Studies dawn on him, and then he was shaken by a fit of rage the like of which he had never known before, not even at the funeral of the landlady, may she rest in peace. It was this rage of his which brought the elegant opening to a violent conclusion, although as far as the entertainment of the audience was concerned it detracted nothing at all, and even added an unexpected turn to the proceedings. "In everything you've said," cried the pharmacist in a loud shrill voice, ending in an ominous gurgle which intimated that he himself would very soon be in need of the Valerian drops alluded to in his teacher's remarks, "you've justified my contention that you have no idea at all of scientific methodology. You yourself openly confess that only once in the whole of your life have you ever set foot inside a laboratory, and therefore you should draw the only possible logical conclusion: not I, but you are the one who needs to go to the biology laboratory. I—I'm a Doctor of Chemistry. I, thank God, already know what a laboratory is. Not I but you are the one to go!"

"It's not I who'll go but you!" shouted the professor in reply; and thus they stood facing one another, each sending the other to the same place with outstretched hands and glaring eyes, and who knows how long they would have remained frozen in these exhortatory postures had not the pharmacist roused himself and passing from words to action, rushed up to his opponent, grabbed hold of him, and dragged him outside. It was thus that the two of them, as has already been mentioned above, arrived at the biology laboratory locked in a close embrace for their final farewell celebrations.

As is also mentioned above, these details concerning the circumstances of his graduation from the Department of Biblical Studies on Mount Scopus I heard from the pharmacist himself some years later at our last meeting in the Café Atara. To be precise, I should point out that this was not only our last meeting in the Café Atara, but also our first, since up to

then I had never seen him in any café at all; evidently he had
been too busy in those frenzied days transferring the Separanda and Toxica departments from one cupboard to another
or else arguing desperately with his professor and his fellow
students about the rightful place of whole offerings and shared
offerings. At first I didn't recognize him, although I sat down
at a table near his and looking in his direction saw a gentleman in a gray suit. Only when the waitress approached him
and he ordered a cup of tea and a plain cake, an echo awakened in me to the sound of the soft pleasing cadence of his
voice. I turned to look at him once more, after having iden-
tified him by the memory of this cadence, and found him as
pleasant and attractive to the eye as he was to the ear, and
this not only because of the tremendous change wrought in
his whole appearance by the light gray suit, but mainly because of the confidence-inspiring expression on his face. His
pince-nez spectacles had at last found their rightful place in
the world in the company of the blue tie peeping out between
the starched collar shining whitely above the well-cut light
gray suit, which made him look tall and broad-shouldered and
lent him an air of respectability and reliability. From the
careful elegance of his attire and the benevolence of his countenance, brimming over with the self-satisfied air of a man
firmly anchored in this world, it was patently clear that he
had at long last found not only the calm of mind and tranquillity of spirit which he had sought in vain in the law
emanating from Mount Scopus, but also a respectable portion
of the goods of this world. He was chatting easily in French,
with a smattering of expressions in Arabic, with a bald, fleshy
man who had entered the café and sat down beside him, and
who looked far more self-satisfied, prosperous, and worldly
than he. From the heavy mustache of this fat bald man, as
well as the gestures of his hands and his appearance in gen-

eral, I concluded that he was one of the Arab Christian merchants from the Nashashibi quarter of Jerusalem, and I proved mistaken only in the address. When he had taken his leave the pharmacist told me that his corpulent companion was one of the wealthiest notables of Beirut, and that he was visiting the country in connection with his business interests, which extended over the whole of the Middle East. The two of them had studied together at the University of Beirut, where a friendship had been inaugurated which had only recently begun to bear fruit, for it was only recently that the pharmacist had finally responded to the persistent propositions of his friend. When they were still students this friend of his had offered him a partnership in his business, which dealt with the production and marketing of pharmaceuticals, and now they were working together. I asked him if he was still a student in the Department of Biblical Studies, and then he told me, in detail and with a good-humored air, the story of the dénouement recounted above, in which he had dragged the Tora professor with him to the biology laboratory. "When all's said and done," he said, "all that miserable creature deserves is a forgiving smile. You'll forgive me, I'm sure, but I must go and speak to that chap sitting and waiting for me over there in the corner all this time. He's still a greenhorn in the hashish trade, and that's why he's so nervous and tense. We're already producing synthetic drugs which are far superior to hashish, but our Palestinian clients aren't used to them yet and still prefer hashish."

He stood up to go over to the nervous greenhorn, and when he gave me his hand in farewell, he suddenly roused himself to look at me and ask, "And Gabriel, how's he? When did you see him last?"

Translated by Dalya Bilu

9

THE POPE'S MUSTACHE

It is not the Pope's mustache which will be spoken of in the story I am clothing now in the language of words and putting down in writing, but the mustache of Mr. Gabriel Luria in the distant days of the past. When all these things had come back to me, bobbing up to the surface of my memory, I went and told them to my wife Shulamith and she said that there was no connection at all between the Pope's mustache and this story of mine. "Right," I said to her, to Shula, "you're right." So I cannot exempt myself from saying something about the Pope's mustache, if only on account of its prominence in the title of my story. And if the manner in which I speak of his mustache pleases neither the sheep in the fold nor the lost sheep, and if it fails too to pass the inspection of the shepherds of the flocks of forms, I will have this consolation at least, which is no mean consolation either, that the words of my Shulamith do influence me, sometimes.

The mustache came before the Pope. Giuseppe Angelo Roncalli, the son of Italian peasants, when he was conscripted into the medical corps of the Italian army during the First World War and promoted to the rank of sergeant, grew himself a fine bushy mustache, hanging over his mouth and drooping downward at the corners. Before half a year was out, the medical corps sergeant shaved off his mustache and became an army chaplain. Many years later, nearly half a century, he was elected to represent Jesus Christ on earth and became Pope John XXIII. He died just recently, while this story was being written, when he was over eighty years old. Pope John XXIII was one of the greatest, the best, and the most beloved popes in the history of the Catholic Church. He had a kind face and a gentle smile, and when in his last years on earth he recalled the period of the First World War, he remarked with a smile that he had grown his wild mustache "in a moment of weakness." This mustache, which due to weakness was not shaved off, lent the Italian medical corps sergeant a bold and virile air, the air of a warrior eager for battle. It was a combat mustache, whereas the mustache of Mr. Gabriel Luria in the distant days of my childhood in the middle of the nineteen-thirties was a salon mustache, squeezed in and fenced off and confined within the borders of an elegant square. He was the head clerk in my father's building goods shop.

In those days, before the troubles between Arabs and Jews broke out in 1936, we lived at the bottom of Mamilla Road opposite the Jaffa Gate and the walls of the Old City. From the balcony of our apartment I could see the nuns dressed all in black with big white three-cornered bonnets on their heads going in and out of their convent gates with quick proud steps. I never once saw a nun strolling at her leisure. They were always hurrying from one secret to another, and never took any notice of the people sitting in the Arab restaurant and café next door. At the entrance to this café a group of three narghile smokers sat permanently on low stools under a green awning. To me they seemed as much a part of the street as the convent building on one side and the lamppost on the other. At whatever hour of the day or night I stepped onto the balcony or looked out of the window I was sure to see them fixed as firmly in their places as nails driven into a wall. Sometimes the man who sold tamar hindi, a drink made from dates, would come to a stop by their side in his pointed colored cap, the burnished copper barrel tied to his stomach lifting its twisted neck like a haughty swan. Although he would enter into conversation with the three seated effendis, his mind never wandered from his task and every now and then, at fixed intervals, he would call out in a brassy voice which burst out of the depths of the barrel itself, "Tamar hindi! Tamar hindi!"

Once an old nun approached him and he poured out a foaming, frothing glassful of the fragrant brown date water for her. She leaned on her stick and drank at her leisure, greedily draining the glass to its dregs before wiping her lips with a handkerchief which she pulled out of its hiding place in the voluminous folds of her dress. The thing seemed incomprehensible to me: this nun, immersed in her distant, hidden world, far above the din of the crowded street and the smells of Arab food rising from the café where it boiled and roasted and fried in all its various spices, her world raised high above the cries of the Arab vendors and Armenian pedlars, the arrogance of the British officials, and the curly mustaches of the Irish policemen, how could she have fallen from such heights and succumbed to the heady sweetness of the tamar hindi like one of the coachmen standing on the corner— the fat one for instance, in the sash and the tarboosh, who had finished drinking just before her? Strange, conflicting feelings rose within me at the sight of the eagerness with which she drank. She fell in my estimation to the level of common humanity, if not lower. For what could be forgiven ordinary flesh and blood could not be forgiven an exalted being, and it was as exalted beings that I saw them, these nuns. And now, lo and behold, this same nun took out her handkerchief and wiped away the sweat which broke out and bathed her whole face, burning from the heat of the day and the greedy zest of her drinking, exactly like the coachman before her.

Therefore, there was no difference between her and this same coachman, who was husband to two wives, except what each did after drinking, he climbing onto the box of his shining black coach to drive important people about, waving his whip in the air and pulling on the reins of his two brown horses, and she hurrying, despite her venerable gray hairs, back to the great iron gates to climb steep stairs and gain the secrets and esoteric mysteries of her exalted world, which was always and forever sealed. Because she had become, with her fall, like any other mortal, she became closer and warmer too, and the uncontrollable thirst she shared with the coachman of the two wives opened my eyes to the special difficulties she must always have to overcome in order to leap up from this inferior base to the heights of her hidden world, difficulties which made me take pity on her. What softened the fall of the woman in my eyes was precisely the fact of her great old age. My heart told me that her advanced years gave her the right to do things which would be quite out of the question for other, younger nuns. If, for example, the fair-faced young English nun, who had only recently arrived in the country and entered the convent, had been the one to give in to temptation and drink the tamar hindi, I would have taken a far more serious view of the matter. It seemed that the fifty years the old woman had spent in the convent had lifted her up to a level so exalted, to a wisdom so lofty and superior that she could now look down from its heights and see that there was really no difference between the world of the novice and that of the coachman, but that in its essence this knowledge was different from the very same knowledge had it chanced to enter the mind of the novice, and the novice was therefore prohibited from receiving knowledge of this degree as yet.

In those days I did not know the meaning of monasticism or of Christian abstinence (to this day in fact my knowledge of these matters is very slight and superficial) and yet, inter-estingly enough, I made no inquiries and asked no questions and demanded no clear answers concerning the mysteries hidden in the convent next door. In my heart I must have realized that any answer at all would be likely to dispel the enchantment that encompassed it, and truly the convent in all its aspects had cast a spell of enchantment on me, with its narrow windows, lengthening to points and filled with colored panes, its blank outer wall circling it protectively about, and its belfry piercing the clear sky. On their holy days the bells would ring out and their echoes shattered off the stone walls into my heart. Sometimes I would wake in a tumult of mysterious dread to the pealing of the bells at midnight and the metallic reverberations of the organ accompanying the singing of the nuns.

The singing of the nuns and the pealing of the bells held Sarah spellbound too. Sarah was one of our two Moslem maids. (I do not know whether Moslem Arabs ever really call their daughters Sarah, but this, at any rate, is what we called her.) I remember how, whenever the thunder of the bells burst, or the singing of the nuns floated gently into the house, this same Sarah would stop washing the floor or beating the mattresses and stand stock-still, frozen in holy awe. As for Mr. Gabriel Luria, who was the most regular and welcome of all the visitors to our house, he too was moved by the magic of the nuns, only in him the magic underwent a subtle change, emerging as a special sort of smile, a gloating smile of lascivious satisfaction. He would feast his eyes on the convent windows and cloisters and on the nuns moving about inside them as he sat taking his ease on our balcony, lord of all he surveyed, leaning back in his chair sometimes for hours on end. The elbow of the hand in which he held his English cigarette he rested on the balcony railing, and in his other hand he held the little cup of Turkish coffee brought him by Jamilla, our Moslem cook, who, unlike Sarah, was quite indifferent to the music of the Christian liturgy, not for reasons of religious fanaticism, but simply because of a total lack of responsiveness to the world of sounds in general, since she was just as indifferent to the Arab tunes which burst forth regularly from the café across the road. In contrast to her musical obtuseness this same Jamilla was endowed with a sharp social sense, and in her delicate sensitivity to the importance of the aristocracy she would apply herself diligently to the service of Mr. Gabriel Luria with the speed and devotion befitting the first son of an important effendi, Luria senior, who had been privileged to receive the Turkish title Bey. Whenever he appeared on our doorstep Jamilla would come running from the kitchen to take his silver-knobbed cane and his white hat banded with a black ribbon—a stiff hat made of woven white fibers, which he called a "Panama hat." My mother, who in her indifference to the world of sounds and her sharp sense of social distinctions was amazingly like her Moslem cook (though as far as any other human quality is concerned, no two women could have been less alike) was always a little offended by the untoward zeal of the slow-moving Arab woman in the service of this ever-welcome guest, who, despite all his charms and the prestige of his father who had a Turkish title, was no more, when all was said and done, than a clerk in my father's shop. After Jamilla had relieved Mr. Gabriel Luria of his silver-knobbed cane and his hard round hat and put them away in their usual place on the rack, she would hurry off to place the wicker armchair and the round three-legged folding table on the balcony, and before he had finished glancing into the mirror which hung in the hallway, adjusting his tie, giving his hand in greeting to my mother and taking a cigarette out of his packet of Players, she would already

have gone to work with a will in the kitchen, preparing his
Turkish coffee and rummaging about here and there to see
what she could provide in the way of delicacies suitable to the
occasion, such as sweetmeats like rahat lakum, for example,
and savory pastries like bureka, to help him, as he sat on the
balcony in the shade of the awning, derive the utmost possible
pleasure from the sight of the convent and its nuns on one of
those days in spring which calm the spirits and broaden the
minds of men.

One spring day to calm the spirits and broaden the minds of
men will always be linked in my memory with the image of
Mr. Gabriel Luria in the days that preceded the troubles of
the year 1936. Mr. Gabriel Luria in white flannel trousers,
called by him "tennis trousers," and in a blue blazer with gold
buttons, lording it over our balcony where he sat solemnly reclining upon the fullness of the harmony that existed between
him and all the world surrounding him. He radiated this air
of glad harmonious solemnity not only when he was looking
down on the world of the Mamilla Road and the Jaffa Gate
from the balcony of our house, but also when at work in my
father's building goods shop in the Commercial Center; and
in his work too he is linked in my memory with a day in
spring, for one whole spring day of my Passover vacation was
spent at his side in the shop. The other clerks, the Jews and
the Arabs, employed themselves in transferring goods from
the warehouse to the shop, and in serving the retail customers,
who were mainly Arabs from Bethlehem and Hebron, although Hurani from Transjordan would also occasionally put
in an appearance in the shop. Gabriel Luria Bey himself
served only wholesale customers, and on the day I am speaking
of he was busy conducting negotiations with Boulos Effendi,
who had grown rich from selling land to the Jews and was
now in the middle of building a big house for his family in

the Talbieh neighborhood of Jerusalem. Boulos had recently returned from a trip to Beirut, and although he had come to us solely for the purpose of purchasing the building materials he needed urgently, since his workers were already sitting idle at his expense and every hour that passed took its toll of his purse, the effendi opened his negotiations with Luria Bey by dwelling on the delightful memories of his trip. They both seated themselves in the office screened off at the rear of the shop, sinking into upholstered armchairs with a comprehensive and noncommittal sigh at the hardship of the times and the state of things in general. After Luria Bey had ordered the messenger boy to hurry to the nearby café and bring Turkish coffee and sherbet and biscuits and a bubbling narghile to revive the spirits of Boulos Effendi from the effort of driving in his new car, a small black Morris, the two began to praise the lovely ladies of the metropolis of Beirut, who could perform and make you perform in the Occidental or the Oriental, the Italian or the French manner, who were so marvelously various and subtle and exotic that they could supply everything needed to satisfy the dearest wishes of a civilized and discriminating man.

When the office was filled with the smoke of the narghile and the messenger boy had been called to take away the glasses and bring another round of delicacies, the conversation took a turn in a different direction and touched on the unemployment that had overtaken the country in the days of Turkish rule. At this stage Boulos Effendi remembered his building workers idling their time away at his expense for the lack of iron and cement. By now it was already past noon and both parties to the negotiations were agreed on the fundamental principle that this matter of tons of iron and cement was too weighty to be lightly discussed on an empty stomach, differing only with regard to the payment of the restaurant bill for their midday meal, since Boulos Effendi declared that he would be the host and Gabriel Bey would dine at his board, while Gabriel Bey for his part insisted that it was the shop which should bear the expense of the honored customer's meal, and it seemed that Boulos Effendi would give way in the end. As for me, Gabriel Bey urged me to join them at the festive board, and it was only after we had climbed into Boulos's car and I begged them to let me off outside my house because my mother had ordered me to be home no later than a quarter past one and it was already twenty past, that he desisted, exclaiming not a little at my extreme anxiety to comply with my mother's command.

As the car drew up outside our house and I opened the door to dismount, the fair-faced young English nun passed by. Mr. Gabriel Luria now had no eyes for me and did not even reply to my goodbyes. He sprang out of the car himself and overtaking the nun with one athletic stride, removed his hat with a gesture of profound respect, fixed his big brown eyes under their heavy brows on her in a look that was at once serious, naïve, and insolent, and said in a low intense voice, "Good morning, Sister Mary Anne, would you allow us to give you a lift to the hospital?" She worked as a nurse in the English Missionary Hospital in the Street of the Prophets. And now too, as at the sight of the elderly nun enthusiastically gulping the tamar hindi, I was overcome by a vortex of emotions at the sight of the fair-faced young nun's reaction to this gallant offer from the good-looking man who suddenly accosted her. A light blush came and went in her cheeks and her two hands clasped and crossed on her bosom in momentary panic at being taken unawares. When she had recovered her composure and considered for a moment, she said with a smile, "Thank you kindly. Truly I am in a very great hurry, and but for your kind offer it is possible that I might even have come late for my shift. It will be a pleasure to drive to the hospital in your car." Yes. Exactly. His lordly aristocratic manner could give rise to no other supposition than that the car was his car and the fat Boulos sitting at the wheel was his driver waiting to do his bidding (this is the way he behaved in the shop too, and new customers, unaware of the true state of affairs, invariably thought that Mr. Gabriel Luria was the owner of the business and my father the shy, retiring book-keeper). He did not trouble to point out her mistake, and she bent down and stepped gracefully into the car. With the same solemn air and serious look as before, and even before returning his hat to his head, he quickly shut the door behind her.

This lift which Mr. Gabriel Luria gave the fair-faced young English nun to her shift at the English Hospital in the Street of the Prophets had unexpected consequences both for his behavior in general and his appearance and the features of his face in particular. When I returned to the shop at dusk on the same day I was confronted by a different Mr. Gabriel Luria, somehow exposed and transparent, and quite unlike the dashing gentleman I had parted from only a few hours earlier doffing his hat so gallantly to the nun and shutting the door of Boulos's black car behind her. The hat—the hard, white, black-banded, round-brimmed straw hat, the Panama hat whose twin sister waving in the hand of Maurice Chevalier, ardently breaking into song for the love of Paris, met my eyes on my visits to the cinema—had vanished, never to adorn the head of Mr. Gabriel Luria again, not on that day nor on the following days of that summer, nor on the summer days of the years to come, until the day he died some twenty years later, which is to say, four years before the writing of these lines. Together with the disappearance of the hat, yet another change had taken place in his person which despite its being more fundamental, profound, and even essential than the first, still kept me wondering for several moments before I comprehended its nature—the mustache! The square mustache which stuck out like a black die adhering to his upper lip was gone, vanished from that day forth, and this is why, when I first set eyes on him, he had seemed transparent and exposed. From that day forth, too, the story of the mustache and the nun came into being and went to join the other stories in his repertoire. "Does Sister Mary Anne know that she is beautiful, very beautiful indeed?" opened Mr. Gabriel Luria, speaking straight to the point without procrastinating or beating about the bush, as soon as he sat down beside her in the little black car, for this was always his way with a girl; if she was a lady, he would immediately address the woman in her, but with servants and other menials he conducted himself like a polite and civil gentleman in the presence of a great lady. Since Mary Anne had retired from the world and accepted the monastic yoke as well as being a lady from the upper classes of English society, he had double cause to stun her with a sudden, strong, deep thrust through the scales of her double armor—that of a lady and that of a nun—into the dark depths of her womanly softness.

"She knows it very well," said she in reply, regarding him coolly with the eyes of a society lady whose heart was hardened to flattery, skilled in the art of brushing off the attentions of importunate admirers, and he who had wished to stun was himself astounded. But if the nun had fallen back on the ploys of previous years in order to deal with Mr. Gabriel Luria, he too had recourse to techniques and ploys of his own and quickly covered up his momentary embarrassment with a bold and scrutinizing look. "If I may be permitted," said he, returning composedly to the attack, "to make a remark of a personal nature to Sister Mary Anne . . ."

"You've already done so without asking permission," she replied, and now he was able to disguise his embarrassment no longer. It was evidently precisely this embarrassment which left him momentarily helpless and melted the scales of her armor that made her speak to him plainly and frankly. And if her first reaction had thrown him into confusion, he was now dumbfounded not only by the degree of frankness with which she spoke, but also and mainly by the tone of her words and the language in which she expressed herself. The proud lady who could nip a troublesome flirtation in the bud with a flicker of her eyebrow had turned into a strange nun. A strange nun, who did not express herself in the common coinage of Christian functionaries (especially those sent out by the Christian churches to convert souls from among the members of other faiths), but formulated her thoughts and feelings clearly and concisely, choosing the simplest words possible (so that they vibrated with the high tension of the load of experience and thought compressed into them), as one might have expected not from a nun who had wandered far afield and come at last to distant Jerusalem to enter a convent and tend the ills of poor afflicted Jews and Moslems in conversation with an insolent clerk in a shop which sold building materials, but from a highly educated, tolerant, broad-minded English girl free from the fetters of provincial morality in conversation with a close friend. "I know from experience," she said to him, "what personal remarks of the kind you wish to make mean. They always have something to do with the nun's habit I wear. Before I put it on, my friends and relations tried to dissuade me, and once I had done so very few of the men I met were able to resist the temptation of cross-examining me about it. Do you know, Mr. Luria, there are two kinds of women who are accustomed to being asked 'What made you choose this path?'—nuns and prostitutes. If you truly and honestly want to know, I will answer you truthfully and honestly and briefly. I will be brief for several reasons, the last of which is that we are already approaching the hospital. This is my answer: saints and martyrs and spiritual heroes need neither external discipline nor social frameworks nor uniforms. I, who am neither a saint nor a martyr nor a spiritual heroine, but wish to find the right way nevertheless, need the convent with its external discipline and social framework and uniform. We have arrived. I thank you for the lift and the pleasant conversation. Good luck and goodbye."

When she had dismounted from the car and he had replaced the hat on his head, he caught a glimpse of his reflection in the mirror fixed to the near-side mudguard. "You know what," he said to Boulos Effendi, "I shall have to get rid of them both, the mustache and the Panama hat as well." The hat he threw out of the window of the moving car, and the mustache he shaved off in the kitchen of the restaurant next door to the convent with the restaurant owner's razor, even before sitting down with Boulos Effendi to dine. Boulos Effendi and the two waiters and the messenger boy and the owner of the restaurant and his wife who was in charge of the cooks, and the cooks, and also the tamar-hindi vendor, who came with a tinkling of his cymbals in at the kitchen door to add water and various spices to the barrel on his stomach which was rapidly being emptied of its contents in the dryness and heat of the afternoon—all of them crowded into the kitchen around Gabriel Luria Bey, who was standing opposite the pocket mirror held up by Boulos Effendi and sweeping the borrowed razor over his mustache. They watched fearfully and wonderingly as the deed was done, a deed expressive of contempt for manhood's crowning glory, bordering on blasphemy and provocatively performed in public. "God the merciful, the compassionate!" said the owner of the restaurant stroking his own curly mustache as if to make sure that his honor was still intact and had not fallen to the destroyer, and the tamar-hindi vendor responded with a nod of silent understanding. "Wait a minute, wait a minute, don't let the hairs fall on the ground!" cried one of the cooks in alarm, hurrying to hold out her apron under Gabriel Bey's chin and catch the felled mustache, which she then cast onto the embers of the fire, whispering to herself the while.

Boulos Effendi hiccupped once and then twice, moved his stool backward to make room for the bubbling narghile brought by the messenger boy, poured another glass of arak down his gullet to appease the dinner boiling inside his stomach, gave vent to one last, loud, comprehensive belch to indicate that he had eaten his fill, sighed a sigh of melancholy satisfaction, and opened with the following words, "It is well known to you, O my friends, dear to me as the light of my eyes"—the owner of the restaurant sucked on the mouthpiece of the narghile in front of him, and the tamar-hindi vendor, who also wanted to hear the terrible tale of the events which had caused Gabriel Bey to shave off his crowning glory but at the same time did not forget his place, listened standing, a pace or two away out of respect, while the mustacheless hero of the story himself sat listening absentmindedly and drummed with his fingers on the table during the entire course of its telling— "that only a week ago I returned from far-flung travels over land and sea. Two whole months I spent in the metropolis of Beirut. Great wonders I saw there which the mouth does not tire of telling and the ear does not tire of hearing, but what happened to me today in my own car in my own city of Jerusalem surpasses all that happened to me in all my travels in the hooting chariots of iron and the great ships which plough the deep seas. It chanced (but God the compassionate and the merciful, He alone is all-knowing as well as all-wise and almighty and all-bountiful) that all the hours of the morning I spent in negotiations with our friend Gabriel Luria Bey in the matter of bargaining and the house which I am building, please God that I may live to see it finished and my sons may live to dwell in it in peace and tranquillity, until the hour of noon came upon us and made us feel our hunger. Now with us in the shop all the morning was also the boy Daoud, the owner's son, and we took him with us in the car intending to drive straight here and eat our fill. But as we were passing by the entrance to his house, the boy entreated us to let him get out of the car and eat at home for his mother awaited him impatiently, and he begged and entreated until we agreed, and neither we nor the boy knew that the hand of God was in it, and that the Compassionate and the Merciful who sees the end in the beginning wanted to spare the child the great trials which were lying in wait for us. Hardly had the boy descended from the car than the nun Mary Anne, may God have mercy on our souls, passed before us on her way to the English Hospital. Gabriel Bey set eyes upon her and lust entered his heart like a white-hot spit, and he reared up and stood erect. I addressed him thus: 'Gabriel O my friend and my brother, restrain yourself and be seated, I pray you. Let us make haste to the restaurant to enjoy our midday repast and do not run after things which are impossible to attain, and do not try to make conquests among the nuns, for you will only lose your soul in the attempt.' Gabriel answered me saying, 'By the hat on my head and by the splendor of my mustache, I swear that I will have this nun and remain master of my soul nevertheless,' and immediately turned to the nun Mary Anne and took off his hat and smiled under his mustache and said, 'Pray, dear Sister Mary Anne, mount this motorized vehicle and it will carry you to the place of your heart's desire.' 'God forfend that I should go where my heart carries me,' the woman replied, making the sign of the cross on her breast, 'but whither I am commanded by our Lord Savior in his infinite mercy, there will I go. And if indeed it is your wish to assist me in doing the will of our Father in Heaven, pray take me to the hospital.'

" 'Even as you say, our Sister,' answered Gabriel Bey, making room for her next to him and closing the door of the car behind her, but what she said he heard not at all because his heart was beating hard with every tremor and quiver of the nipples of her breasts encased in the coarse folds of her nun's garments. To me he said in a whisper in Arabic so that she would not understand, 'Do not drive so fast in the direction of the hospital, O Boulos, for speed is of the devil,' and I, clearly perceiving the reason for his request, said to myself, 'No, my friend, it is not speed but rather your own lust which is of the devil. But if you wish it so, let us turn off in the direction of Talbieh to see how my workers are employing themselves in my absence, for so long as they have to work, they too think as you do that speed is of the devil, but they are all of them as quick and nimble as the sons of the devil himself when it comes to doing the will of the little member of their bodies.'

"So I turn my steering wheel in the direction of Salameh Square and drive on until we behold the scaffolding of my building, which is utterly deserted. I dismount from the car and look about me in all directions and I can see no one. The workers have all disappeared. Even Salim, the boy who hands the bricks, even this insolent child is nowhere to be seen.

" 'To be sure,' I say to myself, 'this it what you richly deserve, O Boulos, you Boulos Effendi, who are so clever in your own opinion, who know very well that workers are lazy even when their master stands over them and urges them on, you deserve to waste your father's inheritance on all the loafers of Jerusalem and Bethlehem and Hebron combined.' I continue looking about me until my eye falls on the olive grove and I see them all, sprawled under the olive trees fast asleep. At the building site itself, there was not a living soul except for the watchman's dog Latif, and he too was sleeping as soundly as if his soul had departed from his body. The nun rose up in her place and peeped out at the scaffolding of the deserted building and the whitewash, which hurt the eyes with its glare, and the whole world swooning in the heat of the sun, and the folds of her dress were disturbed and the nipples of her breasts poked out between them. Our friend Gabriel bent over her as if he too wished to peep out and see where he was in the world, and with an absentminded air he brushed his mustache lightly against the nipple of her left breast.

"And then it happened. The nipple stuck to the mustache and the chain of the cross hanging on her heart came undone and the belt of her garments was loosened and the nipple adhering to the mustache was obedient to the folds of her dress no longer but strained to get out, pulling the whole body after it, and the dress fell off and was buffeted about and dragged out of the window and flew up to the summit of the cypress tree at whose foot the watchman's dog Latif lay sleeping. The mustache adhering to the nipple pulled the body of Gabriel Bey over his soul until the body split open and the naked soul of Gabriel Bey was left quivering in eternity, which is like a ring of radiance. The soul of our friend Gabriel took fright at the supreme radiance and went hither and thither seeking shelter in the material world until it touched on the dress of the nun which was waving from the summit of the cypress and hid inside it.

"Since the body of our friend was no longer occupied by its soul, it was invaded by the soul of the dog Latif, for while the body of the dog was wrapped in sleep under the cypress his soul was free to wander where it would, and the minute the soul of our friend burst out of his body which was possessing the body of the nun, the soul of the dog entered it. Mary Anne, sensing that she was being ravished by a dog, tried to free herself from her body, but without success, for the fetters of the flesh were so tightly meshed about her soul that there was no way out. The soul of Mary Anne, imprisoned in her body which was being ravished by the soul of the dog Latif, languished and pined for the soul of our friend which was hiding in the folds of the nun's habit swelling and billowing on the top of the cypress. And the soul of our friend languished and pined for the soul of the woman imprisoned in the flesh which was clinging and clutching and writhing, but to his body it could not return, for his body was held captive by the soul of the dog Latif. The dog was making vigorous use of the body of our friend and penetrating the body of the nun to great depths, and the eyes of our friend peeping out of the folds of the nun's habit looked and longed. The sufferings of the soul of our friend multiplied exceedingly, its torments increased unendurably, and it found no comfort until our Lord Savior took pity on it. Our Lord Jesus of Nazareth saw the suffering and distress of this soul and in his infinite mercy and his great love, he came to save it. Said Jesus the Messiah to the soul of our friend Gabriel, 'To your body you cannot return so long as it is captive to the soul of the dog, and the soul of the dog will not leave your body so long as it adheres to the body of our sister and bride Mary Anne, and her body will not be separated from your body so long as the nipple adheres to the mustache. It is the mustache adhering to the nipple which separates soul from body and soul from soul. Soul will not be united with body and soul will not merge with soul until the mustache is shaved off.' The soul swore with a mighty oath that the moment it had control of its body the mustache would indeed be shaved off, and our Lord Savior saved it at once. What did the Nazarene do in his infinite mercy? He put the soul of the nun into a trance, and

woke the dog Latif from his deep sleep. The sleeping soul of
the nun flew up to the top of the cypress and merged with
the soul of our friend in the secret folds of the nun's habit,
and the combined force of the two souls merged into one
pulled the garment down from the top of the tree and returned
it to the body of the nun, while the soul of the dog was obliged
to return to its waking body. The dog Latif woke from his
sleep and immediately began wagging his tail and barking for
joy at the marvels which had overtaken him in his dream—
the dream of a dog. And he barked so loudly that all the
workers woke from their sleep and went back to work on the
scaffolding. And I drove the nun to her shift at the hospital,
and the body of our friend Gabriel Bey I brought here to keep
the vow he vowed to our Lord Savior and shave off his mustache, but the essence of his soul remained in the secret folds
of the nun's dress."

From the secret folds of his dress the tamar-hindi vendor
now drew a very large red handkerchief and wiped his face,
which was bathed in sweat, and blew his nose loudly once
and twice and three times. During the entire telling of the
story he had remained standing, leaning slightly backward
with his barrel resting on his belly and his face pouring with
streams of sweat, never daring to make a move. Now that the
story was finished and an oppressive silence had fallen, he
wiped his face and blew his nose with much ado and much
noise and kept on until the restaurant owner, who had started
showing signs of displeasure at the end of the story, caught his
eye. When the trumpeting of the latter had ceased, the restaurant owner coughed shortly and opened with these words:
"In the name of God, the compassionate, the merciful, to this
day we have never heard, and our fathers have never told us,
a tale as strange and terrible as this. Praise and glory be to
the Most High God that our friend Gabriel Bey emerged
safely from the terrible trials and torments of a soul in hell

which overtook him on this day. And you also, our friend
Boulos Effendi, deserve great praise for all that you did, and
above all the mouth will not tire of praising and lauding and
extolling your good taste in the recounting of these things,
which you recounted gracefully and pleasingly and exactly as
they occurred, everything after its fashion, with no detail missing. But please allow me, O my friend and my brother, to
appraise you of one great error in your words, and I beg your
pardon and pray your forgiveness a thousand thousand times
if there is anything in my words to affront your honor in the
slightest degree. For in the cause of the truth I cannot keep
silent, and the truth is, O my friend and companion, precious
to me as the light of my eyes, that you made a great mistake
and committed a grave error in the tale which you have just
unfolded, and God forbid that we should say your words contained a deliberate lie. And for the sake of the truth I myself
will correct all that has been distorted in your story. Now you
have just told us that it was Jesus Christ who returned the
soul of our friend hiding in the secret folds of the nun's habit
hanging from the top of the cypress tree to his body, possessing
the body of the nun, which was captive to the soul of the dog
Latif, and it was not thus that the thing happened but otherwise, and you did not comprehend the true nature of the
events. The thing came about in this manner, that it was
Jesus Christ who removed the soul of our friend Gabriel from
his body, for surely it is known and famed throughout the land
that it was Christ who brought this wizardry to the world of
the soul bursting out of the body and the throwing of the body
to the dogs, and you, O Boulos Effendi, who are a believing
Christian from the womb and the cradle, born in Bethlehem
in the very same street where Christ himself was born, and
named after Paul * the disciple of Christ, how came you to

* Boulos is Paul, or Paulus. There is no "P" in common Arabic pro-
nunciation.

forget this great principle of your faith? Jesus Christ hunted
the soul of Gabriel Bey and removed it from his body, and
into the untenanted body he put the soul of the dog Latif.
Our Lord Mohammed the Apostle of Allah saw the sufferings
of this soul and took pity on it, and in his bounteous mercy he
remembered that Gabriel Bey is named after the angel Gabriel, and it was the angel Gabriel who appeared to him, Mohammed, when he was living as a recluse in the city of Mecca
and its environs, and called him 'Apostle of Allah.' And in his
love and his mercy and his bounty our Lord Mohammed res-
cued him, and it was he who returned the glory of the body
to the naked soul in the manner which you have recounted.
And praise be to Allah, King and Creator of the Universe,
and blessing and peace be on the lord of apostles, our lord and
master Mohammed, and his Family! Blessing and peace for
ever until the Day of Judgment."

Translated by Dalya Bilu

10

FIRST LESSON

To my Shula
in Saint Maur on the River Marne

IN THE BEGINNING was the miracle, and the miracle was, and is, and will be to be marveled at always.

As for me, I have not stopped marveling to this day, to the writing of these very lines in the September of the year 1966 in the French village of Saint Maur des Fossés in Josef's house right on the banks of the river Marne—I can see the tops of the trees on the other side of the river—and I am thirty-nine years old. And not only have I not stopped marveling, but the marveling increases from day to day, against all expectations and even, it might be said, against all ideas of decorum and good taste.

I well remember the first time in my life that I was smitten with the terror of the great miracle. It happened when I was a small child of about three years old. I do not know why I stayed up after my usual bedtime. In contrast to what was to happen later in my life, I remember the hour as a peaceful one in the house. The kerosene lamp burned on the table and its green china shade, in addition to the yellowish-whitish pool of light it shed on the table around the stem of the lamp and its base, diffused a dull green glow. My father sat poring over a textbook on bookkeeping and other books on accountancy in the English language (he had opened a commercial school and there were no books of this kind as yet available in Hebrew, except for two or three which failed to satisfy him). When I approached him he rose from his place, took me in his arms and went outside with me into the night.

This first meeting with the night sky filled me with an obscure terror. I saw the sky and suddenly it was black with tiny points of light in it. "Those are the stars," said my father, and added, "the host of Heaven." Somewhere a door creaked open and a stream of light poured out of the crack which opened in the blank dark wall, reaching the foot of the cypress tree which stood in our yard and wrapping its trunk in a mantle of day. Soft chill tongues of wind whispered between the branches, bringing with them from afar, from beyond the tombs of the Sanhedrin, a smell of damp earth and small humming, cricking, buzzing voices, the voices of night animals suddenly signaling and suddenly stopping, and the existence of the surrounding mountains—the mountains of Nebi Samwil and Sheikh Jarrah and Mount Scopus—was present and breath-stopping and heavy with the weight of an ancient-breathed quality, terrible in its dimensions, which were beyond the dimensions of man, and its eternities which were beyond the eternity of man, and in its indifference to the little men stirring on its back. The same quality of mountains and sky dimly perceived on my daytime ramblings along the mountain paths between the thistles and rocks (we lived then in the old Beth Israel quarter and our house was the last in the street; from it the track continued up to the tombs of the Sanhedrin, and from our window we saw the village of Nebi Samwil astride the hilltop) oppressed me now more strongly in the night world revealed to me. The mountains and the sky at night became more tangible in their distance, more oppressive in their tangible presence in the darkness.

I clung tightly to my father's neck, to the strong pleasant

smell of his tobacco. "Come, Daddy, let's go back," I said to him, "let's go in." He looked at me and said, "Good, let's go inside." I saw in his eyes that he understood that the fear of the elements in the night had overcome its powers of attraction, and with his first surprise had come the understanding that I was not yet old enough to live in both the world of the day and the world of the night. As soon as we had returned to the shelter of the four walls and the soft light of the green lampshade, a heavy weariness fell on me, as if I had just returned from a long journey into an unknown land. After some time had passed—whether it was a matter of days, weeks, or months escapes me—I asked him to take me out again into the mountains and sky of the night. I think I was resentful. I felt a kind of anger, a kind of insult because he had hidden from me until now the other world of whose existence I knew nothing, and in which he continued to live after I had gone to bed to sleep.

The fear of the quality of the elements made tangible in the darkness, which disappeared completely with the love of the night world, came back to me a few years later in a strange form, almost opposed to the first form in which I had experienced it. The fear of the quality of the elements at night, which soon turned to longing (a longing which differed in kind from the longing for the alleys and streets of the town at night, of which we will speak when the time comes), gave way to a fear of the quality condensed into the stillness of a lighted room at night, but of this fear too the time has not yet come to speak.

I have described the first time I was smitten by the miracle. As for the last time, why it has just this moment occurred, with the writing of these very words. If I were a psychiatrist or a psychopathologist or a psychoanalyst or a neurologist or any other kind of diploma-ed soul doctor of our times, and if I

were asked to give an expert opinion on the state of my own
soul, I should be obliged to conclude that in the thirty-six
years which have passed since then my condition has deteriorated steadily and that it is exceedingly doubtful whether any
specialist treatment whatever could bring about a cure at the
advanced and severe stage which it has now reached. For today there is nothing at all in the whole world that does not
arouse my wonder and amazement, and the more I concentrate
my attention on anything the more intense the wonder and
amazement grow: these autumn colors in the garden and the
sky outside, and the coal fire in the grate inside, and the
house, and me myself sitting in it, and my writing hand, and
the writing itself, and the drive to write. If I were living my
life according to my true inclinations and the impulses of my
heart, I would not be sitting and writing now but casting a
line into the waters of the Marne by the side of that slender
Frenchwoman with her hair blowing in the wind. All along
the banks of the Marne there are Frenchmen fishing. Some
fish standing, but most are sitting. Sitting and fishing and
waiting patiently the livelong day with their eyes fixed on the
float at the end of their lines, gazing dreamily at the little
greenish-yellowish-brownish wavelets and the running water
and the dancing specks of light, their thoughts drifting to and
fro over the tops of the trees and the play of light among the
leaves and the warbling of a distant bird, and their hearts
longing for a sudden disturbance of the water and a delicate
tug and the head of a hooked fish appearing on the end of the
line. The fisherman and the fish. Past the fishermen go the
sailors. Some row in rowboats and some are bold and skilled
and sail in sailboats and some, who are rich and desire a maxi-
mum of comfort in their pleasures, drive far out in motorboats.
Where the shore slopes down at the river's bend, at the section
belonging to the village called La Varenne, stand the villas of

the rich and of the singers who have made their fortunes by
becoming public favorites, like Charles Trenet. This elegant
fisherwoman is in all probability one of the mistresses of one
of these rich men, which would of course not prevent me, if
I were living my own life, from wooing her so that she would
lie with me on the riverbanks after the sun had set and the
fishermen and the rowers and the sailors had all gone away.
The trouble is, I know in advance that in the act of lying with
her, and even at the moment of climax, I will be haunted by
longing and tormented by yearning, which is what happened
to me last time with the aging Françoise in her flat on the
Île de St. Louis opposite the cathedral of Notre Dame, and
even before, with her predecessors. All of them fished for fish
in their souls, but she did so consciously. It is the knowledge
after the event that the body is the veil and the limit, and
penetrating it does not lead to the essence beyond, and you
can journey beyond it only in it and through it, and in order
to get everything there is to get out of the journey itself, you
must pay the price of yearning and longing in advance, and
once this obligation has been fulfilled, the difficulties and
obstacles on your way will be eased.

As for me, it seems that I must pay the price in writing,
black on white, and as for the obstacles on the way, I made
their acquaintance at a tender age, in the kindergarten and
before, soon after I was smitten by the miracle of the night.
When I rode around the yard on the red bicycle my father
bought me for a present, the landlord's two sons would place
themselves in my way and bother me; they would grab hold
of the handlebars and hang on and drag along behind me.
The landlord, Mr. Arajun, was a Persian Jew who had a vegetable shop in the market in the Bukharan quarter. His good
apartment he rented to us, while he and his family lived in
the basement below the level of the yard. They had chairs,

but they preferred sitting on cushions scattered about the floor. After Mr. Arajun had given the matter due thought he purchased two second hand bicycles which he presented to his sons, but they still would not leave me alone. They would either place their bicycles directly in my path as I rode around and around the yard, or else they would ride about and bump into me on purpose. At the kindergarten there were always children who got in my way when I was building with blocks, and I liked building with the wooden blocks better than anything. I would sit down in a corner, gather all the blocks into a heap between my legs, and start building a house. There were blocks in the shape of triangles and pillars and supports and capitals, and you could build a real castle with a colonnade of pillars and roofs and pointed towers and steps leading to the main gateway, but before I could finish building it a foot would come down from somewhere and give it a kick, or someone would jump on my back and pull me down and roll on the floor with me and the castle would be destroyed. For some reason I never fought back. I would try to collect all the scattered blocks and sit down in another corner and start again.

All these difficulties and disturbances came as a surprise to me, and this, perhaps, was because of all the love I received at home before the great crises. The love with which my mother and father cushioned my life led me to believe in people in general, and in people older than myself especially, to trust in them and their good intentions. I was thus an easy target for all sorts of practical jokes and tricks, a sort of Simple Simon who believed anything he was told. Whenever I realized that I had been tricked, my cheeks would burn as if I had received a slap in the face, and the truth is that I never in my life received a slap in the face. My father not only never slapped me, he never even threatened to slap me. During the past two years I have discovered that the French are great experts in the business of slapping their children's faces. It is enough for a small French child dragging after his mother in a shop to give vent to one little cry or put out his hand to fondle a pencil lying on the counter, to receive a slap in the face from all five slender, manicured fingers of the hand of his slender, elegant mama. To this spectacle I was a witness two weeks ago while sitting in a little café in the market square of Saint Maur with Josef and listening to him talk, as usual, about Judaism and Christianity and the differences between them. The child put both his hands to his burning cheeks, and Josef said that one of the decisive differences between Jesus of Nazareth and the prophets was that all the prophets prophesied in the name of God: "Thus saith the Lord," whereas Jesus of Nazareth spoke in his own name: "And I say unto you." Ever since this conversation I think of the prophet Jeremiah every time I step into the train in the Métro. This machine hurtling forward along its predetermined tracks is driven forward by the energy of the electric power station many miles away, but Jesus, like the train, thinks the engine is inside his own body. It seems to me that had I lived two thousand years ago, I would have ascribed the words I am writing down now not to myself, but to God. This may seem, on the one hand, like arrogance and impertinence, insolence and unheard-of conceit: here comes a man, some fellow utterly devoid of significance either from the point of view of the amount of space he takes up in the cosmos, or the length of his life span in the dimensions of eternity, or the benefit he has brought, is bringing, or ever will bring to his people or his country or humanity in general, and declares himself to be the apostle of the word of the Lord. On the other hand, it could equally be said that this is nothing but false modesty. This man refuses to take credit even for the words that come out of his mouth. He declares himself to be nothing but a pipeline, a record playing the tune impressed upon it, a kind of medium. However, since I am not living two thousand years ago, but in this day and age, and since my relations with God are what they are, there is no danger of my being accused of megalomania on the one hand or false modesty on the other. I only said that I would have ascribed this writing to God because of the fog, so to speak, in which I find myself, this blurring of the boundaries between what comes from outside and what exists within, the feeling that I myself am only the firmament dividing the waters from the waters, a sort of skin separating two worlds, the inside world and the outside world. If the fence of this garden—a wooden fence covered with a kind of creeping plant whose name I do not know (this business of the naming of plants after their kinds has always been one of the weak spots in my life; there are very few plants which I know by name, despite all Shula's efforts during the ten years of our married life to repair these gaps in my knowledge)—if this fence were to write down its sensations they would surely resemble my own —the sensation of existing between two worlds, of fencing off the garden inside from the road outside. The treetops murmur and sway in the winds blowing into the garden from without, and the birds come flying in from afar, from beyond the river, nest between their branches and fly off again into the distances beyond the river, above and beyond the boundaries of the fence, and their twittering penetrates its crevices, and their singing bursts through its foliage. The stakes of the fence sense the profound tremors rising from the depths of the earth and creak in the silence of the stars in the distant sky.

The faint tremors rising from the depths of the mountains in the darkness and the silence of the stars in the distant sky on my first journey to the edges of the night in my father's arms came to life in me again on my first encounter with the

God-that-is-learned. I was a pupil at the Tachkemoni school in the Mekor Baruch quarter, and when my teacher read aloud during the Bible lesson the words, "In the beginning God created the heavens and the earth and the earth was without form and void, and darkness was upon the face of the deep," the quality of the elements made tangible in the darkness suddenly welled up in me unendurably. "And God said, Let there be light," and in the wall of darkness a crack was revealed and the imprisoned light burst through it to wrap the rocks and clods of earth in a mantle of day. I had sensed the things as they were, from inside myself, and the written and spoken words garbed them in phrases like currency which could be passed from hand to hand, from one man to another. On hearing these words from the mouth of my teacher, Mr. Avisar, for the first time, I waited with a pounding heart for a miracle like the miracle of the first night to happen. A great silence would fall on the classroom and in another little while the voice of God would be heard calling beyond it, and I was already trembling with a terror that grew stronger with every moment that passed. A ripple ran through the class, full of little giggles and murmurs. The teacher seemed to be saying something, and repeating it again, and the laughter of the children behind my back grew louder. Then the teacher spoke again. He called my name and said, "Read," and I didn't understand. My cheeks burned and the teacher started coaxing me to read, and I didn't know what to read because I was waiting for the voice of God. The teacher called another boy's name and he read the same verse in a thin piping voice, and then someone else read the whole story of Creation very quickly as if he were reciting a poem by heart, until the bell rang for a break. All the children pushed and shoved to go outside to play and so did I. When I reached the door Mr. Avisar put his hand on my shoulder and told me to come with him to the teachers' room. There he opened the Bible again and began testing me to see if I knew the letters and their combinations. I was too embarrassed and ashamed to explain what had happened. My voice vanished, and when he pressed me tears started misting my eyes. His eyes showed sympathy for my plight, and he told me in a gentle voice that I needed private tuition in reading at home.

He was a very nice man, with a red face and a lock of hair on his forehead which he combed back severely to one side. He came to school on a bicycle, and on his trouser legs I saw for the first time the metal clips intended to prevent them from becoming entangled in the bicycle chain. This seemed to me the distinguishing mark of an important sportsman, since it was he, and not the gym teacher, who exercised the whole school at the general assembly before the first lesson every morning. He would take up his stance on a box in the playground with a whistle in his mouth and conduct us all. He also had a mustache like the one my father had in those days, and I loved him as I loved most of the teachers who taught me until I went to the university. I did not develop a critical sense, toward either teachers or books, until very late. At this early stage I felt only pain at not being understood, and at his helplessness, in spite of all his niceness, to see into my heart. It is also possible that quite apart from the great shame and embarrassment that tied my tongue, I deliberately chose to keep what had happened to myself and let him think I could not read, despite the pain and humiliation involved, rather than allow him to start fumbling about with the delicately tuned strings inside me. In any case not many weeks went by before I failed in reading aloud in class once more, this time because of the differences between Jehovah and Adonai * and God. When I read the verse, "These are the

* The Lord

generations of the heavens and of the earth when they were created, in the day that Jehovah God made the earth and the heavens," a ripple ran through the classroom again, and I knew that in a little while the derisive laughter of the children would burst out once more because there was something that separated me from them, in this matter of God precisely. Just as I feared and expected, the teacher stopped my reading in the middle and explained at length for my individual benefit what he had evidently explained many times before to the class as a whole without making any impression on me because I was, I suppose, daydreaming as usual: wherever it was written "Jehovah" we must read "Adonai" and the Orthodox read "Adoshem," because it was forbidden "to pronounce the ineffable Name." Even after I had adapted myself to his demands and read "Adonai God" instead of "Jehovah God," I still did not understand either the meaning of the prohibition or the meaning of the words "the ineffable Name." For many years afterward I could not see how there could be any connection at all between "Jehovah"—this word which must for some reason be garbled in reading to "Adonai"—and the words "the ineffable Name," which appeared to me to be some sort of device or stratagem of the kind commonly used by magicians in the performance of their magic spells and conjuring tricks. In contrast to other kinds of magic however, "the ineffable Name" was known only to a certain type of rabbi who guarded it jealously so that it would not, God forbid, fall into the hands of the magicians of other nations. It originated, as transpired from later Bible lessons, in the spells performed by Moses before Pharoah and the magicians of Egypt. In the case of the Golem of Prague, the ineffable Name appeared to me in the guise of a kind of pill which the great rabbi, the Maharal, put into the mouth of the Golem, and which looked like the pills my mother put into my mouth on the orders of Dr. Wallenstein when I was sick, white bitter-tasting pills inscribed with mysterious Latin characters. Unlike me, however, the Golem did not swallow his pill, but kept it in his mouth under his tongue, and having a foreign body rolling around his tongue all the time is probably what made him feel so uncomfortable during the entire period of his activities. As for the ineffable Name which empowered the rabbis to perform their marvels and wonders, this usually seemed to me like a kind of murmured song coming out of the rabbi-magician's mouth to the accompaniment of a strange melody, and made up of mysterious and complicated combinations of nonsense syllables. These were perhaps like the utterances of African witch doctors in films, but I could see no possible connection between them and Jehovah, about whom every single child learned at school.

Between God and my Grandmother, on the other hand, as I gathered from her words and actions, there did appear to be some connection, and the more she stressed this connection, berated and reproached my mother and father in His name, the more rebellious I became and the more strongly I sensed not only the incomprehension of Bible lessons at school, but also a kind of outrage: the kind of outrage Agur ben Jakeh * must have felt on seeing a slave turned king, or an artist would feel if he were compelled to paint according to the dictates of rulers who not only knew nothing about art but were colorblind to boot.

Grandmother, my mother's mother, lived in the Meah Shearim marketplace opposite the synagogue and the big yeshiva, in the same house which we were destined to inhabit some years later after my father's bankruptcy had left us literally without a roof over our heads. Grandmother was not, like the rulers in my parable, colorblind, but quite blind

* Proverbs, 30, 1

owing to the trachoma endemic in the country during the days
of the Turks many years before I was born, and it was in no
other than the sphere of the art of painting that she first chose
to make heard to me the commands of God in Yiddish, since
Hebrew she did not know, and apart from Yiddish she could
not speak or understand anything but a little Arabic and a
little Jewish-Spanish, like other members of her generation.
But before I relate the history of the wars of Jehovah which
I fought in my childhood with my Grandmother—"internal"
rather than "external" wars to use the parlance of our times
(although as will become clear later in this narrative I use
these terms to indicate other aspects of consciousness)—I
must point out that I grew up at home in complete freedom
not only of religious precepts, but from any kind of compul-
sion at all, for example that of going to school every day.
When I refused to go to school because I had not done my
homework and was afraid of what my teacher would say, my
father did not force me to go, and did not even ask the reason
for my refusal. As for my mother, all of whose energies were
directed toward maintaining the health of the body according
to her own unique methods, I had only to say that I felt sick
for her to expressly forbid me to stir from the house. With
every day that passed, my fear of going to school increased
and grew more oppressive. Only after a whole week had gone
by in this manner my father sought me out and explained
persuasively, speaking gently and appealing to the logic of my
own best interests, why it was necessary for me to return to
my desk at school. He also offered to come with me and talk
things over with Mr. Avisar the teacher. This behavior of his
should not be ascribed to pedagogical theories and methods
worked out in advance, for where human behavior was concerned he had no theories at all, and everything he did was
simply the product and expression of the way he felt about

specific situations and the people involved in them and giving rise to them. If he waited for a whole week to pass before persuading me to return to school, this was not because of any educational calculations, but simply because he had not paid any attention to the fact that I was absenting myself from my studies before then, and indeed, from this point of view, so far from crediting him with a particular method of education, he might well be charged with neglecting the education of his only son. At the same time, however, it must be remembered that despite all the vicissitudes of his checkered business career—the circumstances of which will be related when the time comes—for most of his life he himself was a teacher in his own school of commerce and languages, and a teacher moreover who gained the universal love and admiration of his students. To the extent that a coherent view of education stemming from his own natural inclinations did take shape in his mind, it was one that stood for total freedom from any sort of coercion at all, and proceeded on the assumption that what counted was not the teacher or the method, but the pupil and his inherent abilities, and that if a pupil had anything in him it would bear fruit under any educational system, or without any educational system at all, despite all the difficulties and obstacles in the way. In this approach he reached his most extreme position some years later, at the height of the economic and family crisis which took place when I graduated from primary school and the need arose to finance my entry into high school. In one of his quarrels with my mother, which were then a daily occurrence (and were usually conducted in Yiddish, both because of the mistaken assumption that the children, my sisters and I, would not understand what was going on between them, and because of the agitated emotions which caused them to express themselves in the language of their childhood), when my mother accused him, among other accusations of a far graver nature, of neglecting to provide for the continuation of my education, he shouted back that anyone who had anything in him needed neither high school nor universities, and to strengthen his case brought proofs from the history of the people of Israel and the nations of the world, such as the prophet Amos and Jesus Christ, and the Greek Homer and the English Shakespeare and Bialik the national poet, none of whom, so far as he knew, had enjoyed the benefits of modern theories of education as preached by professors at universities, but whose achievements were nevertheless in no way inferior to those of high-school pupils and university graduates.

Father himself, like most of his generation who had abandoned orthodoxy at an early age, had commenced his education in the heder and the yeshiva in the Old City, but soon transferred to the Alliance School, where he learned French, and then to the Ezra Seminary for teachers, where he learned German. At the end of the First World War, under the influence of Jabotinsky, he left the seminary before graduation and joined the Jewish Legion in the British army, although for some unknown reason he actually spent most of his military service not in the Jewish Legion but in an English battalion. Of all the photographs of this period I especially liked one picture, which I still have lying in the recesses of one of my drawers, in which he stands rigidly erect in puttees and short trousers, the uniform of the English soldiers of the time, but without the hat, holding a baton under his arm, looking like a young boy still despite the mustache trimmed into a square and the bold and vigorous expression in his eye. In the days of the wars of Jehovah I fought with my grandmother, he still sported this mustache and went abroad with a walking stick in the fashion of the dandies of the period, and it was only later that they both suddenly disappeared together, the mustache and the walking stick. A number of things acquired during the days of his service in the English battalion he retained for the rest of his life: the always erect posture, the smooth shave every day, even on the days of his deepest depression, and above all the love of what he used to call "the character of the English people"—the patience and the tolerance, the British sense of humor, dislike of comprehensive principles and rigid world views, hatred for dogmatic theories of life, and above all, respect for the personal inclinations unique to each and every man. This is why he was so fond of the English proverb, "One man's meat is another man's poison," and what he referred to as the "mutual poisoning of life" was what he feared above all things. He would often say that Grandmother had poisoned my mother's life and his own life and the life of our family, and it was for this reason that he always tried to avoid coming into contact with her, which was not very difficult in the period I remember, for by then she never left her house at all and in order to see her you had to go visit her. Grandmother in the days of my childhood would still totter from room to room, and especially from her bed to the tap in the passage, where she would stand and give her hands a good scrubbing with soap. Later on she was obliged to give up even this exhausting expedition from her bed to the tap and back again, and she would soak her hands in the basin which my aunt Pnina installed at her bedside instead. It was a wonder to me then how she managed to bend so far forward that she resembled a semicircle from her chin to her pelvis, and her crouching stance at the tap seemed to me an unmatched physical feat. Once I tried to wash my hands with my back curved like hers, and fell flat on my face into the basin. In her zeal for cleanliness, her physical activities were all devoted to washing and purifying herself from the touch of the objects and implements around her, and her daughter Pnina who lived with her and waited on her spent the better part of her life in caring for these needs of her mother's. Aunt Pnina never abandoned Grandmother's washing to the tender mercies of the washerwoman, but did it herself, and when it had dried in the sun she would take the garments that Grandmother wore next to her skin and spread them out in front of the stove standing in the middle of the room to remove whatever dampness remained so that Grandmother's body would not be chilled at their touch. Grandmother's bloomers spread out on the table in front of the stove in all their tremendous breadth were a source of constant amazement to me. Respectable cloth bloomers decorated with lace frills, they were wider than any other pair of panties that I have ever seen, although Grandmother herself was the smallest and most shrunken of women.

On cold winter days and on days when there was linen of Grandmother's to be dried, Aunt Pnina would light the stove, and while she did so with the help of Uncle Kalman, who was responsible for buying the kerosene and filling the container, Grandmother would recall the famous stove which had been lost to her forever in the days of the Turks. This famous stove from the days of the Turks, I was of course never privileged to see for myself, since it was lost about a quarter of a century before I came into the world, but Grandmother lamented it to me so often that in the end I was truly sorry for its loss. To me in particular, because even Aunt Pnina, who in all her years of servitude treated her mother with a quite exceptional forbearance, even she would not allow her to repeat the elegy of the stove, and whenever she set about trimming the wick as a preliminary to the lighting of the substitute stove, she would turn to her mother and say in a commanding voice, "And now wash your eyes and don't start on the business of the stove." I, on the other hand, made an ideal audience, attentive and unlikely to cut the elegy of the stove off short, for during most of the visit I would sit at the table and draw on the brown cardboard boxes with which Aunt Pnina kept me supplied; and the story of the loss of the stove told in Grandmother's hoarse voice, in words threading slowly from her mouth and stopping repeatedly at certain places with a hesitant stammer like that of an epic poet, attempting for the first time in his life and the history of the world to clothe in the language of words a tale great in deeds for the sake of generations to come, this story served me as a vocal background for the pictures I drew in Grandmother's house as against the brown background of the cardboard boxes supplied me by Aunt Pnina. What disturbed me at first was not the voice but rather the color in the background, since it seemed to me that it was spoiling the colors of my crayons: on it the red was not red and the blue was not blue. In later years my mother told me that this supply of cardboard boxes for my drawings was simply one of the fruits of Aunt Pnina's parsimony, for she never in her life threw out a piece of wrapping paper or a shoe box and could never have brought herself to let me spoil her white writing paper with my scribblings. It was this parsimony then which I have to thank for the revelation which took place the moment I was given colored chalks to draw with. The meaning of the color white was now revealed to me for the first time, and then the whole world of colors took on a sharp new reality, and once this world was revealed to me I never wanted to draw on anything but a rough brownish background again. Some years later I was pierced by an intense, throbbing joy, as if encountering fragments of memories from a previous incarnation, when I saw the paintings of Toulouse-Lautrec which retain the cardboard background as part of the colors of the picture and throw the paint as paint into relief.

I drew a round sun at the edge of the sky sending out yellow rays all around it, and two hills touching each other, and on the summit of the one rose the tower of the village of Nebi Samwil, and on the summit of the other stood cypresses around the graves of the English soldiers who fell in the conquest of the land from the Turks, and on the slopes of the hill I drew the opening of the biggest and most impressive of the caves of the Sanhedrin tombs, with an Arab effendi wearing a red tarboosh on his head sitting on the left side of the opening and a mustachioed British policeman riding a horse on the right side of the opening, and in the background I heard the story of the stove which was lost in the days of the Turks twenty-five years ago, six months after my mother came into the air of the world. Grandmother was then living in the big courtyard in the streets of the Bukharans, and Grandfather returned from his first stay in America and bought the house in Meah Shearim in which I am now sitting and drawing. In Mukharram * they moved from the streets of the Bukharans to Meah Shearim, and because of the moving they hired Bulbul the porter to transport their goods and chattels. Bulbul is a Persian Jew who hums to himself Persian songs by the greatest of the Persian poets of long ago. He is called Bulbul because he has a cage and in the cage is a bird and the name of the bird is *bulbul*. Now he has a cart drawn by a mule, but then, twenty-five years ago, he had only a two-wheeled handcart. And on this cart he loaded the parts of the dismantled chests and cupboards and walked back and forth between the streets of the Bukharans and Meah Shearim for four whole days, until all the goods and chattels had been moved. Yes, everything was moved, except for the stove. The stove Grandmother wrapped up and padded very well with

* The month during which it was customary to move from one house to another.

lots of rags so that it would not come to any harm in the jolt-
ings of the journey, and locked it up safely in the built-in cupboard, until its turn should come to bring up the rear. And
after all the goods and chattels had been moved, and also the
children, that is to say, my mother and Aunt Pnina and Uncle
Kalman and Uncle Pinchas called Pinik and Avremele, who
died a few weeks later in Doctor Wallach's hospital of typhoid fever, when all the children and the goods had been
moved and Grandmother returned with Bulbul to supervise
the removal of the stove, and opened the cupboard with the
key she kept in her purse, lo and behold, the cupboard was
empty and the bird had flown. There was no stove. As if it
had never been. As if the earth had opened its mouth and
swallowed it. As if it were a dream. A flame it had had, not
too feeble and not too blazing hot, but giving off a gentle
warmth of life, just what was needed for preserving life, and
the warmth would spread gradually through all your limbs
and infiltrate them and penetrate to the marrow of your
bones, bringing a healing balm for the aches of the body and
a soothing ease for the sickness of the heart. And another
advantage the stove had was that it never emitted smoke or
soot but gave off a delightful scent like that of incense which
filled the whole house, and as if this wasn't enough it also
sang all the time in a nice little murmur of snapping and
crackling coals. From the time that the stove disappeared
she, Grandmother, was beset by all these troubles, may they
fall on the heads of the haters of Zion, amen, may it be His
will. And after the stove was lost, simply disappearing and
vanishing like a dream from the built-in cupboard, the heat
evaporated from the house, and the moment the heat evaporated from the house the cold took hold of her eyes and
darkened them, spreading also to her legs and hips and giving
them such rheumatism that she couldn't take a single step

without being attacked by terrible pains, and her whole world became dark. That was the way of it. She had a stove and it was no more. And all the other stoves were no help at all, but only made her pains worse and added to them also dizziness and nausea from the smoke and the soot they emitted. These modern stoves, there's no warmth of life in them. Move them away from you and you are sure to freeze to death, bring them close and you'll be roasted alive. There's nothing to them but flashy deceptive paint to dazzle people's eyes with.

When there was no one to lend a sympathetic ear to the tale of the stove, and nothing reached her own ears but the commanding voice of Aunt Pnina: "And now wash your eyes. . ." she would repeat it to herself, her lips moving and her voice inaudible but for broken sighs at the most melancholy parts of the recital and fragments of the key phrases such as "warmth of life" or "freeze to death . . . be roasted alive." As soon as I began drawing on the cardboard with my colored chalks I tried to get her to say something clear about the color of the stove and its shape. Was it black or yellow, square or round, high and narrow or low and wide, and a chimney—did it have a chimney or not? These questions aroused her to a frenzy of interest and she repeated them in amazement and admiration: "So, so! A color it had! A shape it had! The warmth of life it gave off! Yes, yes—that was the way of it! I see, Dovidel, that you are a clever boy. You understand what quality of stove it was." And she put out her old shriveled hand, groping blindly for my head, in order to stroke this head which understood so well the quality of the stove and grasped the full enormity of the dreadful catastrophe which had overtaken her with its departure, gone and lost forever. I managed to draw my head back in time to avoid the caress, repulsive even in anticipation, of this blind hand which trembled a little while in the air before dropping back exhausted into the accustomed and beloved shelter of her lap, and took up once more my pressing questions in search of a clear picture instead of these unexpected praises for the depths of my understanding and this amazing outburst of affection, so rare that it could not maintain its course, faltered, and was nipped in the bud.

And again, to my amazement, a peculiar happiness overcame Grandmother at the sound of my impatiently repeated questions as to the color and shape of the famous stove, and she began to tell me again in detail how she had walked to and fro for four days by the side of Bulbul the porter who dismantled the furniture and loaded the parts on his handcart and transported them from the streets of the Bukharans to Meah Shearim, until they had all been moved. I never succeeded in obtaining an answer to this question of mine from Grandmother, just as I never succeeded in obtaining any further information regarding her son Avremele, who died of typhoid fever in the Wallach Hospital. In decided contrast to the catechism of the stove, however, Grandmother showed no signs of interest at all in response to my questions about Avremele, but answered briefly, dryly, and lucidly, "I don't remember. He died many years ago, shortly after the stove was lost." Her false teeth were lying immersed in a glass of water at her side, and she put out her hand to extract them and install them in her mouth in readiness for the buttered rusks brought by Aunt Pnina. In the silence which suddenly fell I returned to the black tassel which festooned the red tarboosh on the head of the effendi sitting at the left side of the entrance to the Sanhedrin tombs. Grandmother champed on her rusks and from time to time gulped a little lukewarm tea to help swallow them down smoothly. "You know"—she turned to me again—"he's to blame for it. The old man." This is how she referred to her husband, my grandfather—

"the old man." "Yes, yes. The old man's to blame for it. As if he thinks I don't know."

"But Grandfather's been dead for ages," I said. I couldn't understand how anyone could speak of someone dead for five years in the present tense.

She paid no attention to my interruption but continued her own train of thought while grinding the rusks with her false teeth. "Oh yes. That's what he thinks! He thinks I don't know—and me, why I know him through and through with all his cunning and his mischief and his tricks! What did he do? While I was here, in the new house in Meah Shearim, helping Bulbul unload the packages, he hurried there, to the old house in the streets of the Bukharans, opened the built-in cupboard, and removed the stove from it. What did he do with it? He went and gave it to Esther, the old Persian woman who lived at the bottom of the road, for a present. The old witch who sat on her doorstep smoking a narghile all day long. He didn't like the stove! Since he came back from America he didn't like anything, but especially the stove. It put him into a fury. A rusty old stove, he would say. A broken vessel. In America you don't see this kind of stove anymore. Today there are modern stoves, beautiful, shining, kerosene stoves. The coal age is over. It's a shame and disgrace to keep a filthy old piece of junk like that in the house, as if he himself in all his filthy doings in filthy America wasn't filthier than all the junk in the marketplace. Yes. Exactly so. And he thinks I don't know! I don't know. I don't know." Her speech, which up to now had been more or less lucid, at this point degenerated into a vague and distant mumble. For some time longer the grinding of the rusks continued to reach my ears, accompanied by little broken sounds whose precise nature and origin were not clear. Perhaps they were the body's contented belches at the filling of its shrinking stomach, or groans of the pain which attends all living creatures as they approach the exit from the body of life in this world, or sighs for sad memories. No sooner had she fallen silent than the sound of her thin whistling snores and heavy rhythmic breathing began to saw the air.

As soon as Aunt Pnina, who came in to remove the tray with the rusks and the tea from the bedside table, had made sure that her mother was indeed asleep and snoring rhythmically (sometimes she would lie flat on her back with all the appearance of being sound asleep and suddenly respond to something said in the room which was not addressed to her at all), she quickly returned the tray to the kitchen and hurried back again to put out the light in the room, although I had not yet completed the drawing of the Sanhedrin caves. She put out the light not because it disturbed Grandmother's sleep, and not because she was unaware of the fact that I was still sitting and drawing, but for reasons of economy. To my cry of protest at the darkness which descended on my drawing she replied, "You can move into the kitchen and continue your drawing there."

I stayed rooted to my chair full of helpless rage at Aunt Pnina. Through the mist of tears which dimmed my eyes I was suddenly aware of the flickering dance of points of azure light rising from the stove which was drying Grandmother's giant bloomers, the same modern kerosene stove which Grandfather had brought back from America, the one she hated which reminded her of the one she loved, the famous stove of yore. In the darkness the stove lengthened to a towering lighthouse with a blueness of soft light flowing through the blue glass of the square window set in its center near its base, and a row of blocks of yellow light shining through the little air vents underneath the cap on its head. The wreath of flames burning steadily on its round wick was reflected through the glass of the window like a sunflower of azure light rising out of the darkness and hovering suspended in a square frame. The square frame became the gateway to a castle far away in the depths of the dark. In the castle was a great light, and its radiance burst out through all the doors and windows and orifices and apertures of its towers and wings and stories and cloisters and halls. The castle walls kept guard on the world of light stemming from within in the calm of the great silence, and I remembered that I had once been inside and wanted to go back, although I didn't have the right clothes to wear and knew that even if I found them I wouldn't be able to put them on because they no longer fitted me. I remembered how I had once stood at the castle gates and I was momentarily overcome by a distressing confusion because I couldn't decide what I wanted to be, a tiger or a deer. When the raging ferment inside me surged up in an overwhelming flood of power, I thought I would put on the striped skin of the tiger, but the next moment all the rage was washed away and I was a deer leaping in high clear mountain air. I glided through the air as if I were a bird. I flew a blue point of light with high-flying sparks of fire in a dance of red and green and gold and blue and lemon-yellow and orange splinters of light, and in the blue light I shed all along the walls of the great hall, a row of idols sat stiff and solemn in their masks, but they all melted away with the dying of my blue light when Aunt Pnina came back and turned on the light in the room.

I saw this row of idols sitting stiff and solemn against the pillars of the temple wall once again, on a night journey from Tel Aviv to Jerusalem. Through the window of the bus I saw in the night sky a row of lighted windows in an airplane about to land in the Lydda airport. This body hovering in the darkness and lit up from within and enclosing its light, which burst forth only from the row of its windows, opened up a window inside me which led directly to my childhood sensations in the presence of the stove burning in the darkness and illuminating it, and it was like a direct continuation of the same sensation without any of the barriers erected by decades of life coming in between. Like those of my dreams which come back to haunt my sleep continuously in the form of a serial story, each of whose chapters follows directly on the one before, without any relation to the thousand and one events of the daily chronicle written all around them on the same page. But unlike the interlocking dreams of my sleep at night, the cycles of memories from long ago which rise up at the sight of light which is imprisoned inside, kindled with the fall of darkness outside and extinguished when the light outside prevails, are always connected with the memory of myself sitting in the gloom of Grandmother's room opposite the square of blue light coming from the window of the stove. The sight of myself as a child precedes the seeing of the vision, gives rise to it and separates me from it, like a double negative of two separate pictures taken one on top of the other.

As soon as Aunt Pnina had switched on the light in the room, I went back to filling in the red tarboosh on the head of the effendi with the continuous steady action needed to complete the picture, without any regrets for the dying of the castle which had been effaced, just as the dreams I saw in my sleep were blotted out when I woke to the morning of a new day, which seemed to me to lead on directly from the one before it. My drawings too I regarded as links in a fixed chain of time and scrupulously observed the sequence in which they had been drawn, the later above the earlier compositions, when I laid them one on top of the other in the old-fashioned coffee tin which I kept on the windowsill next to the coffee mill. In the scenes they depicted too, my drawings sometimes seemed like pages of parchment sewed together in one continuous scroll, for when my piece of cardboard was not sufficient for all the baggage of the effendi sitting by the opening of the cave, I went on to draw his shepherd leading a line of sheep and goats from the cave to the tower of Nebi Samwil on the next piece. Twice a week when she went to do the family shopping at the Meah Shearim market, my mother would deposit me at Grandmother's house, where I would sit and draw, until one Sabbath the war of God broke out between Grandmother and me.

When the war broke out close to the hour of noon, I was alone in the house with Grandmother and we fought locked in hand-to-hand combat. After bringing me to the house, my mother immediately left again with Aunt Pnina to visit a sick friend of their childhood in the Old City. As soon as Aunt Pnina left I discovered, much to my surprise, that Grandmother was perfectly capable of caring for her needs by herself. In spite of her blindness and the pains in her hips she not only made herself a cup of tea but succeeded in bringing it from the kitchen to her bedside table without faltering or bumping into anything on the way. When she had brought this bold project to a close she sank back into her bed and lay for some time indulging herself in a series of well-earned groans of exhaustion and broken hips to boot, and I went up to the old-fashioned coffee tin as usual to get my cardboard and crayons to start drawing. On the tin was a picture of a beautiful Negress with a tray full of coffee beans on her head, and when I first set eyes on the verse, "I am black but comely, O ye daughters of Jerusalem," it was her form which rose before my eyes. I started drawing and Grandmother still lay panting and grunting. Gradually she recovered her composure and soon the only sound heard in the room was the squeaking of my crayon on the cardboard. Grandmother sat up in bed and began to drink her tea, the fruit of her labors, with smacking lips.

"Hah?" She turned to me with a question: "What are you doing there?"

"I'm drawing," I replied.

"So," she said, "drawing!" After considering this for a while in silence she asked what I was drawing.

"The shepherd," I said. "Abdullah, the effendi's shepherd. He's playing on his pipe and all the sheep and goats are walking behind him." As a matter of fact, I had never seen Abdullah playing his pipe. I had only seen him herding his flock with a stick and cries of "Brrr . . . brrr" to the corner of our street, where the women of the neighborhood would gather to buy goats' milk. He would catch hold of one of the goats by its leg, fall onto his knees and begin milking the warm milk into his pail, frothing and steaming. I saw a shepherd piping on the olivewood ornaments carved at the Bezalel Art School though, and from the day that I learned to copy him, my shepherd would always stand with his left profile facing the viewer and his hands stretched out before him playing on his pipe.

Grandmother shook her head. It was evident that my answer had aroused her displeasure. "That's not good," the verdict fell from her lips. "Goats' milk is no good for the health, and besides it has a peculiar smell. Didn't I tell her, your mother, and warn her never to buy goats' milk or goats' meat? A thousand times I've explained to her that she should never let anything into her house but cows' milk and beef, but that girl has never listened to me in her life."

"That's not right," I shouted back, "Mother never buys milk from Abdullah. She only buys milk at the Tnuva dairies." All my protests were in vain, since it was evident from the blinking of Grandmother's eyes that she was deep in an ancient quarrel and my cries were unable to penetrate her ears.

"Your mother," Grandmother continued, "always tried to defy me, and in this she was like her father, the old man, bone of his bone and flesh of his flesh. Enough for me to say 'no' and she would say 'yes.' Just for the pleasure of doing the opposite of what I said she was ready to ruin her life. And she did ruin it too, as you can see for yourself; she went off and married your father—the heretic and destroyer of Israel. And me—I saw what he was when he was still a boy, when he left the yeshiva to go and study at their famous high school. 'There you can learn science,' that's what he said, and I knew very well that from all the science he'd learn there he'd end up in hell. All this science of the goyim, may their name and memory be blotted out, leads straight to crime and abomination and ruination. And that's exactly what happened to him: in the First World War, when the Turks and the British were murdering each other, up he gets and goes to be a soldier in the English army! What's a soldier? A soldier is a murderer, God have mercy on us! It's the one with murder burning in his heart who wants to be a soldier, because the job of a soldier is to murder people. Who's ever heard of such a thing, that a Jewish boy should go to be a soldier?! And all because he went to study the science of the goyim and became a Zionist and listened to the sermons of Jabotinsky, may his name and memory be blotted out! And what is the lore your father heard from this destroyer of Israel? He heard that in order to bring redemption to the people of Israel and the Kingdom to the House of Israel you must take a gun in your hands and make wars, God in heaven help us! And he, your father, who was once a rabbinical scholar and knew that the Holy One Blessed be He will not bring us redemption until we keep each and every one of the mizvoth, was seduced by this destroyer of Israel because his mind was confused, and this happened to him because he studied the science of the goyim! And I knew in advance what would happen to him, and I warned your mother day and night. But she, because she had set her heart on his shaven face like a goy's and his mustache, stuck fast to him and wouldn't let him go, and now you go do something about it. If that's the way things are, I said to her, if your life is no life without this soldat, wait at least until Pnina gets married, since Pnina is the oldest, and who's ever heard of such a thing that the youngest should get married before the oldest? But she shut her ears and because she was so full of lust refused to wait even a single minute, and so Pnina sits in her maidenhood to this day, and my eyes fail me at the sight. And your mother, instead of beating her breast in contrition, instead of repenting and confessing her sins to me and her sister, comes and complains to me that it's my fault Pnina doesn't get married, that I hold her back and won't let her marry because I've made a wretched slave of her. You hear that—I've made a wretched slave of Pnina! When my only aspiration is to live to see Pnina marry and set up a home in Israel, a kosher Jewish home, and bring up Jewish children to Torah and mizvoth and good deeds and not . . . and not . . . and not like her sister who brought you up a proper goy in everything! You, poor child, it's not your fault you're growing up without Torah and without mizvoth, and you don't even know that it's forbidden to draw on the Sabbath, because there's no one to teach you any better. Yes, poor Dovidel, there simply isn't anyone to teach you any better."

Whether because of this melancholy thought, or because of the excitement and exertion of the long harangue she had just delivered, she fell back on her pillows to take a few moments' rest, but it was a troubled rest. Evidently the circumstance of being left alone in the house with her grandson, wanton and lawless because there was no one to teach him any better, made her suddenly feel in all its weight the sacred obligation laid upon her to try to teach me herself, since there was no one else to do it. She sat up in bed and said softly, as if she wanted to take me into her confidence about something, "Come here, Dovidel, and I'll tell you something important." I made no reply and continued stubbornly drawing. I felt calamity approaching fast and ready to strike. As her voice grew sweeter my wrath grew more violent. "You know what, my dear, come to me and I'll teach you so that you'll know. You may not draw on the Sabbath. And now be a good boy and stop drawing and I'll give you a sweet."

She got out of bed and tottered to the built-in cupboard where the sweets and cakes were kept. With a shudder of loathing and a growing suspicion I watched her coming closer, holding up the hem of her nightdress to prevent it from trailing on the floor and picking up dust. And now she was upon me and had placed her hand on my head, and the sweet on the table in front of me. "And now be a good boy and stop drawing at once or else God will punish you. That is what is written in the Torah. Our God, the God of Abraham, Isaac, and Jacob, will be gracious and merciful to you and reward you if you stop drawing at once. And in general, you should know that a Jew is forbidden to draw and make pictures even on ordinary weekends, let alone the holy Sabbath. And here is a sweet for you, too."

I kept quiet and went on drawing all the time, and the more she coaxed and cajoled the more I made the crayon squeak on the cardboard. She began to push the sweet into my hand, and I took hold of it with all my might and threw it far away from me. Without my intending it, the sweet landed on her cup of tea and the cup fell on its side with a loud tinkle of glass and began spilling its contents drop by drop into her sheet, so shining white as to be almost blue.

"Hah!" she cried at the sound of the glass falling. "Please see what this child is capable of! Things he throws in the house! Today just things, tomorrow he'll learn to throw knives! And what's the wonder, isn't he bone of the bone and flesh of the flesh of his father the soldat? Why it's mortal danger just to be in the same room as him! And now, you little savage, give me the page!" And she seized it with unexpected strength. I grabbed it out of her hands and began tearing my picture to pieces with all my might, tearing and scattering pieces on the ground, tearing and throwing the crayons in all directions, tearing and crushing and grinding to powder with my feet. Tearing and crying. At first she shouted criminal, destroyer of Israel, robber! But her shouts soon turned to cries for help, to the thin piercing hysterical scream of an old Jewess with a sharp sword at her throat: "Gewald! Gewald! Jews, to the rescue!" Had she sensed the curse I was cursing her within my heart, "I wish you were dead, I wish you were dead, I wish you were dead"?

I fled for my life. I took the steps in two jumps and sped like a deer through all Meah Shearim with two opposed emotions pounding in me as I ran. Now the curse has hit her, split her heart like an arrow, now she's lying dead among the torn shreds of my picture and the broken pieces of crayon. Trampled and trodden and squashed beyond recognition. No. I wasn't sorry for the murder—I was only afraid. Horribly afraid that in a little while the Jews in their Sabbath streimelke would catch me and wreak a terrible vengeance on me. And when I was dead Father would be sorry. He would be so very sorry. And I couldn't bear his sorrow and couldn't endure his bereavement. Dear Father, for his sake I must not be caught and killed. I must try to stay alive simply to keep his heart from breaking, and no sooner had this feeling abated than I was seized by a fit of trembling which started in my throat and spread down my spine with the certain knowledge that she was pursuing me with both hands outstretched, one groping for my head to embrace me and the other trying to push a sweet into my mouth.

For a long time after I had gained the shelter to which my flight had carried me and was sitting on the rock outside the cave, safe from the persecutions of Grandmother and her God, I went on spitting and retching and shaking my head— spitting out the sweet which had not succeeded in entering my mouth and shaking off the repulsive embrace which had not materialized because I had managed to avoid it in time. And over and above and below these head-shakings and retching coughs, my cheeks burned as if I had just received a slap in the face, burned as they always did when I found I had been cheated. "Grandmother's lying," I said to myself, and the lie I meant was not only, or mainly the lie of the blind hand outstretched to embrace my head and the lie of the hand holding out the sweet. It was the lie of the prohibition that angered me mortally. I knew then what Grandmother didn't know and never learned until the day she died, four- teen years after waging this godly war on me, that the God who created the heavens and the earth and said, Let there be Light and there was light, did not forbid me to draw on the Sabbath.

I haven't painted for many years now, not on the Sabbath and not on the days of the week. In fact, I stopped painting two years before Grandmother died; not because the urge to paint had died inside me—although it had certainly grown so weak and faint that it would sometimes lie dormant for weeks and even months at a time—but because my energies were absorbed by other needs, mainly, to my sorrow, external needs dictated by the requirements of existence in the external world, which pressed upon me so that I consciously helped in the suppression of this urge, which was at a low ebb in any case. But ever since then, at unexpected times and in unexpected places, it has come vividly to life in me again, especially recently: these autumn colors which have overtaken the garden on the banks of the Marne—the trees kindled into candles with whispering flames flickering through the spectrum, starting with green and passing through all the shades of yellow and orange and red and crimson and purple and brown until at last they die down and fall off and leave their wicks charred branches against the soft fleece of the clouds. I go down the gloom of the staircase to the dark cellar in the depths of the house to add a shovelful of coals to the rusty, old-fashioned iron stove. Above the murmur of the glowing embers with their warm smell, tongues of pure blue hover and dart up, despite the coal which comes piling down on top of them. Mosquitoes and moths dance in a circle around the grate of the stove shining in the darkness. Drunk with desire one moth darts into the grate and is immediately transformed into a glowing red spark haloed with orange in the heart of the blue flame which writhes about it and licks a way up in the darkness with its tongue. I heaped another shovel of coals into the grate and thought that now there was nothing to prevent me from painting, not even the nuisance of existing in the external world, and yet, although the drive is there and the means of realizing it, I do not paint but yearn and marvel instead—and pay, it seems, the price in writing, one installment after the other.

Translated by Dalya Bilu

11

BRURIA

BRURIA died at five in the morning, a week after she was brought to the hospital, unconscious from the morphine injected into her in Haifa three hours earlier.

Thin white snow was falling outside. Greti looked out of the window, delighted. "You know," she said to me, "it's just like Switzerland." She smiled. "I would never have thought that it snowed in Palestine, too." I went to the window, bent over her and took her hand in mine. A pure, soft, and fragrant fall of snow had covered the rooftops, the pavements, and the streets, the Moslem cemetery, the walls of the Old City, and the towers of Mount Zion. White wreaths hung from treetops and from the drainpipes. The snow covered everything.

We went down to the hall. At that hour, neither night nor day but between the two, the hall was spacious and deep, filled with secrets and tranquil. Greti went into the kitchen to make two cups of coffee and I sank into a chair.

The hospital was in an old and spacious Arab house, surrounded by a high stone wall. A mulberry tree pushed up out of the wall, twisting and winding its many branches toward the road. A wide balcony standing on iron pillars ran the whole length of the upper floor. In the tall arched windows were panes of colored glass. Thick iron bars were set in all the windows and doors of the upper floor. They completely enclosed the square balcony at the back of the building. Three male and twenty-five female patients spent their lives on the upper floor. They helped the cook to prepare their meals, they washed up, cleaned the floor, made their beds, and mended their own clothes. In the summer, they had permission to spend time in the enclosed yard. They were mostly "quiet" patients.

The hospital was run as a private business. It belonged to two partners. One was a small bachelor, bald and fat, in his forties, who hated women passionately. He made a point of talking to them as little as possible, and fired his nurses regularly. He spent his days smoking thick English cigarettes and eating. His partner was a God-fearing Jew, burdened with a wife and family. This man had no sexual relations with his wife, who suffered from every kind of complaint, and sinful thoughts bothered him day and night. To fight against this evil inclination, which threatened to drive him mad, he always kept at his side a book called *A Statute Unto Israel*. He spent all he had on doctors and medicines, but there was no doctor in Jerusalem who had not told him that his only hope was to get a woman. This alone did not satisfy him, until he obtained rabbinical permission to live with a woman, even though only separated from his wife. He showed this document to no one, but hinted that he had it in his pocket. Once he had it, he needed only to find a woman. This he tried to do but failed.

The medical director of the hospital was a German Jew who cut his beard in the French style. He wore glasses, and the curved stem of his pipe was never out of his mouth. He visited the hospital for half an hour a day, between ten and ten-thirty. At the very same time, also for half an hour, the two partners were to be found on the premises. All three would retire into the office and discuss financial affairs until their curses and imprecations resounded through the house and the telephone on the office table shook under the impact of their pounding fists. Once the commercial debate was over, the doctor went up to the top floor to visit the patients. He scanned the beds and peeked into the medicine cupboard to see if there was enough sleeping powder and morphine solution. Then he would give a few orders to the nurse and leave the building in a hurry. Once he had gone, the bachelor partner would make for the kitchen to fry himself an omelet of three eggs, golden onions, and lots of pepper. The other partner pored over *A Statute Unto Israel,* commiserating with himself for being without a woman. When the one had finished his omelet and the other had put down his book, they both left. Then the stillness would return and fill the rooms and halls until the next morning at ten.

I was the night watchman. I got to work at ten each night and drank the cup of tea Greti prepared for me. She ended her shift at ten. Once out of her white uniform, she spent a long time in front of the mirror making up. Then she would rise and, with a "Good night" to me, step lightly out into the street.

Night after night I sat in the corridor on the upper floor and read by the light of the table lamp until one in the morning. Then I climbed up the wooden staircase to the attic, made my bed, and slept till the morning. Only rarely did any shouting wake me. If the screaming went on for too long, I came down, prepared a morphine injection and gave it to the screaming patient. I knew the patients by name, but nothing else about them, as we had no contact. However, I did get to know one well, and we became good friends. He was a small man, with smooth gray hair which he combed back from his forehead. His features were pleasant, and his eyes were small, blue, and wise. He was a neat, clean man and his name was Kagan. He paid no attention to me the first night I was there. Then one night he came over and informed me, apologizing for the trouble he was causing, that Alex, his roommate, was about to have an attack. Alex was given two injections of morphine a day, one in the morning and the other in the evening. That night he had missed his dose. We heard the first moans before I had managed to fill the hypodermic syringe.

When I came back to the corridor, I saw Kagan leafing through the book I was reading. It was McDougal's *Elements of Psychology*. At that time I was studying for my finals. "I see"—he turned to me laughing—"that you are interested in psychology. I was also interested in that subject once. I used to lecture on the psychology of peoples at the Teachers' College." He stopped talking and frowned, thinking I did not believe him. In fact, social psychology had once been known as "the psychology of peoples" and it was his use of just this term, reminiscent of the heavy volumes of Wundt, that made me believe him.

Kagan had been the director of the Alliance Israélite Universelle schools in the Levant and North Africa. He spoke a correct Hebrew, perfect French, and knew English. He had even kept up to date with the achievements of social psychology until committed to the hospital. During his ten years in the asylum, he had learned German, Ancient Greek, and Arabic, all from reading the Bible in those languages. He claimed that his wife had robbed him of his property and committed him, so that she could stray more easily with her lovers. This kind of talk could have indicated either madness or the truth, and I was almost ready to believe him because of our friendship and the respect I had for this pitiful man. However, Greti told me that Kagan suffered from hallucinations, which used to afflict him at mealtimes. Greti gave out supper, and during the meal Kagan would claim that he heard the voices of his daughters. He could hear them trying to get up to see him, but their mother was stopping them. He would also smell the fragrance of the roasted chicken that his wife was preparing for her lovers. During the ten years he had spent in the asylum, none of his family had visited him. He often asked that books be sent him from his library, but none arrived. Apart from the Bibles in various languages which he had brought with him into the hospital, he possessed no books.

One night Greti told me that a new woman patient had been sent in from Haifa, by the Social Welfare Bureau there. She had no relations or acquaintances and was completely alone. As she had arrived from Vienna a few years before, it was hard to consider her a new immigrant. Her age was unknown, but she seemed to be close on thirty, perhaps younger. She possessed no clothes but the dress in which she was admitted.

The doctor took her gold watch off her wrist while she was still unconscious, in case it got lost or broken. He intended to return it, of course, when she recovered. She neither spoke nor ate. When a day had passed without food, the doctor decided to feed her through her nose. This practice he called the "Zonde." When a patient had to have the Zonde, the orderlies would tie him to a chair. Then a rubber tube was introduced through his nostrils to his stomach, and the doctor would pour milk and lemon juice through a funnel and into the tube. By the time it reached the stomach, the milk was usually curdled, and sometimes, when not enough lemon juice was used, the patient would vomit. After we had given Bruria, as we called her, the Zonde once or twice, she decided it would be better to eat like everyone else. It was clear, however, that eating made her suffer. Food sickened her.

The details on her card had been written in a hurry, and

no one in the hospital could decipher them. Only three letters could be made out, once "beth" and twice "resh," so we called her Bruria.

Bruria did not sleep at night. On her first night, a week before her death, there was a heavy downpour of rain, and a wintry wind blew at the window. Kagan, enveloped in a woolen blanket, was sitting close to me explaining a French text. While I was trying to grasp the nature of an irregular verb, I heard soft footsteps from Bruria's room. The whole building was in darkness. Only the light of the desk lamp lit up the table and threw the corridor into deep shadow. Bruria slowly left her room. She walked along the wall till she came to the table. For a long while she stared at the lamp, her hands pressed to her sides. Then she sat down. Kagan looked at her with pity, and said, "Poor girl." Outside it rained without stopping. Occasionally a blue flash of lightning lit up the windows, followed by thunder breaking the silence. Kagan stood up. "Cold," he said, and a good-natured smile lit up his tired old face, furrowed with wrinkles. "Good night," I said, "Good night. Pleasant dreams." "Yes, pleasant dreams," he repeated with a sad smile, and went into his room.

Bruria sat withdrawn into herself and stared at the lamp. Her face was pale and her smooth, long, brown hair fell down her back. Her eyes were large and brown, with long lashes. I shut my book and prepared to go up to the attic. First I took my books up and made my bed. Then I went down again to the corridor. Bruria was still there, staring into emptiness. I shivered. The night air had penetrated into the house, and the curtains were stirring in the cold breeze. Bruria shrank into herself even more, but did not leave her place. "Bruria," I said, "go to sleep. You'll catch a cold." But Bruria did not stir. She looked at me and said nothing. I took a woolen blanket out of the cupboard and wrapped it around her. Then

I went back to my attic. I tried to fall asleep, without success.
Should I give her an injection? I turned the sheet over, re-
arranged the pillow, turned to the wall, but did not fall asleep.
At three-thirty in the morning, Bruria was still in the same
place, but her eyes were closed. I picked her up and put her
in her bed. She was hot.

"What's happened?" said Greti, drawing out the sounds of
her sweet, guttural French. "It's only twenty-five past nine."
"I was seized by a terrible longing for you," I said.
"Liar," she said with a broad smile.
Greti had been in the country for eight years but she spoke
no Hebrew and did not understand a word. She usually
spoke French, but with the doctor she conversed in German
and with the owners in Yiddish with a clear Galician accent.
The French vice-consul used to come each evening in his
shining car and patiently wait for her at the gate. While she
was still inside the entrance, five wide stone steps away from
him, he would open the door of the car with a gentlemanly
flourish, fling out his arms, and say in a cajoling voice, "Step
in, my little girl." She had other suitors, most of them middle-aged. They were well-mannered, possessed round stomachs and wealth, and held solid opinions.
A cold wind blew through the streets, scattering white
scraps of paper. The trees swayed to and fro and the gray
clouds came down low and hung themselves on the rooftops
and street lamps. "It's colder here than in Switzerland. It
gets into your bones," said Greti.
"I'm afraid it will snow," I said, and a great sadness settled
on me. It was soft, pale, and silent, like Bruria.
"Bruria is sick," said Greti.
"I know, she had fever yesterday." Again I felt Bruria's
back burning in my arms. "What does the doctor say?"

"A slight cold," said Greti. "I forced her to take some aspirin."

As Greti poured my tea we heard the hoot of the vice-consul's car. "He can wait," said Greti. She sipped her drink with pleasure, then she took her time making up in front of the mirror, finally she stepped out.

Bruria came again at midnight. She was very pale and her eyes were sunk into dark rings. Her walk was unsteady. Exhausted, she sat down at the table and fixed her eyes on the lamp. It was cold, and although Kagan had wrapped himself in two woolen blankets his shoulders were shivering. At the sight of Bruria dressed only in a thin blue robe, a shudder passed through me. Kagan got up. Whenever Bruria appeared, he would hurry off to his room.

"Poor girl," he sighed. "Poor girl. She's very sick. See how beautiful she is." He went into his room wrapped in two blankets, his white hair wild and gleaming in the dark.

I had not noticed Bruria's beauty until Kagan mentioned it. After her death, I met Greti one afternoon in a café. It was about a month after she had been dismissed from her job at the hospital and when she saw me her face lit up. She stood up and without any hesitation or warning gave me a big resounding kiss on my mouth. At that moment it seemed to me that all the waiters had stopped dead in their tracks and the customers had interrupted their eating and talking just to stare at us. However, the earth did not open up to swallow me and I did not have enough determination to make my escape, so I sat down at the table with a look of distinguished apathy on my face. That was just like Greti. She was always gay, always pleasant, and she liked men. She did not refuse presents and people gossiped about her, but she earned her keep by hard and fatiguing work at the hospital. As my earnings were no larger than hers, she refused to allow me to pay for her at the cinema and bought her own ticket. Gradually, our conversation came round to Bruria. Greti's expression became grave and she spoke about her for a long while. "Bruria was a wonderfully beautiful woman," she said. "Any man might have fallen in love with her at first sight." She glanced at me and I hid my face in the coffee cup.

When Kagan had disappeared into the darkness and closed his door, I was terrified. Snow began to fall softly without a sound. The wind had died down and the trees had stopped swaying. The silence was intense. Bruria sat staring at the lamp. Her expression was neither frightened nor pitiful. There was a sadness and a weariness about her eyes. The fear that gripped me kept me from moving. I did not even have the courage to turn my head. Bruria loomed over me like a threatening wall, like an imminent catastrophe. Her presence was like the mark of Cain, like the Day of the Lord. Her eyes did not leave the lamp, her lips were pressed together, and her hands tight against her body. In the last week of her life she said nothing and made no sound. That night I could no longer bear her heavy silence. I had to do something, something big, important, necessary, a duty that my life depended on. But I was glued to my chair in the darkness of the house with Bruria's pale face lit by the light of the table lamp, with her silence and with her eyes staring into the glow.

I watched her and the fear that overcame me did not allow me to move a muscle. "How awful," I said. "How awful!" The keys fell to the floor with a metallic clang. I jumped after them, opened the door to the stairs and ran through the dark to the hall. In a cupboard in the doctor's room there was a bottle of brandy. I put the light on. The room was quiet and undisturbed. I found the bottle in its place. It was two o'clock in the morning. Bruria was burning with fever. She shrank from my touch. Weak and fragile as she was, she did not have the strength to resist. I laid her on her bed; she looked for the light. I brought the table lamp into the room and sat by her and looked at her. She stared at the light. I spoke to her and the words came of themselves, spilling out like coins out of a hole in a bag. They were worn and dull coins, things that were ancient in the days of Enoch, Erad, Mehujael, Methusael, and Lamech. I spoke of injustice and wickedness, of good and evil, of life and death, and of life after death. I spoke about love. I spoke about the sky and the earth and the sun and the moon and the distant stars. I spoke about war and peace. I spoke about myself and about her. She stared at the lamp and kept silent. Her fever was burning. I talked on and on and told her everything. She stared at the lamp and kept silent. When the dawn came a white layer of snow had covered everything.

On the last night of Bruria's life the vice-consul did not come to fetch Greti. The snow had frozen over and cars could not move. Greti was gay and flushed. Her face shone.

"Pierre won't come tonight."

"Walk, it's wonderful out."

"I'm not walking as late as this. I'm sleeping here tonight."

In my bed in the attic there was only one mattress and two woolen blankets. When I climbed up the stairs I noticed that an eiderdown quilt had been added to them and Greti had not forgotten to bring two pillows. She liked her comfort.

We drank our tea.

"How is Bruria?" I asked.

"She still has the fever."

"What does the doctor say?"

"It'll pass. There's no reason to worry."

"You look beautiful tonight," I said to her. "You look good."

"I'm always good-looking," said Greti, "only you don't notice and hardly see me at all. You only care about your examinations and you are getting thinner every day. Did you eat any supper?"

"Yes," I said, "I ate a very good meal."

"What did you eat?"

"I don't remember, I don't remember what I ate tonight." Greti laughed. She climbed up the stairs to the attic and went to bed. I sat in the corridor and stared at my book but the letters began to dance about and lose their shape. Kagan was beside me telling me about something that happened to him when he was a young student at the university. He fell in love with a French girl, a devout Catholic, and they decided to marry. First she told him that it would be better for him to convert. Then she changed her mind and decided that she would convert. This story dragged on till midnight. Bruria did not appear. I went to her room and looked at her. Her eyes were closed and her breathing was heavy. When I got into bed, Greti was deeply asleep and snoring softly.

I woke up suddenly and jumped out of bed. Greti opened her eyes, startled, and muttered something angrily. It was five in the morning. I ran down the stairs to the corridor and made for Bruria's room. I opened the door and hurried over to her. She was lying just as she had been at midnight. Her eyes were closed, her hands pressed to her sides. She was dead. Greti was standing in the doorway rubbing her eyes. "She is dead," I said to her. "Bruria is dead." We carried her out, put her on the floor and covered her with a sheet.

We drank our tea contentedly. "I've got some cakes," Greti remembered. She took some biscuits out of her bag and arranged them on a tray.

"This is the last night," Greti said, "I'm not coming to work tomorrow, I'm fired."

"Why?" I asked, feeling sorry, sorry that Greti had been fired and sorry for myself now that she would not be waiting for me at ten each night.

"Sondelsohn came up to me today and told me that he had permission to live with other women because he was separated from his wife. He tried to kiss me and promised me two pounds extra a month. I slapped him, and then Wunschel turned up shouting at the top of his voice that I was a whore, that all women were whores and that all I wanted was to lead men on. I knew that was it. There was a tray full of food on the table. I picked it up with both hands and brought it down on his bald head." We both laughed.

"You're beautiful," I said. "I love you."

"You're lying," she said. "You know you are." Her look was of someone who was about to reveal a secret no one else knew. "I'm older than you by—"

"Three years," I suggested.

"More—seven years. If I were younger, I'd marry you and we'd live in a pretty white villa surrounded by a large garden and a high wall. You'd go to work in your car each morning and in the evenings we'd give parties and dance. You'd love me very much. You'd love only me and I'd love only you."

"I do love you," I said. "I want you to be my wife." I got up and she put out her hands toward me. I bent over and kissed them. When I looked up at her eyes, I saw that they were full of tears and smiling at me.

Translated by Zvi Jagendorf

12

THE PROPOSAL

ALONG WITH the slight itch in his nostrils came the memory of the smell and the taste of blood and that apprehensive fore-knowledge of the red trickle that would shortly issue from his nostril. This sort of thing had not happened to him since his childhood days. The last time his nose had bled had been when he was a youth of thirteen and that was twenty years ago. In that former time, the blood would flow because of the hot dry sharav and would not stop until he went to the Italian doctor, who inserted into the sensitive nostril a round stick anointed with some mercurial medicine and with it dabbed the tiny vein with an impermeable sheath. Twenty years had passed since then, and the apprehension that now the blood was about to ooze forth revived in clear and sharp recollection the feeling of those days. He at once lay down flat on his back on the floor of the room and the cool touch of the tiles on his neck made him feel better. To his gaze, Esther's legs up to and above the knees were revealed with their blue network of veins outlined on them. "There you are—in addition to everything else, she's got veins on her legs." And he thought to himself, "After she gives birth she'll probably need thick bandages." If he had noticed it previously, would he have acted differently? No, he would not have acted otherwise even if she were actually deformed. On the contrary, if she were deformed, the weight of responsibility toward her would have been sevenfold more burdensome—that feeling of excessive responsibility which, as was now apparent, had made him seem to her impertinent, insulting, and now ridiculous into the bargain because of this bleeding nose of his. Had she not been so confounded, she would have burst into laughter. But she had not yet grasped what had happened. At first she was stunned, then angry, and before her anger could subside she was alarmed by his sudden fall to the ground. As yet the blood had not issued from the region of the nostrils. He only felt it coming and was stretched out on the floor as he used to stretch out in the days of his childhood. She shrank back with a cry. A shrill cry, somewhat hysterical and hoarse and rather helpless, like the cry of an old woman. For a moment she thought of dashing out and calling for the neighbors, but then she approached him carefully to see what was wrong. He sent her a wan apologetic smile and wanted to tell her. "It's nothing, it will pass. It's twenty years now that I haven't had a nosebleed. Then it used to happen on account of the sharav but now there is no sharav, it's really the middle of the winter now, isn't it? It's probably because of the rapid change from the outside cold to the heat inside. It's really cold out too, a real frost, while in here the central heating has made the room like a bathhouse." And, indeed, the vapors in the chamber hung about heavily like the vapors in a bath after a woman had washed, full of the smell of woman and soap. He would have said this to her except for the fear that on opening his mouth the blood would trickle forth. The idea was to lie still and hope and pray that the blood would congeal in the nostrils before it could flow out upon the curve of the upper lip.

The unexpected appearance of the blood seemed to bring out his weakness in all its nakedness, showed up his own helplessness. Always it had seemed to him forbidden to be weak and in need of help; he had to be the strong one, the pillar of strength in a crumbling world. Yes, the crumbling of the world about him had oppressed him for many years now. From the age of seven his eyes had been opened to the dangers threatening the whole world. He had been in the second grade and the teacher had read to the class out of a book about the earth, the sun, and the planets. He had listened with concern and had trembled at the explicit statements that the sun would one day cool, and the whole world would freeze and perish from the cold. The teacher, who thought that seeing was believing, showed them pictures of snowy mountains and frozen tundra. He had revealed his anxiety to his mother and with her sought to find some means of overcoming the perils of a world growing cold. She could not help him much because she had been so absorbed in her own cares and troubles. Her husband was quite lost to her there in America, and she was sure that he spent most of his fortune on gentile women, whereas to her he only sent what was left over, although it was not to be denied that these leavings were adequate to provide nicely for her and her son. All through the years, she had lamented her bitter fate, warily putting aside most of the money sent to her from America against the eventual days of scarcity. Her son Pinik used to join her in her sorrow and try to help her as much as he could. All through these years, a chafing complaint against his father had accumulated in his breast, and when he reached the age of eighteen he decided to go to America to persuade his father to return to his mother.

When he went to America, his mother was left alone in the large house. Even in those days, when many houses stood empty and owners of property were begging for tenants and even the poor could afford a two-room flat, even then their house was considered large. It had a big broad hall, like a dance hall, and four rooms led out of it, two on each side. The ceilings were arched and the walls were so thick that on the windowsills you could stand and dance to your heart's content when and if the spirit of gaiety took you. I, myself, have danced on the windowsill of the hall on the side facing Sheikh Jarakh when my cousin came to visit us. She had been born in Tel Aviv and never before this visit of hers to Jerusalem had she seen such large rooms and windows so high and walls so thick. "But everything looks so miserable . . ." she said to me. "That's not so," I answered, "everything is really very jolly." And forthwith I leaped onto the windowsill and began to dance before her. I had hardly taken three big hops when she too jumped up and joined me in the dance. Thus we danced, opposite one another, until old Shprintza came, Pinik's mother, and told us, "Quiet, quiet. Stop that noise. My eyes hurt me." Noise would bring on her headaches, and the headaches would make her eyes hurt, and the pain of the eyes was worse than the headache. But all this occurred later, close to the time of Pinik's return from America, on the eve of the Second World War. By then she was no longer living alone. She had let us two rooms and half the hall, which in turn was larger than any of the rooms.

Old Shprintza had received the house as a gift from her husband at the time of his last stay in Jerusalem. He had bought it from Yussuf Effendi and had signed the deed over to his wife in order to appease her, but she was not appeased. She was full of bitter remonstrations, grumbling about everything and sighing for the good old days that were gone. These good old days that were gone forever were the days of the Turkish rule in the land when a woman would go out and buy meat by the rotel and eggs by the dozen and hire an Arab woman at the Damascus Gate to work for her from sunrise to sundown, all for a single napoleon, from which there would still be lots left over. Even "pioneers" from Poland could be hired cheaply and they would know their place. Then they hadn't dared as yet to raise their heads. Shprintza disliked

Poles thoroughly. Had we been from Poland we should never have been able to rent a flat in her house.

After old Shprintza had been left alone in the large house for three or four months, she permitted her sister Gitel to come and live in the little room at the far end of the courtyard. This room, which hugged the stone wall that protected the entire house against the four winds, had previously been used as a sort of barn or just as a storage shed. Its windows, torn out of the stone wall, were very low, hardly reaching the knees of a passerby on the other side of the wall, and were protected by iron gratings. Children would sometimes grab hold of the grating and look in, especially after Gitel moved in and the light of her little lamp unexpectedly shone out from the wall, lighting up the street below like a meteor. To enter this room you had to go down seven steps made of Jerusalem stone. Pinik used to implore his mother in every letter that he sent her to urge his Aunt Gitel to come and live inside the house. He did this out of concern for his mother and because of some strange things that had happened to him in America. On the night of his arrival in New York, when he was staying at a hotel, his dead sister had entered the room and had sat down on a chair at his bedside. She was wearing a white blouse and a blue skirt and short white stockings folded over her brown shoes. "Pinik," she said to him, "I think you ought to learn something practical, something productive. Study building construction or electricity or irrigation. We need men of action."

"But statistics is also a practical profession!" Pinik had cried out to her, and he jumped out of bed. Awakening, he groped with beating heart for the switch and snapped on the light. After a while he tried to go back to sleep but couldn't. He dreaded the dark and yet in the light he couldn't fall asleep. Ever since then he had been troubled by night fears. From about midnight on, if he were sitting and writing, he would begin to shiver all over. A figure would be standing behind him. This figure was not a menacing figure, nor one of horror. It was just a figure, a formless sort of figure, whose very presence filled him with dread. At such times he was too frightened even to leave the room to go to the bathroom, lest some ghostly hand reach out toward him. Needless to say, he never mentioned his night fears in his letters to his mother; he merely hinted that it was quite unwise for her, an elderly lady, to be alone in the big house. If a young man like himself could be given to such night fears, how much more an old woman like her. For some reason, he could not grasp that she had absolutely no fear of ghostly figures or any other such silly products of the imagination. Her fears were of an entirely different sort. These were fears of a quite tangible, practical nature such as, what if the old man, her husband, stops sending these checks from America; what if we, her tenants, stop paying the rent; what if the old man leaves his fortune to the gentile woman he's keeping?

Before moving in with her sister, Gitel had lived in a cellar of one of the houses in the Greek colony, where Shprintza never saw her; indeed she took care to avoid any contact with her, except for the one that had been imposed upon her from without. Every three months, when the money order for Shprintza would come from America, there was an additional sum of fifteen dollars enclosed for Gitel. Thus Gitel used to come to her sister four times a year, sign her name on a previously prepared receipt, and go home. Shprintza never forgave her sister for wasting her portion of the inheritance from their mother, and she saw her sister's wretched life of penury as a sort of punishment from heaven, and God forbid that she should interfere with that which Providence had ordained. It seems that Gitel lived on these five dollars a month that she received from her brother-in-law, making no effort whatever to increase this income; that is, unless one cares to mention that single disastrous attempt shortly after the coming of the English to the country, when Sir Herbert Samuel was appointed High Commissioner. Gitel had weighed the matter carefully and had decided that she was eminently suited to serve as his cook. She sent him a letter and in it listed her various qualifications. His secretary answered with that well-known British politeness, thanking her for her good will and promising her that as soon as her services might be required, she would receive notification. She waited two weeks and when the expected notification failed to arrive, she sent another letter. To this letter she received a similarly worded response. This did not seem to satisfy her and so she sent a third letter. Thus an exchange of correspondence continued for some months, until one day an Arab policeman appeared and warned her that unless she stopped writing letters to the High Commissioner, she would end up in the Central Prison. In such fashion were Gitel's endeavors to better herself concluded, but her spirits did not fail.

Gitel was by nature a happy person. She cheered her life by singing songs and telling herself stories. Some of these latter were so funny that she would burst out laughing even in the middle of the street. As a matter of fact, almost everything amused her. She never reached the kitchen of the High Commissioner, but she did manage to serve in the kitchen of her sister Shprintza, in return for room, board, used clothes, and twenty-five piasters a week. Every Friday afternoon before the lighting of the Sabbath candles, Shprintza used to pay her her weekly wages and Gitel would burst out laughing. So it continued until Pinik returned from America.

Pinik spent twelve years in America before he came back. The ship on which he made the voyage arrived in Haifa harbor on a Saturday, and he reached Jerusalem on Sunday. During the whole of the week prior to his return, Shprintza was in a bad temper and on Friday she vented her spleen on Gitel. In fact, she threw the whole plate of soup that Gitel had prepared in Gitel's face and hurled after it a volley of insults and curses on her head such as I had never heard before. Then she went to sit on the stool by the gate in order to get some fresh air and collect herself, except that the sight of the Polish shopkeeper opposite whetted her anger all the more.

"Do you see that Polish 'paskudniak' there," she said to me. "When he came to the country he roamed the streets like a hungry dog and was ready to do any work whatever for fifteen piasters a day, and now he owns a whole building and is still not satisfied. He had the nerve to send a real-estate agent to me with an offer to buy my house, the house that was bought with the money of my dear late husband." Tears came to her eyes. The sound of a laugh broke out of Gitel's room. "That crazy woman is becoming the death of me," Shprintza continued. "I give her a room, board, and clothing and twenty-five piasters a week, besides all the money she steals from me when I send her to the market, and all the thanks I get are sneers and insults. Why she's worse than all the Poles, the Rumanians, and the Sephardim together." Only the Rumanians and the Sephardim seemed able to compete with the Poles in iniquity. Gitel, her head and shoulders popping up out of the depths, stood at the door of her room and looked at us. As soon as Shprintza turned her head in the direction of the Polish "paskudniak," Gitel motioned me toward her with her finger. Frightened as I was of her adversary, I only dared come to her later on. Gitel's room was permeated with the odor of ancient wooden cabinets, dust-laden curtains, and mint leaves whose fragrance is like that of arak. The actual smell of arak was also present in the room sometimes, from the bottle of liquor on the table or from her mouth.

"Do you know why that witch is so mad?" she asked me. "Because her son is coming back on Sunday. She doesn't want him back. She wants him to stay there and send her money every month. Like his father used to. She made his life so difficult for him that he had to run away from her to the ends of the earth. And now, all of a sudden, she's become so righteous! 'My late husband, my poor late husband.' Her late husband wasn't even allowed to have dinner with her when he returned from America because she couldn't stand the noises he made during the meal. He had false teeth that used to grind away like those machines that make gravel out of stone. He also had to wash his own clothes, because his wife refused to do his laundry . . ."

"Gitel! Gitel!" Shprintza called out loud. "Come here, right away!" Gitel climbed the few stairs and locked her door. "Let her yell," she said to me. "First she throws the soup I made for her in my face and now she probably wants me to wash the dishes for her. Poles! Poles! Her husband was a Pole and she wasn't fit to kiss his feet. He was a wonderful man. A real saint. And I don't know why God punished him with that cursed bitch. Now she has become so devout. As though I didn't know that she used to cook and mend on the Sabbath—and now she keeps sending letters to her son to keep the Sabbath in America. I tell you—no one can live with her. They all run away. Her husband ran away from her to America and died there; her daughter ran away from her to the kibbutz and died there, and her son ran away and he's coming back now. I don't know why he decided to come back. What's waiting for him here? And I won't stay here any longer either. I'll go back to my own room. I won't be her servant and I won't let her raise her voice at me! I came here only because she told me that Mendel—Mendel was her husband, a very dear man was Mendel—only because Mendel asked me to come and live with her and I just couldn't refuse

Mendel anything. But now Mendel is dead and I won't live with her anymore. I'm going away from her. I'm off!"

When her calm was restored she began to prepare for Pinik's return. All of Saturday Gitel spent ransacking the great iron-bound wooden trunk, until she found a suitable garment in which to welcome him. On Sunday she cleaned the house thoroughly and even watered the two cypress trees in the yard and then she hurried to the market to purchase all that was required for the table. To her chagrin, Pinik appeared while she was away at the market.

He entered the courtyard with measured steps effusing the smell of neatness and order. On his head, the American straw hat he wore sat straight and rigid without any of your cavalier tiltings, and his blue American cloth suit was new and well pressed. He had even had his shoes polished on Jaffa Road by Mustapha Khalil. His hands gripped a suitcase each and behind him an Arab urchin, breathing heavily, was bringing the rest of his suitcases along on his pushcart. In all the twelve years of his stay in America, Pinik had not forgotten his street Arabic and he parted from the young Arab with a suitable blessing and sizable baksheesh. He then wiped his pince-nez spectacles with a carefully folded white handkerchief and set them back on his broad nose and at once a look of importance gleamed from his eyes. When he entered the hall, he took off his hat and revealed a large bald spot in the center of his scalp surrounded by thin, well-combed hair. An air of importance radiated from him, the air of an official who had not yet reached that highest post which, he believed, was still coming to him. When his mother appeared from her room, he let go the suitcases and hastened toward her with arms outstretched and trembling. This momentary quiver of the arms, accompanied by the anxiously apologetic look of his eyes, thrust aside the air of importance and all that was left was a rather bewildered and agitated person who was not quite sure what awaited him, and did not even exclude the possibility of sudden violence.

"Shalom, Mother!" he said, with the trace of an American accent in his speech. It was not clear whether he would continue the impulse of his movement ending in an embrace and a kiss or whether he would check it and rest content with a verbal greeting. His mother extricated him from the dilemma by going up to him and placing a dry kiss on each of his cheeks.

"You've grown old in America," she said to him. "I wouldn't have recognized you in the street. And you're already bald! My God! So young and already bald! And what a sharp smell of tobacco. You probably smoke like your father, may he rest in peace, two packs a day. That's just the way to undermine your health."

Having greeted him in this forthright way, his mother ushered him into the inner room. "And your eyes are so red from the smoke. If you don't stop smoking, you'll go blind altogether," she kept saying as she closed the door. As soon as he saw his mother, a lump formed in his throat and his eyes became moist. When he had met his father in America twelve years ago, he had also wanted to burst into tears. He had seen a sick old man, trudging along with his final strength to keep making a living instead of lying in a hospital. He had wanted to help him, but had come too late. And only two months after Pinik's arrival the old man died. And now again, the same familiar old helplessness gripped him in all its bitterness, an inability to fulfill the obligations imposed on him which he knew so well from childhood on, when those quarrels in the house used to begin. Even then, at the age of ten, he knew that he was the one who had to subdue the domestic storms and repair the cracks of the crumbling home. He had

no idea who was guilty or what was wrong. There were times
when he felt his father was a wicked-hearted man dealing
harshly with his mother, and at other times he felt that his
mother irritated his father needlessly, and that somehow his
aunt Gitel was involved in their squabbles. He used to run
from father to mother and plead, "Quiet, please be quiet." He
would have been ready to do anything to restore peace, but
he never succeeded. How well he remembered his mother's
pulling Aunt Gitel's hair and yelling, "You whore you, get
out of here or I'll kill you." And it was then that his father
had fled the house and had not returned for many days. Afterward it turned out that he had rented a room in the Greek
Colony and his mother had said to him, to Pinik, "You may
as well know that your father is an old lecher." All this occurred just before the old man's departure for America, and
even at that time Pinik had wondered about the matter and
had come to the conclusion that all the troubles came because
no one was willing to give in just a little to some one else. If
only Rachel his elder sister had been home, she might have
been able to help him quiet the storm and make peace. But
Rachel was not at home. She had run away before that to the
kibbutz and had no wish to return and did not even answer
the letters her mother sent her. Only he was left with his
mother.

When the news came of Rachel's death from stomach poisoning—several of the kibbutz comrades had been poisoned
from something eaten in the settlement's dining room, but
only Rachel had died—when the telegram came, his mother
had beaten her breast with her fists and shouted, "The old
lecher caused her death, he is the one to blame . . ." And
when Aunt Gitel came running in distractedly and crying,
"Where is her kibbutz? I'll go there to help her . . . Let me
go to her!" her sister yelled at her, "You whore you, get out
of here! You're the one to blame for her death! You and your

old lecher—go to him in America." And all the time Pinik
knew that it was he, Pinik, who was guilty of her death. Only
two weeks previously he had received a letter from Rachel
urging him to join her in the settlement. "Pinik, my darling
little brother," she wrote to him, "why not come and live with
us. It's a different life here, a new life and finer and more
just." And he had answered that it was not right to leave his
mother alone. This had been a cry of help on her part and he
had not responded to it. He was convinced that had he responded to the call and gone to her, she would not have died.
She was the only one of all those whose stomachs had been
poisoned who had failed to recover. That was because she had
a stomach ulcer which she had not bothered to take care of.
She had kept it secret, not wishing to burden the others or to
demand any special conditions for herself, just as she always
used to work beyond her strength.

"And how do you expect to make a living here in Jerusalem?" his mother asked him after he had finished telling her
a little of his life in America.

"I don't know yet," he said.

"It's hard to find a good job nowadays without pull. You're
not from Poland and you've got no chance of being accepted
in the Jewish Agency . . ."

"I don't think I'll work at first. I want to see the country
a bit."

He restrained himself with difficulty. He wanted to shout,
to beat his head against the wall, to pack up and to go back
to America. To do anything but remain in the same room
with her.

"What do you mean, see the country?" she asked. "Why
you've been wandering about for twelve years."

"But I haven't wandered around the country here. I want
to see it, to get to know the land."

"What is there to see here?" the old woman said irascibly.

"Stones, rocks, sand, and good-for-nothing pioneers. Every day Jews are being murdered on the roads and you want to go wandering about. And how will we live? Tell me. How?"

"I've accumulated a little money in America. It will last us for two or three years."

"What are you saying, Pinik? Have you gone out of your mind? The little money we've got we'll set aside in Barclay's Bank, against a rainy day. I don't agree to using any bank owned by Polish Jews. They'll skin you, and you won't be able to utter a word. Barclay's Bank, that's the gentile bank and the goyim don't know any tricks. As of tomorrow you go out looking for a job."

Shivers began to make their way up his body, from his navel upward. He lost control over them and the waves reached his mouth and burst out all at once in a mad roar of laughter. His mother shrank back and with dull eyes watched her son writhe with laughter.

"Stop laughing," she shouted at him. "Stop it. My God, you laugh the way your aunt Gitel does."

"Aunt Gitel. Ha ha ha . . ." His outburst rolled along the length of the hall. With a quick impulsive movement, his mother took the jug of water on the table, which she always had ready for when she should feel faint, and dashed all of its contents in his face. He became still, and she went down on her knees and began to weep. "Mother," he said, fastening his gaze upon her and talking softly. "Forgive me. I didn't mean to upset you. I've come from America in order to be near you. To take care of you. To make sure you won't be lonely in your old age. The way it's written in the prayer book, 'Cast me not out in my old age.' How could I stay there in America when I read in the papers that Jews are being waylaid and murdered on the roads."

"If you've come to help me, then put your money in Barclay's Bank and don't waste it on anything silly."

"You're right, mother. I won't waste it."

Slowly she was pacified, but her peace of mind did not last long. That very night she thought she heard his voice, talking to himself in his room. Before morning she was awakened again by the sound of repressed laughter in the adjoining room. She rose from her bed trembling, and peeked in through the keyhole. He was sitting fully dressed and with a handkerchief to his mouth to keep the laughter from bursting forth. "My God," the old woman murmured, "Pinik has lost his mind in America. He talks and laughs just like Gitel."

In anticipation of his return home from America, Pinik had purchased many gifts and things for his mother as well as for Gitel and for himself; but the manner of his welcome had made it absolutely clear to him that he could never even show them to her. She would take it is an unredeemable waste. He also canceled his plans for a trip. On that very first night, he decided to look for a job as soon as possible. "That's the biggest test," he kept telling himself. "The biggest and the hardest test of all, and I've got to stand up to it." For years now any definite position was a kind of test, and for some reason or other, he had been found failing in all these tests. Before morning, Gitel made her appearance in his room and asked him to come to see her at eleven o'clock. Her appearance stimulated him to another fit of laughter, the one which his mother had witnessed through the keyhole. In any case, he waited impatiently for his mother to leave the house. That day, a Monday, was the day when the eye doctor received at the Hadassah clinic and she used to be punctual about seeing him every week. She left the house at a quarter to eleven, and fifteen minutes later Pinik descended the steps to Gitel's room.

"Pinik, Pinik," Gitel called, and her eyes filled with tears of emotion as she rushed to him with open arms and kissed him on both cheeks. He felt the touch of her withered skin and the moistening of his face with her tears. He had to over-come a certain shrinking in order to let himself be kissed, just as he had held back from his mother's embrace. This made him wonder why one would shrink from the kiss of the aged. On the clean tablecloth a round cake had been carefully cut into neat slices and nearby was a bottle of wine and little glasses and a plate of sweets. She poured him some of the wine with shaking hands and said, "Come drink to your health and to life and to your return home," and again tears began to stream down her face.

"What about you? Won't you drink? Come along, drink with me."

She poured for herself, not wine but arak, and kept urging him to eat and drink. While he was thus occupied, she asked him questions about his life in America, and amongst others, inquired about Mendel's last days. When he told about his father, she again began to weep. "Your voice is so like your father's," she told him.

When he finally glanced at his watch, he saw that a whole hour had passed and that his mother would be arriving any minute.

"Look," he said to her, "Father asked me to keep sending you five dollars a month. Just so there won't be any complica-tions, I'll give you now sixty dollars for the whole year . . ." And he took out some bills and placed them on the table.

"I'm going back to my room in the Greek Colony," she said. "Visit me there."

"Yes, I'll come," he promised and hastened up the stairs into the courtyard before she could catch him with another kiss.

At the doorway, he met his mother returning from the clinic. "I'm going to look for a job," he said to her and felt that he was involved in some intrigue against her.

"Don't forget your papers. I hope you succeed," she called

to him. She harbored no suspicions whatever of him and her innocence made him feel sorry for her.

"Come along and let me show you what I've brought you from America," he said, regarding it somehow necessary to compensate her and feeling at the same time that this need was in itself something underhanded.

"No, no. Go to your business first," she urged him.

"My business can wait. First let me show you your presents." And he took her arm in his and directed her steps indoors. The smell of medicaments rose from her, mixed with the odor of clothes which had lain for a long time in camphor. In the other room, he opened one of the suitcases and began to extricate kerchiefs and scarfs.

"How much does this shawl cost?" she asked, examining the cloth with her fingers.

"Three dollars," he said and felt sorry he hadn't purchased a more expensive one.

"Three dollars wasted on a shawl! Why, here you can buy a rag like this for twenty-five piasters. Too bad I didn't write to you not to throw away money on such things. Why, you don't understand anything about women's clothes, and they've cheated you there."

Once again the shivers rose up from his belly and he could barely restrain the outburst of laughter. Everything seemed so marvelously absurd.

"This you call waste? Why it's nothing compared to the hundred and fifty dollars I spent on the big pieces of nonsense." And with this he opened the heavy suitcase and showed her that it was not a suitcase at all but a large portable radio-phonograph.

"And you don't know what's hidden inside, no one knows, neither the customs officials nor the police," he said and, removing the cover, drew from among the wires and tubes a small pistol. "You see," he remarked, waving the shining weapon before her, "I thought about this too. I figured everything out in America. Every Jew has to be armed with a pistol and that's the way we'll overcome the attacks against us."

At the sight of the pistol, the last of her doubts about him vanished. She was now certain, beyond any doubt, that Pinik had gone out of his mind and that she had to handle him with extreme care, just as one deals with dangerous lunatics.

"Yes, yes, of course. Now run along to your business. And don't take the pistol. It won't really be of any help to you."

"Sometimes I feel that this is just what will be of help to me, more than anything else maybe," he answered. "You have no idea how useful it can be." And unable to restrain himself any longer, he burst out laughing. At his departure, he waved to her clownishly with an American flourish and said in English, "Bye-bye, honey."

She went out after him and watched him until he disappeared from sight, and then she hurried back to the pistol on the table and wrapped it in one of the kerchiefs. Having so swathed it that it lost all shape she took the weapon out to the courtyard and threw it into the cistern. After having disposed of the pistol, she began to work out a story in her mind to cover the act of pillage. But Pinik had been quite sure, when he left the house, that his mother would get rid of the weapon in one way or another and he did not really care. "The loss of a pistol is neither here nor there. In the long run, all is lost." And this very thought, that all was lost, made him feel strangely jubilant.

After two weeks of search, Pinik found a job with an Office for Translations and Applications. He could easily have obtained a far more lucrative and respectable position, being a graduate of an American university and able to maneuver freely in English as well as Hebrew and Arabic. He was even offered the management of a subdepartment in the Jewish Agency, but he refused. At first he sought a job for the night hours. Failing to find such a place, he agreed to work in the afternoons or evenings, but under no circumstances in the morning. His explanation was that he was busy during the morning hours. The truth of the matter was that he required the morning to sleep in, being unable to fall asleep before the early hours, two or three o'clock in the morning, and just as unable to get up before nine or ten . . . The translation office was also open only until five in the afternoon; but the owner, unwilling to relinquish such a find as this, agreed to let Pinik begin work at two in the afternoon and continue into the evening, either in the office or at home, as he chose. This owner happened to be a lady, a distinctly blond type, around fortyish or so, with bobbed hair and protruding ears and rather energetic, decisive movements. She was polite even in her irritability or even in anger, restrained in her courtesy, and efficient in whatever she did. In short, a woman quite capable of taking things in hand. She was punctilious about preserving all the formalities in her relations with one Mr. Pinchas Cohen-Hayerushalmi, Pinik in other words. And only after a considerable time, when her sense of righteousness began to trouble her about the pitiful salary she was paying him, did she draw up one of the curtains of distant formality and say in a cordial tone which was meant to be nonchalant, "You know, from the first moment I saw you, I knew we would work together in . . . complete understanding. I realized at once that you were a man . . . a . . . a serious and solid person . . . respects the profession and likes it. Yes, that's the main thing . . . solidity and respect for one's profession. Yes. Here in this country, no one seems to respect his vocation. I realized at once that I . . . that you . . . yes . . ." Her face suddenly froze in confusion and a blue vein stood out on her forehead.

"Miss Simon," Pinik answered, "I have thought well of you from the very first moment." And to his dismay those familiar shivers began to move upward from his belly, quavering and surging forward. From the very first moment, he had detested the smile she bestowed on her customers, the seriousness with which she discussed every silly detail—that solidity which she valued so highly. He hated those things in her which he despised in himself,. for he did despise himself. The pince-nez spectacles, this carefully groomed hair. If she only knew what was going on behind his respectable exterior! At their first meeting, after they had decided on the conditions of his employment, and she had stretched forth her hand to shake his, he had been seized with a desire to pull the ears which protruded from her bobbed hair as' one would lift one of those large vases with two curving handles. Fortunately he had been able to control this impulse, but ever after that he was careful to keep his glance lowered whenever they spoke and thus observe the freckles on her forearms. The skin of these arms was a bluish white and was somewhat flaky besides being extremely sensitive. Any kind of pressure on this skin would cause yellow-green bruises to appear. A sharp perfumed smell exuded from her. The perfume itself was probably expensive and of choice quality; Miss Simon could not conceivably buy any other. Yet when the perfume combined with the profuse perspiration odors of her body, the result was a sourish smell like that of parsley in a salad. Her palms were of the kind that easily become clammy.

He tried to convince himself that Miss Simon was repulsive to him because he detested the work in the office. Most of this work consisted of translating letters, the majority of which were requests for money from relations in America or South

Africa, or letters of thanks for money received which were intended to stimulate further contribution. Eventually he took over the whole correspondence of a respectable institution whose entire existence was based on shnorerei, on contributions from abroad, and he came to know the wording of every letter by heart. He learned how to address an important contributor and how to address a minor one, how to express appreciation for a contribution of ten dollars, and how to voice gratitude for a hundred. The more he despised his labors the more he succeeded in them, and Miss Simon showed her gratification. "Look," she called to him one day, "they're showing a movie at the Zion Cinema based on a story by Stefan Zweig . . . Stefan Zweig is a great writer . . ." An hour later she informed him of her solemn determination to raise his salary; and he naturally invited her to the Zion Cinema. Of course, their celebration could hardly conclude with that, and when he took her home after the show, she permitted him to come into her room. The walls of this room were decorated with the pictures of Kaethe Kollwitz and the bookcases were lined with fine German editions of Stefan Zweig, Arthur Schnitzler, Peter Altenberg, Herman Hesse and Emil Ludwig, while on shelves nearby defiantly heavy and complicated stood the works of Marx, Engels, Lenin, and even Edward Bernstein.

"I am not acquainted with the socialist thinkers," Pinik said, pointing to these latter heavy volumes when he became weary of her precisely detailed analysis of the film based on the book by Zweig. In her speech the expression, "A woman's soul in all its nakedness" kept popping up like carps' heads in a fish pond. "I couldn't really reveal my soul, my own soul in all its nakedness, my heart's depths, any more precisely than did Stefan Zweig in his book."

"I have long been intending to read Marx and Engels,"

Pinik interrupted her, dreading to hear more of this laying bare of her soul, which he pictured to himself as looking something like the bluish-white freckled skin of her arms.

"You have never been a socialist?" She lunged at him with an impatient cry as soon as she realized the futility of her literary speculations.

"I don't know," Pinik said and endeavored to order his thoughts. "From the little I know about socialism, I have always been a socialist at heart. I have wanted justice in human relations, that people should be fair to one another, that they should try to act in kindliness and pity . . . that's what I've always wanted," and he smiled in perplexity and continued, "except that I myself have always failed in this."

"Nonsense!" This word exploded from her lips with a decisiveness that left no room for argument. "It's pretty evident that you don't even know the very simplest principles. What you say sounds like bourgeois philanthropy, and bourgeois philanthropy is worse than bourgeois tyranny.

"The important thing is the exactness of the socialist system, the scientific theory which proves the inevitable collapse of the present regime. That has nothing whatever to do with hypocritical philanthropy," she continued as soon as her agitation subsided and the blue vein on her temple fell back to its normal place beneath the skin.

The evening, however, was not thereby spoiled, for she managed to ride the crisis, returning after a while to the original theme. While they were having coffee, he was brought to realize, with her help, that she had succeeded in effecting harmony, not only between Marx and Peter Altenberg, but also between these two and all the good and the beautiful in Eastern art.

Only now did he notice the huge Turkish sword mounted on the wall in the far corner, not far from a Kaethe Kollwitz,

and the Persian rug on the floor and the Yemenite embroidery
on the table. The coffee had been prepared in an Arab finjan
and served in little cups in true Eastern fashion. At around
midnight the discussion narrowed down from the literary soul
to the particular soul of the one sitting opposite him. He listened to what she had to say about all that was taking place
beneath the outer mask and began to feel the slimy perspiration of her hand clutching at his arm in a paroxysm of frank
and searching self-exposure. Her heart had belonged to a man
for twenty years; she had given him her whole life. She had
not even hinted that he leave his wife, being prepared to remain the backroom sweetheart. All she had wanted was to be
sure that his heart was devoted to her and not to his lawful wife.
She had had many opportunities, extraordinary chances to
marry "first-class gentlemen," handsome and highly respectacle,
but she had refused them all for his sake. She had even sup-
ported him, secretly, at times. But how did it turn out in the
end? It turned out that he was a low and cunning traitor. Yes,
a Jew of Polish origin, even though he polished his German
with sayings from Goethe and Schiller. Of course, she was
not the sort, heaven forbid, to believe in any theories about
origins or racial types, still she couldn't resist the thought that
there were certain contemptible traits associated with Polish
Jews. However, she had succeeded in overcoming the crushing blow, and she still believed in love. Yes—she was still able
to love with all the warmth of her heart, with all the woman-
liness of her soul. At this stage, the tip of her ear was already
touching his cheek, and her eyes were moist before his gaze
like two candles seen through a wet window. "Now, I'll pull
her up by the ears," he thought. And this ridiculous notion
so gripped him that he had to clench his fists to prevent himself from acting accordingly. At the same time, to his dismay,
those waves of laughter began to tickle his belly. "I've got to

get out of here fast, or else something awful will happen."
And he began feverishly to contrive schemes of flight, such
as "Ah, did you hear that? Shooting. Yes, some gang has
probably broken into the neighborhood and they're beginning
to kill Jews . . ." No, that was silly; there was no sound of
shooting—or of anything. Maybe he could just jump up and
tell her that he had some serious stomach trouble, diarrhea or
something. And he did indeed make a motion as though to
leap up, and in doing so stretched out his hands toward her.
His fingers were actually touching her ears. But then, at the
critical moment, he managed to convert this into some awkward caress. Her head lay between his arms, and the smell of
the perfume from her hair made his nostrils twitch and made
him want to sneeze. She lifted her head and as her left ear
passed his lips, he planted a light biting kiss on it. A tremor
passed through her body. In a trice, the pincer movement of
her fingers on his arm tightened, but then she pulled herself
together and said to him in a weak, hushed voice, "We've gone
too far, Pinchas. We . . . ought to control our feelings."

"No . . . no . . ." Pinik cried passionately, and the thin
hairs on his head waved and stuck out of the sides of the head
like quills. "We've got to cast off restraint. Let go . . ." And
in fact, he did let his foot go and it slipped back in an effort
to support his body against the weight of Miss Simon, and in
doing so kicked the little table. The finjan and the two little
cups and the plate of salt crackers all fell over. A turbid stream
of coffee liquid wound its way down the table and over Miss
Simon's dress and dripped from the dress to the floor.

"Mr. Cohen-Hayerushalmi!" she cried out, unable for once
to hold her anger in check. "Look what you've done! This is
my best dress!" And before he could recover his balance, she
was in the bathroom and out of her dress, rinsing and cleaning
it with her usual energy and then she was back again, clothed

in another garment, industriously mopping the floor. He stammered his apologies, and when order was restored she was already in a more conciliatory mood and was able to bid him farewell in an almost affectionate tone of voice. She also warned him that next time, which would be the following evening, he should not be so impetuous. After all, she wasn't alien to deep feelings, as he knew, but still they had to try to keep these feelings under control.

When he went to bed at three in the morning, he wondered whether the logic of the situation had not required him to give her a good-night kiss. Then, out of sheer physical and emotional weariness, he fell asleep at once without any of the usual night fears. In his sleep, Miss Simon came to him and shouted that she hated Poles, and then she turned into his mother who was yelling at him, "You're a rotten Pole. An old lecher." She approached him with slow measured steps and with threatening countenance, and he knew that she was about to strangle him. Then he remembered the pistol, ran to look for it with fluttering hands, and the danger of death came nearer. When he finally found the pistol, Miss Simon said, "Mr. Cohen-Hayerushalmi, you really must control your feelings!" And he shouted back at her, "I'll choose my own way of dying and the time of my death." Upon which she smiled at him as she was accustomed to smile at her lesser customers, and her ears lengthened out frighteningly. "That's a primitive way of looking at it," she said to him. "There are scientific laws, and they decide what's what."

In the morning, he had to admit that there was a certain resemblance between his mother and Miss Simon, and this in addition to and besides the dislike of Poles. It was something that was not connected with physical appearances or even with "the soul in all its nakedness"; it was something unbearable and yet requiring and arousing pity. "Miss Simon is a woman who is incapable of arousing any feelings of love. Simply an unbearable and unlovable woman." So he decided that evening on his way to her, as he was preparing himself for their second encounter. "Why, it's awful, awful. The most awful thing that can happen to a woman." The more he thought about it, the more his pity for her grew, and he became convinced that he ought to console her, compensate her somehow for all the shame she had undoubtedly suffered in the forty years of her life.

In the light of what had happened the previous evening, Miss Simon was careful to wear a house robe. And when she opened the door for him and the wind blew at the skirts of the robe, her legs were revealed in all their bluish white glory, and she told him that she was sure that tonight he would be careful not to spill coffee over her. "Still, I took precautions. It's easier to launder the robe . . ." She beamed at him and closed the door behind him. Clouds of hot moist air hung about the room and he took off his coat and still felt warm.

"It's warm here," he said to her. Were it not for the need to maintain certain formalities, he would have loosened his necktie.

"The central heating in my apartment is excellent," she replied, as she sat down and primly folded the skirts of her robe about her legs lest more be revealed than was warranted by good taste. "I simply cannot live in an apartment that doesn't have central heating. We have been told that the climate of the country is subtropical! But in Jerusalem I feel colder in winter than in Berlin. I can't understand why the cold here so gets into your bones. You would probably like a cup of coffee to warm you up."

With the coffee drinking, she returned to her literary mood and began to read him some inspired notes she had jotted down while reading Peter Altenberg. When she finished, they both sank into a silence pregnant with meaning.

"Aren't you afraid of sleeping alone?" he asked suddenly. She sent him a knowing and reproachful smile.

"But Pinchas, what absurd ideas you have. You're really going too far."

"But, Miss Simon . . ."

"Please don't call me Miss Simon. My name is Esther."

"But, Esther, I really think about it seriously."

"What do you think seriously?"

"I, personally, am afraid to sleep alone. Strange fears come to me in the night."

A gust of rain began to beat the windows outside and the wind made the tops of the cypress trees sway to and fro. Pinik told her about his fears and the visits of the dead in the night. On account of the cold outside and the fearful tales within the room, she cuddled up to him while he spoke. And once his tongue was loosened, he was no longer able to restrain it. He even told her about his aunt Gitel and the seizures of laughter which came to him, apparently, from her.

"You see," he said, "sometimes everything seems to be so ridiculous. I just can't stop laughing. It begins in a sort of quiver in the stomach and goes up, up. It made its appearance only about half a year ago, when I came back from America. Lucky for me, I've never yet had such an attack in the middle of the street."

"But what's so funny to you?" she asked, wondering at him.

"Everything," he answered. "And myself most of all. Suddenly I see myself as being extremely funny, like a living joke. And when I'm not ridiculous in my own eyes, I'm hateful to myself."

"But you're not hateful to me," she said to him.

He looked at her and it seemed to him that she was really excited and blushing. From lying on his shoulder, her hair had become deranged and her ugliness pinched his heart by its sheer wretchedness. "I am a misanthrope, misanthrope!"

And he realized that this was the hour of decision, the truly great decision. He had now to request her hand willy-nilly, or miss the chance forever. Why, it was so simple really. All he had to do was to take up her slippery, sweating hand, peer into the moist lights in her eyes, and ask her softly, "Will you be my wife, Esther?" And then a wave of happiness would sweep over her. There is no man who does not have his hour. And this was Pinik's hour. For thirty-three years he had never in spite of all his efforts managed to make anyone happy. Now his chance had come. The feeling of the possibility of giving satisfaction to a living creature made him feel satisfied with himself. And with the suspicion that this self-satisfaction was liable to arouse a self-hatred which would exceed even the hatred he felt toward others who were overcomplacent, he hastened to take the decisive step before he could regret it. In a twinkling, he planned the whole action. He would rise from his place, take a few steps up and back like one who deliberates on an extremely important, epoch-making decision in his life, and then, stopping short before her, with manly courage, he would address her in a deep restrained voice. "Esther, will you be my wife? Please don't refuse!" And without further delay, he proceeded to carry out his plan. He leaped to his feet, and in the act his nose struck against Esther's arm, which had been resting on him. As the pain receded, he felt the itch in his nostrils and with it the memory of the smell and taste of blood, and he knew that soon the red trickle would issue from his nose. "Now that's an unanticipated obstacle for you at a decisive moment—a nosebleed." He immediately stretched out on the floor, as he had used to do twenty years ago and more, in his childhood, when the cool touch of tiles would help him to recover.

Esther jumped to her feet in alarm. At the sight of the man who had unpredictably cast himself down on the floor at her feet, she became convinced that all those stories about night fears and seizures of laughter, all those odd tales of his were not by any means the amusing pleasantries of a man in love, of one so taken by passion that his heart was about to be rent open and its deepest truth was about to emerge—but they were sober truth.

"What's happened to you, Pinchas?" she cried out. He tried to answer, but anxious lest the blood would flow if he began to speak, he simply smiled at her with gaping mouth. He had to breathe through his mouth in order to let the blood in his nose congeal. And then to calm her, he sent her a kiss and caressed her heels with the fingers of his outstretched left hand. She shrank back with a cry. A faint cry, a little hysterical and hoarse and rather helpless, like the cry of an old woman. For a moment she thought of dashing out and calling for the neighbors, but then she approached him carefully to see what was wrong. He sent her a wan, apologetic smile. The blood finally congealed; with it came the ability to stand up on his feet. As he was about to do so, however, those familiar quiverings began to leap about in his belly. And then with a final effort to control the laughter, he called out to her from the floor, "I love you, Esther. Will you be my wife. Say yes. Say yes. Say yes."

In the grip of near panic, she shrank back even farther. When at a safe distance, she called back to him, "You're mad. Absolutely mad. Get out of here before I call the neighbors."

"I'm going," he said and rose to his feet. "You needn't call the neighbors."

Outside the rain had ceased. In the light of the street lamps, the washed houses and the trees glittered with a cool, healing freshness. Pinik walked along and laughed and walked, and with every burst of laughter the knotted tangle of his tension unwound until he was all loosened and calm was restored. As he put increasing distance between himself and her house, it became even more clear to him that the first epoch of his life was now terminated. True, it had happened late; but he still felt himself a young man. Actually he felt younger than he had ever felt before. He waited impatiently for the morrow, for the new morning. He would rent a room for himself, perhaps that would make it easier. He would leave Miss Simon to her own devices, let his mother look after herself, and begin to seek the meaning of his own life.

Translated by Yehuda Hanegbi

13

THE CLOCK

Miss Tide had come to spend the spring on her uncle the younger Lord Timer's estate one and half kilometers south of Tel el Wakf. Summer after summer the younger Lord Timer would return to this Palestinian estate and devote himself to his archaeological excavations on the tel. He had already spent seven consecutive summer seasons in this way without obtaining any real results. He would appear about a week after Passover, hire Arab workers from the neighboring village, and begin excavating the tel in a characteristically English manner—systematically, patiently, and with a restrained and lasting enthusiasm unlikely to lead, in the end, to the frayed nerves and fits of melancholy and despair that tend to overtake archaeologists of a more impetuous temper when their impatient digging in the graves of past generations fails to bring anything significant to light. He paid all the expenses of these expeditions from his own pocket and made no attempt to attach himself to any academic institution or government body, either in Palestine or abroad. Toward the Jewish scholars who were beginning to replace the gentiles in the field he showed no signs of affection, or of hostility either for that matter, maintaining toward them the same attitude of calm indifference which marked his relations with his gentile colleagues. On one occasion only he remarked to his niece, Miss Tide, that these Jews with their complicated Talmudic subtleties took all the relish out of the work and spoiled the fun of the thing.

It was in his last season, the eighth in number and the first year of the State of Israel, that he brought Miss Tide to the tel. By then the neighboring village had been abandoned by its inhabitants and all that remained of it were the few huts which had not disintegrated in the shelling, standing there in all their loneliness, nakedness, and misery. So the lord was obliged to hire Jewish workers for the dig. Except for me, all seven were archaeological students, and the head of the group was already a qualified archaeologist, who from the day he started working with antiquities had begun to call himself Atikai. If it hadn't been for this Atikai I myself would never have landed up on the tel. One day, when I was hurrying as usual to get hold of a ticket to *Ohel Shem,* Atikai suddenly appeared before me with the glad tidings that Lord Timer the younger, whose coming we had all been so anxiously awaiting, had arrived at last. At that time I didn't yet know exactly who or what this Lord Timer the younger, whose arrival we had all been so anxiously awaiting, was. And how could I possibly have known? I was far too busy running after tickets to *Ohel Shem,* and in my spare time I was busy hiding from the old man who was pursuing me with an unpaid bill in his hand. True, I would have to pay up in the end, and when the day of reckoning arrived I would have to settle my accounts with the old man. But until then I wanted at least to be free of his irksome presence, which oppressed me so much that it prevented me from tackling the question of how to get hold of an entrance ticket to *Ohel Shem* with a clear mind.

"Is that so?" I exclaimed as if I too were a party to the general excitement. "So the lord has arrived at last!" Because I was hurrying on my way, looking forward to the long queue

in front of *Ohel Shem* and backward to see if the old man
were following me, because of this mad, frantic rush, I didn't
stop to ask who this lord was or why his arrival was so eagerly
awaited. If I had, Atikai would have grabbed me by the arm
and embarked on a long lament as usual about the deplorable
ignorance of people like me who didn't know the most elementary things, before going on to expound in detail and with
scientific precision the history of the said lord and the history
of his fathers and his fathers' fathers back to Adam.

Atikai gave me a penetrating look, and because he knew
how to put two and two together saw at once that I wanted
to join the group of diggers. He placed his hand on my shoulder and said, "Don't worry. I've already put your name down
on the list." This being the case, I had no choice but to go
with him, and because I went with him my worries went with
me, jumping from the old man to *Ohel Shem,* and from *Ohel
Shem* to Lord Timer the younger—until it suddenly occurred
to me that by cultivating this lord I might be able to get hold
of an entrance ticket before the old man finally caught up
with me.

So we pitched our camp consisting of three tents on the
slopes of Tel el Wakf and Atikai introduced us to the cele-
brated English archaeologist. Lord Timer the younger was
far from young. He was a red-faced, white-haired Englishman
of about sixty or more with a strong body, an erect bearing,
and twinkling gray eyes. He looked us over like an old sea
captain with a bunch of new recruits and even Atikai, who
was already a fully qualified archaeologist as mentioned above,
quailed beneath his appraising eye like a guilty child. The
lord then delivered a short speech in which he said that he
hoped the work on the tel would go forward in a spirit of good
humor without any friction or disagreement, and expressed
his firm belief that we would all derive great pleasure from

these archaeological labors, which for the past forty years had been the source of the most marvelous enjoyment and happiness in his life. It was obvious from his healthy body and glowing face that he was telling the truth, and that he had indeed derived a lot of satisfaction from his life. His niece Miss Tide was a woman of about twenty-eight or thirty. She went about the tel in a checked shirt and riding breeches, entering enthusiastically into all the details of the dig, which she understood as little as I did. Her eyes were big and brown and wild, and when she stood on top of the tel in her riding breeches with her chestnut hair blowing in the breeze, rhythmically slashing at her thigh with vigorous movements of the whip in her hand, she was like a beautiful wild animal holding back in a potent, panting fury before pouncing on its prey. Every movement of her body was full of a restrained power, and her manner of speaking too expressed the same forceful restraint.

The atmosphere when the dig began was charged with a tense expectancy which put us all nervously on edge. On the second day we were inundated by a heat wave and on the following day a hamsin descended like a solid body of burning air which pressed down on us and did not let up even at night. For a whole week the air burned around us with a dull yellow light and the cracked earth breathed heat from its rocks and fissures and scorched thorns and bitter nettles. The old man disappeared from view and even the entrance ticket to *Ohel Shem* stopped beckoning to me. Everything I had ever learned from books was forgotten too. I took off my shirt and then my vest and dug in the ancient bricks, which clung to my sweating body in layers of fine gray dust, penetrating my every pore, clinging to my eyelashes, clogging my nostrils, suffocating my throat, and leaving a taste of wormwood in my mouth.

On the seventh day of the dig the expectation exploded into a fever of excitement. Atikai and his friends flew from one side of the tel to the other trembling with agitation, like men in the middle of a gold rush suddenly catching sight of something glittering on a riverbank. They were all talking about levels and potsherds and buried scrolls and the First Temple and royal dynasties and military hierarchies and priestly castes and prophetic sects, and I knew that all these things had once meant something to me too. I wanted to find out what all the excitement was about but my eyes were dazzled and my ears were ringing and I neither saw nor understood anything, for the fever had seized hold of me too and every fiber of my body was trembling violently in anticipation of the fulfillment of a desire as ancient as the antiquities whose meaning I could not comprehend. I stood in a rectangular pit which reached down to a vein of rock in the ground and tried to look around me and determine the plan of the tel and understand the meaning of the excavations, but I saw nothing except gray dust rising from the fissures of the cracked earth and a murky yellow descending from the sky and the wheel of the sun sawing through my head with a whispering of dusty streams of sweat in my ears, and the agitated excavators running back and forth sniffing like mice in a cage. Suddenly Miss Tide's riding breeches appeared above me, and then her checked shirt, the column of her neck, her mouth pursed like a bell-button, the nostrils of her snub nose, and above them her two eyes penetrating me with the force of the burning sun and her curly hair tumbling down her back. She stood there in the whirling dust, which never seemed to cling to her, and there was a fever in her eyes. I was surprised to see that nobody was taking any notice of her and she was wandering around the tel getting under everyone's feet without attracting any attention at all from the excavators. I lifted the pick and brought it down with all my strength, and the rock crumbled like a lump of clay, leaving a cloud of dust in the air.

"Stop!" cried Miss Tide with a savage joy. "Stop, you're destroying the wall!"

"There's no need for the wall," I replied from the bottom of the pit. To tell the truth, I couldn't see any wall and as for her, she knew no more about what was happening on the tel than I did. From the moment the excavators had discovered whatever it was that they had discovered, I was the only one who paid any attention to her, and from the moment I started paying attention to her everything else vanished from my head and I felt a kind of lightness and power and a wonderful happiness. I went on brandishing the pick and planting it in the rock and the rock went on crumbling.

"Barbarian!" cried Miss Tide, with a note of exultation in her voice. "These are your antiquities and you're destroying them with your own hands." She was almost dancing for joy, and her words reached my ears from a distance, through a veil of dust. Although I didn't raise my eyes to look at her, her presence seeped into my veins and pounded in my head like wine.

I dug on in a frenzy and she lifted her whip and struck it across my bare back. The whip whistled through the air, twisting around me like a snake. Its tail flicked my eye with a searing, white-hot pain, and my pick fell to the ground.

That night the hamsin gathered force until it was like the flaming breath of a giant bending over the earth, but no one seemed to feel it. Everyone had gathered in Atikai's tent to take trembling stock of the day's rich haul, like a gang of robbers counting their spoils by candlelight. The joy of the first moment of discovery had given way to a tension vibrating in the air like a net with a trapped animal inside it. Atikai sat opposite Lord Timer the younger and both of them recorded the day's finds on large sheets of squared paper, according to the order in which they were drawn out of the sacks. From time to time they shot suspicious glances at each other, like a couple of gamblers who had staked their entire fortune on a game of chance and were constantly on their guard against being cheated. All the excavators sat around them in a circle, as if watching to see how the dice would fall. Miss Tide stood on a bench behind her uncle with her eyes fixed on the flame of the field lamp standing on the table, and I stood with my eyes fixed on hers. The whip marks were still burning in my flesh and I couldn't bear the touch of shirt or vest. I stood there in nothing but my shorts looking at Miss Tide's eyes looking at the lamp. Suddenly she tore her eyes away from the flame and discovered me, whereupon she jumped off the bench and ran outside.

For a moment I stood looking at the table on which the entrance tickets to *Ohel Shem* were lying scattered; I could have stretched my hand out and taken one of them with no trouble at all, but I couldn't be bothered. All I wanted was Miss Tide. I left the tent and went out after her, and the tel loomed up in front of me like a primordial beast in heat, squatting down on spread-out legs ready to mate. I made a detour around the back of the tel and walked down the path leading to Lord Timer's house. Miss Tide ran in the dark of the night and sparks flew from her feet. I ran after her with drops of sweat falling onto the welts made by her whip and burning my flesh like live coals. Before the door she paused for a moment and turned her head, and I seized her arm and pulled her toward me. She freed herself with an abrupt, energetic movement and bursting into the house with a moan, threw herself down on the leather sofa. I ran in after her and found myself face to face with an antique black clock standing on the floor next to the sofa and reaching almost to the ceiling. A long pendulum swung to and fro between two weights and the sound of the clock's ticking was as metallic and melodious as the peal of a bell. I went up to the sofa and placed my hand on her neck. She looked up at me with a strange surprise in her big wild eyes, and with every tick of the clock I felt the pounding of her heart sending waves up the vein in her slender neck. She closed her eyes and slid her hand over my body, and an exquisite yearning sensation, the like of which I had never experienced before, surged through me. She was alive and breathing to the point of pain, to the limits of endurance, to the heart's bursting. There was nothing left over: no time, no sky, no earth, no sun or moon or stars. And then the clock started ticking inside my head. At first with a faint, muffled drumming coming from a long way off, from behind a curtain. The drumming came closer and turned into a hammering and the hammering grew louder and louder until it thundered in my ears with a terrible violence.

"Say something to me," she whispered. "Tell me that you love me. Tell me that it's good for you with me. Tell me that I make you happy."

"Until I found you I didn't know what happiness was," I said, and my voice echoed in my ears with a foreign, superfluous sound. "Until I saw you I didn't know what a woman was, and until I knew you I didn't know what love was."

For a moment she seemed to be smiling at me and saying something. I jumped up and started pacing the room and the hammering in my head didn't let up for an instant. I dropped into a chair and she rose from the sofa. Her body shone like a statue in its nakedness and called to me. She approached me and sat down in my lap and took my head in her hands and her lips moved and her eyes spoke to me, but I didn't hear her voice. The strokes of the clock grew louder and louder, pursuing each other in a demented fury. I suddenly realized that in addition to losing my hearing, I was blind to everything but the big face of the clock and the long pendulum which glinted metallically every time it reached its center between the two suspended weights.

"I have to get that clock out of here," I said. "Its hammering's splitting my brain." She smiled and said something, and I felt that if I didn't get the clock outside I would go out of my mind. I went up to the clock and lifted it onto my back and turned toward the door. The touch of the smooth cold glass sent a shiver down my spine. I went down the path leading to the tel and the hammering in my head turned into a continuous liquid murmur like that of a waterfall. The clock writhed and twisted on my back until it melted and seeped into me and merged with my blood. I remembered the entrance tickets to *Ohel Shem* lying on the table in Atikai's tent, and picked up my feet and ran for my life in the direction of the tel. The field lamp lit up the entrance to the tent, and the shadow of the old man standing there holding the unpaid bill in his hand stretched and lengthened until it merged with the darkness of the surrounding night.

Translated by Dalya Bilu

14

THE EMPTY PACKET
OF CIGARETTES

THE EMPTY PACKET of cigarettes was to blame. It happened some years ago when the British were still in the country, and it was raining. When I stubbed out my last cigarette at about two o'clock in the morning the empty packet confronted me in all its horror. It opened its mouth and gaped at me, exposing its naked cardboard and a few twisted shreds of tobacco. Outside the rain fell steadily. It had been coming down in sheets since early in the evening and it seemed as if it would never stop. The empty packet lay on its side against the ashtray and outside the rain poured down from the heavy black clouds with a low, continuous, murmuring sound.

If I had found one single cigarette I would probably have calmed down and gone to sleep. As it was I started searching the room feverishly. I had a habit of leaving cigarette ends on the book shelves and in the pockets of my clothes. I scanned the bookcase and then turned to the wardrobe, removing jackets and trousers from their hangers and turning their pockets inside out. I looked under the bed and rummaged in the desk drawers. I looked inside a vase that had been standing empty for months, and found nothing but cobwebs and the desiccated corpses of two brown cockroaches. The sight of these blighted brown bodies enraged me beyond reason. Whatever happened, I had to get hold of some cigarettes. All the shops and cafés had long since closed for the night, and the curfew in the southern part of the town made it impossible for me to reach my friends there. Suddenly I knew what I had to do—I had to rob. To rob an Arab. I saw the precise image of my victim—a respectable rich Hawaga who would be returning at this hour from one of the brothels near the Damascus Gate. An old boy of St. George's College who spoke a polished English and smoked Black Cat cigarettes. Perhaps he would have some cigars and a Ronson lighter as well. "I won't let him get away with the lighter either," I said to myself as I lifted my raincoat from the pile of clothes heaped on the bed with their pockets turned inside out. I put on the coat and an old cap and went out into the darkness and the rain.

I walked down to St. Paul's Road. Torrents of water poured down the Street of the Prophets and parted at the intersection, one stream flowing down St. Paul's Road and the other continuing all the way down the hill to Mussrara. At the intersection a street lamp illuminated the statue of the Virgin Mary standing above the entrance to the Italian hospital. Drops of rain gleamed on the shawl covering her head and wrapping the baby in her arms. The rain came pouring down and Mary inclined her head with a modest, dignified grace, serene and tranquil in her immunity to the rain and wind and cold. I crossed over to the hospital doorway and pressed myself against the wall. Big drops of rain dripped down from the cornice above my head.

St. Paul's Road was the border; there were no Jewish houses beyond this point. In the immediate vicinity were the houses of the British officials and a little lower down, the police station. Beyond these the Arab quarter of Mussrara extended all the way to the Damascus Gate.

There was a deep silence, the kind of silence that only

exists after midnight. The only sound was the low incessant murmur of the rain. After a while I heard footsteps. They came from the direction of Mussrara, and they came quickly. I tensed myself, pressing my back against the cold wet stone, and saw a man coming toward me. He seemed in a desperate hurry. I heard him panting and saw the breath steaming from his mouth and nostrils. Instead of turning into St. Paul's Road he went straight on up the Street of the Prophets. After he had passed me and disappeared into the darkness beyond the intersection, I set out after him. The distance between us grew greater and I lengthened my stride. He started to run and I found myself running after him. When I was close enough I shouted in English, "Hey, you—stop!" I did not recognize my voice—it was thick and coarse and cruel. He stopped and stood still, too frightened to turn his head. I took the key to my room out of my pocket—it was a big black thing made of iron—and jabbed it hard against his back until I could feel it pressing against his spine. "Keep moving," I said and directed him into Abyssinian Road. Once in the alley, I stood him with his face to the high stone wall. From the moment I had heard his footsteps I had known he wasn't an Arab, let alone a Hawaga, but the die was cast. "Hands up," I said, trying to sound like a British policeman. He raised his arms and rested them against the dripping wall while I searched his pockets. The first thing I found was a packet of cigarettes. They were a cheap Arab brand called Badour. In those days you could buy a packet of forty for three and a half piasters. "What are you doing in the streets at this time of night?" I asked him while I opened the packet and took out a handful of cigarettes, which I put in the pocket of my raincoat. "Doctor," he said in an imploring, trembling voice. "Doctor!"

I put the remaining cigarettes back in his pocket, and in order not to arouse his suspicion continued to search him. I pulled out an old, worn leather wallet. It contained two pound notes, some yellowed documents, receipts, promissory notes, and an identity card. I looked at the identity card and learned that he was a Jewish plumber, aged thirty, that he was married and had a daughter, and that he lived in the Arab quarter of Mussrara. I returned the wallet.

"What do you want a doctor for?" I asked him. His face was still turned to the wall and my question was superfluous, but with the cigarettes in my pocket I felt relaxed and free to take an interest in him.

"For my daughter," he said in Hebrew, "for my daughter."

"All right," I said. "You can go."

When I told him to go I spoke very kindly, with the benevolence of an absolute dictator. I felt like an omnipotent being who grants and pardons not because he is obliged to do so by the demands of justice, but because he is powerful and good and fully aware of his power and goodness.

"Thank you," he said. He said it in English. "Thank you very much." And I knew that he really did thank me from the bottom of his heart. He was grateful to me for allowing him to continue his search for a doctor.

I took one of his cigarettes out of my pocket and lit it. The rain went on falling with a thin, liquid murmur, and I walked down the Street of the Prophets to Mussrara. I turned to the right and walked along the façade of the Notre Dame Church until I reached his house. He lived in the basement of a house owned by a Doctor Nasser Krikorian. The lights were on and his wife was looking out of the window. When she heard my footsteps she came outside in a dressing gown, with a shawl tied around her head. Before she had time to turn back I called out to her.

"Excuse me please," I said, "but I can't find my way. Could you tell me how to get to the Street of the Prophets?"

She was evidently relieved to hear me speak Hebrew. All

around her lay the Arab quarter of Mussrara, and above her rose the threatening walls of the Old City. It was night and it was raining, the silence was hostile and her child was sick. "God in heaven," she said, pulling the shawl tightly around her head and thinking of her daughter. "This is an Arab quarter and you could easily lose your way and find yourself in the Old City. Who knows what might happen to a man around these parts at this time of night?" We both thought of her husband who had gone to look for a doctor. "My husband will soon be here and he'll show you the way."

Inside the house the child began to cry and we both went in. The child, a pretty little girl of about three years old, was lying on her bed. "Imal'e, Mummy," she cried. The woman wrung her hands despairingly. "Imal'e, imal'e," the child cried again, and the mother picked her up and started walking about the room, hugging the little girl in her arms. It was raining and her husband had gone to call a doctor with only two pounds in his pocket and it was not yet the middle of the month. The child clung to her mother's neck, exhausted. Her head drooped helplessly and she kept up a steady whimpering. The woman walked up and down until she was tired out and put the child back in her bed. She went to the window and looked outside. "I can't stand it any longer," she whispered to herself. "God in heaven, I can't stand it." She was a young woman and the little girl was her first child.

"Is there any news?" she asked me abruptly, trying to take her mind off her daughter's suffering. The child cried out again imploringly, but there was nothing the mother could do to alleviate her suffering. I went over to the bed and looked at her. She lay on her back, red and burning with fever. Her eyes were shut tight in pain and two trickles of tears ran down either side of her little nose, which she wrinkled up as she cried. I looked at her but could not penetrate her being.

"The Anglo-American Commission of Inquiry has decided to partition the country into two states, one Arab and one Jewish. Jerusalem will be proclaimed an international city," I said in reply to her question, and she stared out of the window and waited for her husband and the doctor to come and save her.

"God in heaven," she said, and she couldn't understand why the child was suffering and why it was impossible to help her, and why God in Heaven saw her suffering and kept silent, and why she lived in an Arab quarter and stood looking out of the window at the walls of the Old City and the rain.

"Here they come!" she cried and ran outside. I took one last look at the small feverish body on the bed and slipped away. I went around the back of the house and hurried down the Notre Dame alley and up the Street of the Prophets to the intersection.

When I reached the Italian hospital I lit another cigarette and thought of the plumber and his wife and his little daughter. "She'll recover," I thought. "She'll get better and grow up to be a beautiful woman." And then I saw him—the Hawaga. He had a fat cigar in his mouth and leather gloves on his hands and he looked at me with a mocking, contemptuous smile. I lifted my eyes to the statue of the Virgin Mary, but she averted her face and inclined her head with a modest, dignified grace, serenely indifferent to the ravages of the rain and the wind and the cold.

Translated by H. M. Daleski

15

THE DEATH OF
THE LITTLE GOD

AT TEN TO SEVEN the shamash of the hospital, a bearded Jew with side-curls, knocked on my window. I don't know why he knocked on the window and not at the door. Perhaps he wanted to see whether I was in, or perhaps it was a habit that he had carried over from his days as a beadle at the Central Synagogue when he had had to summon the "good Jews" (as he called them) to midnight prayers. At all events his knocking shattered my dream. The moment I opened my eyes and saw his big head pressed close to the windowpane I knew that the meaning of his visit was that the Little God was dead, but looking at his abundant, untidy beard and at his blinking eyes I refused to believe it.

Startled, I jumped out of my bed and hurriedly opened the door. He came in without uttering a word and, nonchalantly sitting down on a chair, he smoothed his beard with both his hands and placed its tip in his mouth, chewing it with his false teeth. At the same time his eyes roamed over the room till they rested on a picture of a naked woman reclining on her elbow and staring indifferently at the world. The expression on his face hardened and he quickly looked away from the picture to the bookcase. Next to the gaudy pocket books there stood six heavy, old, calf-bound volumes worn at the edges with years and use. For a minute he hesitated, but then he got up and looked at the volumes. I glanced at him sideways, ready to see on his face an expression of wonder mixed with disappointment, for the six calf-bound volumes were neither Talmudic commentaries nor prayer books but the first edition of Hugo's *Les Misérables*, which appeared about one hundred years ago in Brussels.

He pulled out the middle volume, wiped the dust off the cover with his sleeve, sniffed at the smell of old books which it gave off, and glanced at me to see whether I was ready to go or whether he had time to look at the book. I prepared two cups of coffee, one for him and one for myself. He opened the book in the middle, frowned at the sight of the Latin characters, shut it, and returned it to its place with a dry and bored face, like one accustomed to all sorts of oddities. He recited shehakol over the coffee and drank it slowly and deliberately. After I too had finished my cup it suddenly occurred to me to sweep the floor, but I did not do so because I did not want to delay him too long.

We went out and only after we had started walking was I seized by a hot and cold fever and by the need to hurry. I had to make haste lest I should be too late. I walked quickly, taking big strides, till we reached the bus stop. We both jumped onto the bus without paying attention to the people who were standing in the queue. Perhaps they did not protest or shout at us because they could see that we were agitated and pressed for time. If there had been any young people in the queue, people who stand up for their rights and who are quick to get angry, they would doubtless have tried to prevent us from boarding the bus, but in fact there were only some old and weak Jews, experts in suffering and accustomed to being deprived of their due, and they did not say a word. They looked at us with their sad eyes and murmured, "Ay, ay." Perhaps they even understood that we were hurrying to the chamber of the dead, on the floor of which the Little God was lying cold and silent, covered with a white sheet and with candles burning all around him.

In the bus the shamash took out a tin box which had once been ornamented with colored pictures but which now showed a white, worn-away, tinny nakedness. He opened it and took out half a cigarette—all the cigarettes in the box had been cut in half. He put the cigarette in an amber holder and lit it. Looking at him, I wondered what was going on in the head of the old Jew. He was wearing a black hat, his face was wrinkled and brown like old parchment, and his red, flattened nose dipped into the sea of his mustache and beard. The holes in his socks peeped above his heavy boots and even from afar he gave off a smell of stale sweat mixed with Turkish tobacco. All in all he looked old and calm amid sorrow and disasters and many funerals—the funerals of my generation and of the generation which preceded mine. It was he who had seen my grandfather to his grave, and now he would accompany the Little God, who had died in his very prime if not in the bloom of his youth.

On the way to the hospital we passed many people and they all looked strange and distant and absorbed in their own business. Only a few of them walked calmly; mostly they had tense and worried faces and the children alone seemed happy.

I ran into the hospital and the shamash hurried after me. I wanted to go up into the ward where the Little God had been lying and to ask the chief nurse, "How's the Little God? Is he any better? I am here, ready to do everything that's necessary." But he drew me to the chamber of the dead. Before I entered it he held me and rent the lapel of my jacket and then took out of his pocket a small black skullcap, which he put on my head. I knew that he would do everything that was necessary—that he would conclude the business with the Chevra Kedisha, decide on the site of the grave, and handle all the other funeral arrangements. He was the only solid basis in the void and formlessness, around which the darkness was in flux on the face of the deep.

When I went into the chamber of the dead I saw the long body of the Little God, enshrouded in white sheets, stretched out full length on the floor. My tremulousness vanished completely and one great wish took hold of me—to run out and to escape from the place as quickly as possible. Most of the candles around the corpse had already burned out and only a few were still flickering in the stench of the room. In a corner an old blind man was sitting and reciting psalms—a task which had occupied him for the last forty years, ever since he had been hired for the job. The shamash put an end to the silence in which he had been immersed since he knocked on my window at ten to seven, leaned toward me, whispered in Yiddish, "A finever," and then went out to collect the ten men needed for the minyan.

"That means that this minyan is going to cost me a fiver," I said to myself. "Half a pound each." I went to the corpse, lifted the white sheet a bit, and saw a thin cold arm on which death had spread a greenish yellowness. "That's forbidden, that's forbidden," somebody suddenly called out. The man who had stuck his red face into the chamber nodded at me as if I were a naughty child. I hurriedly covered the arm and went outside.

"You," he said to me, "are you a relative of the deceased?"

I did not know how to answer him satisfactorily so I started to fumble in my pockets, looking for my cigarettes. The man stuck the red swollen fingers of his left hand into the packet and nimbly extracted a cigarette. He jingled the collection box which he was holding in his right hand. I remembered him from my early childhood. He always followed funerals with a sad face, rattling his collection box and calling out,

"Charity wards off death, charity wards off death." It was said that he owned two buildings in the Mahne-Yehudah quarter and one in Nachlat Shivah. His daughter was a nice buxom girl and all the boys used to talk about her reverently till she married an English policeman and went with him to England when the British left the country.

"I was a lodger in his apartment," I answered him.

"Ah?" He threw out the syllable like a question mark while he lit the cigarette.

"I lived in his apartment," I repeated.

"He was a good man," he declared, after blowing out a cloud of smoke through the nostrils of his big red nose, which was pitted like a sieve. He looked around and, seeing no one nearby, put his face close to mine and whispered confidentially, as if we were two old friends, "A good man, but a bit touched . . . too much thinking."

Only after the second cigarette did it occur to me to put a coin in his box. Since the coin was safely in the box, and since none of the deceased's family—or anyone else, for that matter—had come, as people say, to pay their last respects, and since the minyan of beggars whom the shamash had gathered were the only people in sight, he fluttered his eyes, made a curtsy in the French fashion of all things, and went on his way. After he had gone one of the minyan of beggars approached me, inspected me from head to foot, and finally murmured sympathetically and compassionately, "A small family, eh?" Then as a consolatory afterthought of a more philosophical order he added, "It is not good that a man should be alone."

"I am not one of his family," I answered him. "I live in his apartment. He had a two-room apartment and I live in one of the rooms."

"So. . . so. . . And what did he die of?"

"A brick fell on his head," I told him.

He rolled his eyes in wonder, as if I had told a joke in bad taste, turned his back, and rejoined his companions.

"It really is like an odd joke," I reflected. "He was walking along harmlessly enough past the scaffolding of a seven-story apartment house under construction when a brick fell on his head; he instantly lost consciousness and died two days later. And that's that. All over. And indeed he once told me in a moment of confidence that his whole life was nothing but a joke. 'All in all,' he said, 'I am nothing but a practical joke of somebody else's making.' "

And who was that somebody? He certainly meant his Little God. He had a sort of theory that God was small. Once he had gathered a couple of students around him and for two hours he had expounded his views about the divinity—ever since, he had been nicknamed "The Little God." In his big, lucid, somewhat childish handwriting he had even left a paper entitled "Reflections on Man's Concept of the Dimensions of God in Time and Space." Several days before the brick fell on his head he had started to translate the paper into English. "It seems," he told me, "that not until the gentiles accept my views will Jewish scholars listen to my system." He was a physicist by profession, and until he dedicated himself to his idea about the dimensions of God, which are, according to him, much smaller than we can imagine—indeed so small that our minds cannot grasp their smallness—up to the time he sank into big thoughts about the smallness of God, he was, one might say, like everybody else, or at any rate like any other man of science. He was tall and thin and stooped, his eyes were gray and slanting, deep wrinkles ran down from his longish nose to the sides of his mouth, flaxen tufts flapped from the sides of his bald head, and all in all he looked as if he were constantly apologizing for his long figure and big arms and awkward hands and, in general, for occupying space in the world. One could not tell how old he was. Sometimes, when he smiled, he looked like a giant baby. But usually he did not smile and sadness flowed down his face, an ancient sadness.

It's strange that he was happy—when he wasn't sad. He would sing and even dance and drink heavily—but it's perhaps as well not to go into the details of his behavior when he was happy, for at the end of each attack of happiness he would fall into the hands of a Greek prostitute and talk lovingly to her, in Yiddish of all languages, till he fell asleep on her lap. On such occasions he would also wave his fists and shout at the top of his voice that he hated humanity. "I love men, and better still, women, but humanity, dear God, I hate humanity. I can love Yankil or Shmeril or Beril"—he would hit the table with his fists—"but giwald, geschrien, I hate Jewry." Even when he sobered up and was in control of all his faculties he would avoid any human contacts, and things came to such a pass that he was often attacked by a fear of crowds. Then he would shut himself up in his room, close the shutters, draw the curtains, plug his ears with cotton wool, and cringe on the edge of his couch, praying silently to his Little God to save him from humanity.

When I came to rent the room in his apartment about a year before he died, his condition was already pretty serious—or so his colleagues and other people who knew him thought. He himself was sure he had climbed as high, in spirit, as a man could. By then he had already abandoned his work in the Physics Department "in order to dedicate myself to philosophical contemplation," as he said. His colleagues nodded sagely and talked of the "attacks" which more and more often laid him low. For a long time he had gone out of his way to avoid people and disdained to enter buses or restaurants or cinemas.

Apart from going out in the early morning or late in the evening to do his daily shopping, with which even he could not dispense, apart from these excursions which he undertook as if compelled by the devil, he would sit shut up in his room sailing on his thoughts about the concepts of God. He would sit for two or three weeks, or sometimes even for a month, until happiness started to ferment in his limbs. The hummings and whisperings that emanated from his room at an ever increasing tempo gave me advance notice of such happiness. Like a volcano on the verge of bursting out, he would walk up and down in his room, turn on the radio, open the curtains, and lift the shutters to let in the sunshine and noise of the street like an overflowing river. Finally he would wash, shave his month-old beard, put on a white shirt, don his Sabbath suit—the only one in his cupboard—and run out like a prisoner escaping from jail.

During the last year of his life his whole income consisted only of the rent he received from me and of a small allowance made to him by one of the Zionist institutions. Throughout the time I lived in his apartment he only once told me about his life in the past and about his family—and that was when he was brought home by the fat, aging Greek prostitute. I learned from him that his father had been a Zionist of some standing, important enough to have a settlement named after him. He had two sisters, one a communist who had married a gentile, and the other, who had remained single, a doctor who had specialized in tropical diseases and had gone to care for the Negroes in Central Africa. Had he told more, perhaps I could have found some clue to the way of life of the daughters of the Zionist who had not had the good fortune to immigrate to Israel and who had been murdered by the Nazis, but the Little God was not communicative and I had to content myself with what he divulged.

And so during the last months of his life he was driven from seclusion to the most dubious and strange friendships, and from elation and belief in his original thinking, a belief bordering on a strange boastfulness, to the depths of despair. Then one night, some two weeks before that brick fell on his head, he gave me a terrible fright.

From eleven o'clock that night a wintry cold had prevailed over the sleeping world and a silent wind had brought layers of low cloud which completely covered the sky and the sickle of moon. I had closed the window and made my bed. I had fallen asleep a few minutes after I had gone to bed and would have gone on sleeping happily till morning had I not been woken by a muffled cry of fright which set my nerves on edge.

The Little God was groaning in his room like a wounded jackal. Then suddenly he came and knocked faintly at my door. I braced myself, overcame my fear, and even remembered to arm myself with a ruler before I slowly opened the door, ready to strike him over the head if he jumped at me in his madness. His long body was clad in pajamas which were too short for him and his feet were bare. As soon as he appeared in all his shame and awkwardness I let the ruler drop and pushed it under the bed with my foot. He stood in the middle of my room like a man fleeing a catastrophe and urgently in need of shelter who suddenly finds that the anticipated shelter is illusory.

"Excuse me," he muttered, "please excuse me. I shouted in my sleep. I must have given you a real fright. I myself was frightened to death—otherwise I would not have shouted. But now it's all over and I must go back to bed. Yes, I must go back to sleep, but really I'd prefer to remain here with you a little while, a little longer, for I'm afraid to go back to sleep. These nightmares are worse than hell. Perhaps you'd like to come to my room and I'll make you tea? Till I calm down?"

"No," I said to him, "I'll make some tea. You just sit down here."

He obeyed me and sat down on a chair. He knew he could not have made tea, for his hands were still trembling. He held his cup with both hands but it shook and tea dripped onto his hands and knees.

In his dream his father had come to him. He was wearing only a sleeveless vest and short underpants, and the Little God burst out laughing and his heart wept and his teeth chattered and his eyes shed tears. "How is it, Father," he said, and he pointed at him, but his laughter and the chattering of his teeth choked his voice, "how is it that all of a sudden you decided to put on short underpants like a modern dandy? All your life you have worn long woolen underpants because of the chronic cold you have had since your youth."

"Here in Eretz Israel," said his father, "one does not need woolen underpants."

"What are you saying, Father? This is not Eretz Israel! Look, the fields around us are covered with snow and the trees are standing naked and a frosty wind penetrates to the marrow."

"Stuff and nonsense, my boy, you're talking nonsense."

While the Little God was talking to his father the scene changed to the father's study. A blue Keren Kayemet collection box was standing on the table with the carved legs. A map of Palestine, with all the Keren Kayemet land colored green, was hanging on the eastern wall. Opposite the map, on the western wall, the faces of Herzl and Nordau stared down from within their golden frames. When the Little God approached the pictures in order to examine them more closely he was confronted by the faces of his two sisters. The sisters, he saw, looked as they had when they were in their first year at the gymnasia. His father went to the table and spread out on it an issue of the *Welt*, the Zionist organ, which grew and grew till it covered the whole table. Then his father sat on the table, crossed his arms over his chest, which was covered only by the thin vest, and said, "Now tell me what's going on in the world."

"The world is growing bigger, Father, and God is growing smaller." His father jerked his head back and laughed heartily in the way he used to laugh when he was in a good humor. Protruding veins twined on his forehead and his belly heaved as he laughed and laughed until tears came to his eyes and his voice choked and one could not tell whether he was laughing or crying.

"God is growing smaller, Father, and now, already, compared to an ant, God looks like a flea compared to an elephant. He is still alive, wriggling and writhing under the weight of the world He created, but it is only a matter of time before His death agonies cease."

"And how long will it take before He disappears?" asked his father, his face becoming serious.

"Two or three weeks, perhaps less."

"Then this is the end."

"Yes, this is the end."

On hearing this his father jumped off the table and started to knock his head against the map of Israel. He knocked his head and cried out with pain, knocked and cried, and with each knock his body became smaller, and his son knew that only he could save him but his whole body became stiff and numb and he could not move a limb. He froze with cold and fright and saw how his father was becoming smaller and smaller, knocking his head against the wall and vanishing, till nothing remained of him but the reverberations of the knocking.

Translated by H. M. Daleski